A YEAR WITH GOD

Also by Renovaré

Connecting with God
by Lynda L. Graybeal and Julia L. Roller

Contemplative Compassion
by Sarah Butler Berlin

Devotional Classics
co-edited by Richard J. Foster and James Bryan Smith

Embracing the Love of God
by James Bryan Smith

Learning from Jesus
by Lynda L. Graybeal and Julia L. Roller

Life with God
by Richard J. Foster with Kathryn A. Helmers

The Life with God Bible
edited by Richard J. Foster and others

Living the Mission
by Lynda L. Graybeal and Julia L. Roller

Prayer and Worship
by Lynda L. Graybeal and Julia L. Roller

Spiritual Classics
co-edited by Richard J. Foster and Emilie Griffin

A Spiritual Formation Workbook
by James Bryan Smith with Lynda L. Graybeal

Streams of Living Water
by Richard J. Foster

Wilderness Time
by Emilie Griffin

A YEAR WITH GOD

Living Out the Spiritual Disciplines

RICHARD J. FOSTER
GENERAL EDITOR

COMPILED BY
JULIA L. ROLLER

HarperOne
An Imprint of HarperCollinsPublishers

Contents

Foreword

Spiritual formation is writ large across the pages of Scripture—so large, in fact, that it's often easy to miss it altogether. In C.S. Lewis's *The Silver Chair*, from *The Chronicles of Narnia*, Eustace and Jill search for a sign in a ruined city of giants, but are disheartened to find themselves wandering through a confusing maze of rock trenches without uncovering any message. The following morning, while looking out from a high window, they are astounded to see the words "UNDER ME" carved in huge, deep letters on the stony hillside—and they suddenly realize they had spent the previous day stumbling through the very words they had been seeking. They had simply lacked the vantage point from which to read the sign.

Some of us experience the same problem reading the Bible. We have become accustomed to examining the text through a microscope: seeking the underlying principles of key passages, making a focused examination of the structure of individual sentences, delving deeply into the original meaning of Greek and Hebrew words. This detailed study can be wonderful, but it also has its limitations. Many of the Bible's greatest themes are seen only in the sweeping landscape of the divine story; they are expressed more in vistas than in verses. To catch sight of these themes we need a different perspective, a shift in viewpoint. Rather than a microscope, we need a mountaintop.

A Year with God provides that vantage point. This twelve-month journey through Scripture reintroduces us to the great characters, passages, and themes of Scripture and helps us understand how they consistently reveal and illuminate God's passion to renew us in the likeness of Jesus Christ. One by one we look at some of the key practices and disciplines through which we are able to throw our lives open to the transforming grace of God: practices such as prayer, worship, study, confession, silence, simplicity, and celebration. We learn how to intentionally trim our sails to catch the wind of the Spirit, and so find ourselves taken in wholly new and unexpected directions. And in the spiritual renewal we experience as a result, we find ourselves becoming "in every aspect a dwelling place of God."

Along the way we are reminded of the great high points of the biblical story: the creation and the fall, the exodus and the conquest, the judges and the monarchs, the prophets and the exile, the coming of the Messiah and the birth of the Church—and, of course, a look ahead to the great day of Christ's return. At each point, we see how God has been working to create, as expressed in *The Life with God Bible,* "an all-inclusive community of loving persons with God himself at the very center of this community as its prime Sustainer and most glorious Inhabitant."

This book is not a year-long course on spiritual formation from which we can graduate and move on. Formation into Christlikeness is the work of a lifetime, so we need to develop a measured stride in our walk with Christ that can be sustained across decades—what Friedrich Nietzsche described as "a long obedience in the same direction," from which "results, and has always resulted in the long run, something which has made life worth living."

A Year with God can help set a good pace. It is not a hearty meal to be devoured at a single sitting, but provisions to sustain you on a lengthy journey. Savor each morsel. Read slowly and reflectively. Take time to meditate on both the passages of Scripture and the commentary. Allow your reading to develop into prayer, to entice you into God's transforming presence. Then—and only then—begin to explore ways to allow your life to be reshaped by what you discover. If read quickly, these pages will yield a few nuggets of insight, perhaps some interesting quotes to share with friends at church, but little more. Absorbed slowly and thoughtfully, *A Year with God* will continue to bear fruit in your life long after the book itself has been placed back on the shelf.

A tremendous journey lies before us. Every day in this coming year will present us with an opportunity to draw a little closer to the Father's heart, to open ourselves a little more to the gracious, reforming Spirit of God, to become a little more like Jesus. You hold in your hands the ideal guide for such a journey. *Tolle, lege*—take up, and read!

Christopher S. Webb, TSSF
President, RENOVARÉ
Castle Rock, Colorado

The Bible and the With-God Life

The Bible is all about human life "with God." It is about how God has made this "with-God" life possible and will bring it to pass. In fact, the name Immanuel, meaning in Hebrew "God is with us," is the title given to the one and only Redeemer, because it refers to God's everlasting intent for human life—namely, that we should be in every aspect a dwelling place of God. *Indeed, the unity of the Bible is discovered in the development of life "with God" as a reality on earth, centered in the person of Jesus.* We might call this the *Immanuel Principle* of life.

This dynamic, pulsating, with-God life is on nearly every page of our Bible. To the point of redundancy we hear that *God is with* his people: with Abraham, with Moses, with Esther, with David, with Isaiah and Jeremiah and Amos and Micah and Haggai and Malachi, with Mary, with Peter, with James and John, with Paul and Barnabas, with Priscilla and Aquila, with Lydia, Timothy, Epaphroditus, Phoebe, and with a host of others too numerous to name.

Accordingly, our primary task is to learn to see and understand the reality of the with-God life, to enter the process of the transformation of our whole person and of our whole life into *Christlikeness.*

Opening Ourselves to the Life
If we want to receive from the Bible the life with God that is portrayed *in* the Bible, we must be prepared to have our dearest and most fundamental assumptions about ourselves and our associations called into question. We must read humbly and in a constant attitude of repentance. Only in

this way can we gain a thorough and practical grasp of the spiritual riches that God has made available to all humanity in his written Word.

When we turn to Scripture in this way, our reason for "knowing" the Bible and everything it teaches is that we might love more and know more of love. We experience this love not as an abstraction, but as a practical reality by which we are possessed. And since all those who love through and through obey the law, we become ever more obedient to Jesus Christ and his Abba.

Our goal is not to try to control the Bible—that is, to try to make it "come out right"—but to simply seek to release its life into our lives and into our world. We seek to trust the living water that flows from Christ through the Bible, to open ourselves to it and to release it into the world as best we can, and then get out of its way.

NURTURING THE INTENTION: THE BIBLE

God remains with the Bible always. It is God's book. No one owns it but God himself. It is the loving heart of God made visible and plain. And receiving this message of exquisite love is the great privilege of all who long for life with God. *Reading, studying, memorizing, and meditating upon Scripture has always been the foundation of the Christian Disciplines.* All of the disciplines are built upon Scripture. Our practice of the Spiritual Disciplines is kept on course by our immersion in Scripture. And so it is, we come to see, that this reading, studying, memorizing, and meditating is totally in the service of "the life that really is life" (1 Tim 6:19). We long with all our hearts to know *for ourselves* the with-God kind of life that Jesus brings in all its fullness.

And the Bible has been given to help us. God has so superintended the writing of Scripture that it serves as a most reliable guide for our own spiritual formation. But as in its authorship, so in its presentation to the world, God uses human action. So we must consider how we can ourselves come to the Bible and also how we can present it to people in a way that does not destroy the soul, but inducts it into the eternal kind of life.

We begin by experientially finding, day to day, how to let Jesus Christ live in every dimension of our being. We can open our lives in Christian community to the influx of God's life by gathering regularly in groups of two or more to encourage one another to discover the footprints of God in our daily existence and to venture out *with God* into areas where we have previously walked alone or not at all.

But the aim is not external conformity, whether to doctrine or deed, but the reformation of the inner self—of the spiritual core, the place of thought and feeling, of will and character. The psalmist cries, "You desire truth in the inward being; therefore teach me wisdom in my secret heart. . . . Create in me a clean heart, O God, and put a new and right spirit within me" (Ps 51:6, 10). It is "our inner nature" that is being "renewed [*renovare*] day by day" (2 Cor 4:16).

Although the many Christian traditions differ over the details of spiritual formation, they all have the same objective: the transformation of the person into one of greater Christlikeness. *Spiritual formation* is the process of transforming the inner reality of the self (the "inward being" of the psalmist) in such a way that the overall with-God life seen in the Bible naturally and freely comes to pass in us. Our inner world (the "secret heart") becomes the home of Jesus, by his initiative and our response. As a result, our interior world becomes increasingly like the inner self of Jesus and, therefore, the natural source of the words and deeds that are characteristic of him. By his enabling presence we come to "let the same mind be in [us] that was in Christ Jesus" (Phil 2:5).

UNDERSTANDING THE MEANS:
THE SPIRITUAL DISCIPLINES

The with-God life that we see in the Bible is the very life to which we are called. It is, in fact, exactly the life Jesus is referring to when he declares, "I am come that they might have life, and that they might have it more abundantly" (John 10:10, KJV). It is a life of unhurried peace and power. It is solid, serene, simple, radiant. It takes no time, though it permeates all of our time.

But such a life does not simply fall into our hands. Frankly, it is no more automatic for us than it was for those luminaries who walk across the pages of our Bible. There is a God-ordained means to becoming the kind of persons and the kind of communities that can fully and joyfully enter into such abundant living. And these "means" involve us in a process of intentionally "train[ing] ... in godliness" (1 Tim 4:7). This is the purpose of the *disciplines* of the spiritual life. Indeed, the very reason for this book is so that Scripture itself will be a primary means for the discovery, instruction, and practice of the Spiritual Disciplines, which bring us all the more fully into the with-God life.

The Spiritual Disciplines, then, are the God-ordained means by which each of us is enabled to bring the little, individualized power pack we all possess—the human body—and place it before God as "a living sacrifice" (Rom 12:1). It is the way we go about training in the spiritual life. By means of this process we become, through time and experience, the kind of persons who naturally and freely express "love, joy, peace, patience, kindness, generosity, faithfulness, gentleness, and self-control" (Gal 5:22–23).

Many and Varied

What are the Spiritual Disciplines? They are many and varied: fasting and prayer, study and service, submission and solitude, confession and worship, meditation, guidance, and silence, simplicity and chastity, secrecy and sacrifice, fellowship and celebration, and the like. We see such Spiritual Disciplines cropping up repeatedly in the Bible as the way God's people trained toward godliness. And not only in the Bible; the saints down through history, even spilling over into our own time, have all practiced these ways of "growing in grace" (2 Pet 3:18).

A Spiritual Discipline is an intentionally directed action by which we do what we can do in order to receive from God the ability (or power) to do what we cannot do by direct effort. It is not in us, for example, to love our enemies. If we go out and try very hard to love our enemies, we will fail miserably. Always. This strength, this power to love our enemies—that is, to genuinely and unconditionally love those who curse us and spitefully use us—is simply not within our natural abilities. We cannot do it by ourselves. Ever.

But this fact of life does not mean that we do nothing. Far from it! Instead, by an act of the will we choose to take up disciplines of the spiritual life that we can do. These disciplines are all actions of body, mind, and spirit that are within our power to do. Not always and not perfectly, to be sure, but they are things we can do—by choice, by choosing actions of *fasting, study, solitude,* and so forth.

The Purpose of the Disciplines
The Spiritual Disciplines in and of themselves have no merit whatsoever. They possess no righteousness, contain no rectitude. Their purpose—their only purpose—is to place us before God. After that they have come to the end of their tether. But it is enough. Then the grace of God steps in, takes this simple offering of ourselves, and creates out of it the kind of person who embodies the goodness of God—indeed, a person who can come to the place of truly loving even enemies.

Again, Spiritual Disciplines involve doing what we *can* do to receive from God the power to do what we *cannot*. And God graciously uses this process to produce in us the kind of person who automatically will do what needs to be done when it needs to be done.

The ability to do what needs to be done when it needs to be done is the true freedom in life. Freedom comes not from the absence of restraint, but from the presence of discipline. When we are on the spot, when we find ourselves in the midst of a crisis, it is too late. Training in the Spiritual Disciplines is the God-ordained means for forming and transforming the human personality, so that when we are in the crisis we can be "response-able" —able to respond appropriately.

Grace, Grace, and More Grace
It is vitally important for us to see all this spiritual training in the context of the work and action of God's grace. As the apostle Paul reminds

us, "It is God who is at work in you, enabling you both to will and to work for his good pleasure" (Phil 2:13). This, you see, is no "works righteousness," as it is sometimes called. Even our desiring the with-God life is an action of grace; it is "prevenient grace," say the theologians. You see, we are not just saved by grace; we live by grace. And we pray by grace and fast by grace and study by grace and serve by grace and worship by grace. *All the disciplines are permeated by the enabling grace of God.*

But do not misunderstand, there *are* things for us to do. Daily. Grace never means inaction or total passivity. In ordinary life we will encounter multiple moments of decision in which we must engage the will, saying yes to God's will and to God's way, as the People of God have been challenged throughout history.

The opposite of grace is works, but not effort. "Works" have to do with earning, and there simply is nothing any of us can do to earn God's love or acceptance. And, of course, we don't have to. God already loves us utterly and perfectly, and our complete acceptance is the free gift of God through Jesus Christ our Lord. In God's amazing grace "we live and move and have our being" (Acts 17:28). But if we ever hope to "grow in grace," we will find ourselves engaging in effort of the most strenuous kind. As Jesus says, we are to "*strive* to enter through the narrow door" (Luke 13:24, emphasis added). And Peter urges us to "make every *effort* to support [our] faith with goodness, and goodness with knowledge, and knowledge with self-control, and self-control with endurance, and endurance with godliness, and godliness with mutual affection, and mutual affection with love" (2 Pet 1:5–7, emphasis added). It is our hope that this book will assist you in your efforts to support your faith.

Adapted from The Life with God Bible, *Richard J. Foster, Editor; Gayle Beebe, Lynda L. Graybeal, Thomas C. Oden, and Dallas Willard, General Editors,* © Copyright 2005 by Renovaré, Inc.

How to Use This Book

The aim of this book is to assist you, through study of Scripture and practical application, on your journey of discipleship to Jesus Christ. Each of the eighteen sections of *A Year with God* focuses on one Spiritual Discipline practiced by the People of God in the Bible. For each day we present a Scripture passage, then a commentary on the passage from *The Life with God Bible* or a spiritual practice followed by a quotation, prayer, or reflection relating to the passage. Of course, these sections are not meant to be completely comprehensive, including every passage about the given discipline. In the case of the first section, The With-God Life, we would have to include the entire Bible! But we include the passages we thought would be most helpful for thinking about, understanding, and practicing each discipline. In each Spiritual Discipline section you will find Scripture passages from a wide range of biblical books, from the Old Testament to the New, from the Prophets to the Letters.

It is of course somewhat of an artificial distinction to separate the disciplines in this way. Most of the disciplines flow together and are meant to be practiced that way too. Indeed, it would be difficult to practice service without submission or to celebrate without worshiping. Often we find that the practice of one discipline serves to help us understand and practice another. You will find this kind of overlap in many of the sections.

The readings are designed to be started at any time; it is not necessary to wait until January 1 or even to go through day by day. The days are numbered, not listed by date, so if you miss a day or two, you can pick up right where you left off. Similarly, it is not necessary to start with The With-God Life section and work straight through, although we have ordered the disciplines with an eye toward balance between inward and outward spiritual practices and in a progression that we think makes sense for spiritual formation.

Each section focuses on a particular Spiritual Discipline and begins with a definition and introduction, which you can read on the first day of that section and/or refer to throughout the days you are studying that discipline. Each section (with the exception of The With-God Life, which has twenty-five days) has twenty readings for twenty days. Since an essential part of spiritual formation involves action and practice, we have incorporated two spiritual exercises in each section. These are introduced on the first and eleventh day of each Spiritual Discipline section (again, with the exception of The With-God Life, where the exercises are given on the first and fourteenth days). The first practice in each section is one that you can do a little of each day while you are working through that section, and the second practice is one that will require a single, usually longer, time commitment. You can do that exercise anytime within that ten-day period.

It may be helpful for you to use *A Year with God* in the context of a small group. You and the individual members of your group might do the daily readings and perform the spiritual exercises on your own, perhaps while keeping a journal of responses to the questions and other reflections. Then your group could meet every ten or twenty days to talk about the spiritual practices, the readings, journal entries, and other pertinent topics. In so doing, through mutual accountability and encouragement, you would be creating a relational space to help you get the most out of *A Year with God*. At RENOVARÉ we refer to this type of connecting as a Spiritual Formation Group.

It is our great hope that you will find this resource a helpful one in your journey with God and that it will enhance your understanding and practice of these disciplines. May God bless you richly in your study and practice.

Julia L. Roller, RENOVARÉ

A YEAR WITH GOD

The With-God Life

The Bible is all about human life "with God" and how God has made this "with-God" life possible and will bring it to pass. The name Immanuel, meaning "God is with us," is the title given to the one and only Redeemer, Jesus the Christ. It refers to God's everlasting intent for human life—namely, that we should be in every aspect a dwelling place of God.

From Genesis to Revelation we see how God has been with us in a variety of ways. God created us and wants to be with us in relationship. Throughout the Old Testament we see God being with the chosen people as individuals and as a family, through the judges, through the monarchy, through the words of the prophets, even through exile. Then, just in case there was any lingering doubt about how much God wants to be in relationship with us, we have the coming of Jesus Christ, the Immanuel, literally "God with us." God is with us through the physical presence of Jesus and then, after Jesus' death and resurrection, through the Holy Spirit and the Church.

As we move through these passages, we catch a small glimpse of how much God loves us, as evidenced by God's divine compassion, mercy, tenderness, loving care, and blessings given to the chosen people and, yes, also by the discipline given us when we rebel, disobey, and turn away from what is good. What response can we have but to seek God, to do as much as possible to be in relationship with our Father, who loves us so much?

And remember, I am with you always, to the end of the age.
—Matthew 28:20b

The With-God Life

Looking for God

Then God said, "Let us make humankind in our image, according to our likeness; and let them have dominion over the fish of the sea, and over the birds of the air, and over the cattle, and over all the wild animals of the earth, and over every creeping thing that creeps upon the earth." / So God created humankind in his image, / in the image of God he created them; / male and female he created them.

God blessed them, and God said to them, "Be fruitful and multiply, and fill the earth and subdue it; and have dominion over the fish of the sea and over the birds of the air and over every living thing that moves upon the earth." God saw everything that he had made, and indeed, it was very good.

Genesis 1:26–28, 31a

WITHIN THIS VAST creation God wants human company and conversation partners. Humans, both male and female, resemble the Creator and were created to share a unique relationship with God. Human beings are spoken to directly by the Creator, given capacities to be stewards of creation, and entrusted as caretakers of God's goodness. Upon the completion of all that God has created, culminating in his relationship with us human creatures, the order is proclaimed "very good."

God is still with us, just as on the day human beings were created. For the next thirteen days, as you read through the selections and ponder the different ways God has been with various individuals and groups of people, look within your own daily life for God's presence. Each day as you are able, perhaps once at midday and once at night, ask yourself, "Where did I see God?" or "Where did I meet God?" Your answer may be in a friend or a person you met, in a Scripture passage or something else you were reading, in a feeling of calm or peace, in a flower or tree or other aspect of nature. Challenge yourself to look for God in new places. For example, if you most often see God in the actions, words, or smile of another person, try looking for God in nature or in a time of solitude.

Spiritual Practice

Sin Enters the Picture

They heard the sound of the LORD God walking in the garden at the time of the evening breeze, and the man and his wife hid themselves from the presence of the LORD God among the trees of the garden. But the LORD God called to the man, and said to him, "Where are you?" He said, "I heard the sound of you in the garden, and I was afraid, because I was naked; and I hid myself." He said, "Who told you that you were naked? Have you eaten from the tree of which I commanded you not to eat?" The man said, "The woman whom you gave to be with me, she gave me fruit from the tree, and I ate." Then the LORD God said to the woman, "What is this that you have done?" The woman said, "The serpent tricked me, and I ate."

Genesis 3:8–13

WE ARE CREATED with the freedom to resist the will of God, and the resulting human sin leads rapidly to cover-up, embarrassment, fear, guilt, blame, and confrontation with the Creator. The man blames the woman, the woman blames the serpent, and God curses the serpent, but God never abandons the relationship with humankind. Indeed, as a gesture of reconciliation God himself fashions more appropriate clothing "of skins" (3:21). Despite their disobedience, man and woman never cease to be conversation partners with God. Although they are given a new vocation to till the land beyond the garden (3:23), they are never fully expelled from the presence of God. Even when sin removes us from close proximity with God, God is ever in pursuit of renewed relationship with us.

As you reflect on how you saw God today, think also about any times you felt especially separated from God. Was sin involved in your separation? If so, ask God for forgiveness.

God Makes a Covenant with Abram

Now the LORD said to Abram, "Go from your country and your kindred and your father's house to the land that I will show you. I will make of you a great nation, and I will bless you, and make your name great, so that you will be a blessing. I will bless those who bless you, and the one who curses you I will curse; and in you all the families of the earth shall be blessed."

Genesis 12:1–3

AS IN THE beginning of creation, God's powerful word creates something new. Against a backdrop of (Sarah's) barrenness (11:30), by dramatic summons, hope for the future is born by God's speaking. God calls Abram into relationship, and life with God begins anew. The promise that follows assures Abram that when God gives such a radical command, he journeys forth not alone, but with God, who is leading him. The blessing includes what we still seek: a place to live and thrive, the security of community, prosperity, and prominence. The text reminds us that these are not acquired by our own doing, but are gifts from God—divine grace, divine blessing.

As you seek God's presence today, reflect on the covenant God made with Abram. How has God blessed your family?

Father God, so often I prefer to dwell on everything in my life that I would like to change rather than thanking you for all of the blessings you have given me and my family. Thank you, Lord, for the tremendous gifts you have given each and every one of us, and especially for the greatest gift of all—that you journey through life with us. In your name I pray. Amen.

The Lord Will Fight for You

As Pharaoh drew near, the Israelites looked back, and there were the Egyptians advancing on them. In great fear the Israelites cried out to the LORD. They said to Moses, "Was it because there were no graves in Egypt that you have taken us away to die in the wilderness? What have you done to us, bringing us out of Egypt?" But Moses said to the people, "Do not be afraid, stand firm, and see the deliverance that the LORD will accomplish for you today; for the Egyptians whom you see today you shall never see again. The LORD will fight for you, and you have only to keep still."

Then Moses stretched out his hand over the sea. The LORD drove the sea back by a strong east wind all night, and turned the sea into dry land; and the waters were divided.

Exodus 14:10–11, 13–14, 21

OUR CHOICE IS either to trust our plans with all our heart or trust our God. Not only do the best-laid plans fall to pieces, but often enough God prompts us to act without any plans in place and with no guarantee that everything will come together as it should. No one knew what God was going to do to rescue the Hebrews from pursuit by the Egyptians. They could only trust that he was going to do something. Suppose they had insisted that, before they left Egypt, scouts sent in advance report back that the route was clear, the Red Sea parted and waiting? They would have remained slaves. The water was only parted once they had acted in faith and followed God. They could not count on any plans, because God gave them none. He only gave them himself. God was the plan.

As you look for God today, reflect on when in your life you have been able to trust in God wholly when things fell apart. If you cannot think of a time, how do you think you might come closer to allowing yourself to step back and let God fight for you?

Do Not Fear

Do not fear, for I am with you, / do not be afraid, for I am your
God; / I will strengthen you, I will help you, / I will uphold you
with my victorious right hand. / But now thus says the Lord, / he
who created you, O Jacob, / he who formed you, O Israel: / Do not
fear, for I have redeemed you; / I have called you by name, you are
mine. / When you pass through the waters, I will be with you; / and
through the rivers, they shall not overwhelm you; / when you walk
through fire you shall not be burned, / and the flame shall not consume you. / For I am the Lord your God, / the Holy One of Israel,
your Savior. / I give Egypt as your ransom, / Ethiopia and Seba in
exchange for you. / Because you are precious in my sight, / and honored, and I love you, / I give people in return for you, / nations in
exchange for your life. / Do not fear, for I am with you; / I will bring
your offspring from the east, / and from the west I will gather you.

Isaiah 41:10; 43:1–5

THESE PHRASES ARE characteristic announcements of divine presence.
The recurring promise of God's presence is the most fundamental assurance given in gospel faith. God *is* with us: ours is a with-God life.
The announcement itself radically transforms situations by inspiring
an awareness of God's presence. In the Gospel presentation of Jesus'
life, the same "Do not be afraid" is used at key points. The birth and the
resurrection of Jesus are decisive events in the history of the world that
evoke from God the transformative announcement of his presence (see
Luke 2:10; Matt 28:5).

Too often we forget that we are precious in God's sight, honored, and
loved. Read these words again. See what they do for your sense of security in God's love.

Learning from Jesus

And the Word became flesh and lived among us, and we have seen his glory, the glory as of a father's only son, full of grace and truth. From his fullness we have all received, grace upon grace. The law indeed was given through Moses; grace and truth came through Jesus Christ. No one has ever seen God. It is God the only Son, who is close to the Father's heart, who has made him known.

John 1:14, 16–18

Spiritual Practice

GLORIOUS MYSTERY: THAT God should become human! Imagine if a shoemaker would become a shoe! The Greek word translated "lived" literally says "pitched his tent" or "tabernacled," which invites us to ponder all the biblical passages about God's glory descending upon the Israelites' tabernacle in the wilderness to signify his presence among them. Compare Revelation 21:3, which extends the hope that someday we will know God again as intimately, face-to-face, as the disciples did being with Jesus. How can we learn to live that hope more deeply now?

The theme that the Son makes the Father fully known is fleshed out throughout John and the rest of the New Testament. As you read the passages that follow over the next eleven days, ask yourself what we learn about God from what Jesus does and says, from how he treats people, and from the words and actions of the members of the early Church, the Body of Christ. How do these insights change the way you respond to situations in your own life?

~ *Learning from Jesus*

The Birth of Jesus

Now the birth of Jesus the Messiah took place in this way. When his mother Mary had been engaged to Joseph but before they lived together, she was found to be with child from the Holy Spirit. Her husband Joseph, being a righteous man and unwilling to expose her to public disgrace, planned to dismiss her quietly. But just when he had resolved to do this, an angel of the Lord appeared to him in a dream and said, "Joseph, son of David, do not be afraid to take Mary as your wife, for the child conceived in her is from the Holy Spirit. She will bear a son, and you are to name him Jesus, for he will save the people from their sins." All this took place to fulfill what had been spoken by the Lord through the prophet:

"Look, the virgin shall conceive and bear a son,
and they shall name him Immanuel,"

which means, "God is with us." When Joseph awoke from sleep, he did as the angel of the Lord commanded him; he took her as his wife, but had no marital relations with her until she had borne a son; and he named him Jesus.

Matthew 1:18–25

GOD'S COMING IN the person of Jesus Christ, from the babe and the carpenter to the cross and the resurrection, was totally unexpected and incomprehensible to human ways of thinking. In human history and in individual lives, God is always entering at unexpected times and in unexpected ways. Not only is Jesus born by means of virginal conception, but the Messiah will bear a divine throne name—Immanuel, meaning "God is with us." God is personally present with his people in and through Jesus—Wisdom in the flesh.

How has the reality that God took on human flesh and lived among us changed your life?

I Am the True Vine

"I am the true vine, and my Father is the vinegrower. He removes every branch in me that bears no fruit. Every branch that bears fruit he prunes to make it bear more fruit. You have already been cleansed by the word that I have spoken to you. Abide in me as I abide in you. Just as the branch cannot bear fruit by itself unless it abides in the vine, neither can you unless you abide in me. I am the vine, you are the branches. Those who abide in me and I in them bear much fruit, because apart from me you can do nothing."

John 15:1–5

JESUS' METAPHOR OF vine and branches reminds us that our spiritual life is entirely dependent upon God's grace. This metaphor is one of seven "I am" metaphors for Christ in the book of John. Jesus says, "I am the bread of life" (6:35, 48), "the light of the world" (8:12; 9:5), "the gate" (10:7, 9), "the good shepherd" (10:11, 14), "the resurrection and the life" (11:25), "the way, the truth, and the life" (14:6), and "the vine" (15:1, 5).

John reveals several divisions of the people over who Jesus is. The same is still true today. Some want to make him simply a good man, model, teacher, prophet, or preacher. But the "I am" statements continually force us to ask, "Is Jesus who he says he is?" Is he the Bread of *my* life? Do I live by *his* Light? Do I enter through him as the Gate to salvation, or do I keep trying to rescue myself? Do I trust him to Shepherd me? Do I depend on him as the Resurrection, or do I keep trying to lift myself up? Do I let him be the Way for me or do I keep asking for directions? Is he the Truth by which I judge all other lesser truths? Is he my Life, or do I employ entertainments to bring me life? Do I abide in him, cling to him as a branch to a Vine, and draw all my spiritual nourishment from him?

Pick one or more of the above statements and spend several minutes meditating on it during your prayer time. What do Jesus' "I am" statements reveal to you about God?

May They Also Be in Us

"I ask not only on behalf of these, but also on behalf of those who will believe in me through their word, that they may all be one. As you, Father, are in me and I am in you, may they also be in us, so that the world may believe that you have sent me. The glory that you have given me I have given them, so that they may be one, as we are one, I in them and you in me, that they may become completely one, so that the world may know that you have sent me and have loved them even as you have loved me. Father, I desire that those also, whom you have given me, may be with me where I am, to see my glory, which you have given me because you loved me before the foundation of the world."

John 17:20–24

THROUGHOUT JOHN 17 and especially when Jesus prays for us, we join the beloved disciple in eavesdropping on the conversation of the Trinity. John's Gospel is crucial for reminding us how integrally connected the Persons of the Trinity are and how thoroughly involved the entire Tri-unity is in all dimensions of our creation, redemption, and sanctification. The Trinity is not simply an abstract doctrine made up by the Church. It is the way God is and works. The triune fellowship of God invites our participation; we are embraced in the co-inherence of the three Persons of the Godhead. By the intercession and redeeming work of Jesus and by the Advocate's witness, we can know the Father.

> *Eternal Trinity, you are a deep sea,*
> *into which the more I enter the more I find,*
> *and the more I find the more I seek.*
> *The soul ever hungers in your abyss, Eternal Trinity,*
> *longing to see you with the light of your light,*
> *and as the deer yearns for the springs of water,*
> *so my soul yearns to see you in truth.*

—St. Catherine of Siena

I Am with You Always

Now the eleven disciples went to Galilee, to the mountain to which Jesus had directed them. When they saw him, they worshiped him; but some doubted. And Jesus came and said to them, "All authority in heaven and on earth has been given to me. Go therefore and make disciples of all nations, baptizing them in the name of the Father and of the Son and of the Holy Spirit, and teaching them to obey everything that I have commanded you. And remember, I am with you always, to the end of the age."

Matthew 28:16–20

AFTER JESUS' RESURRECTION he appears to the women at the tomb and tells them to tell the disciples to go to Galilee, where they will see him. The Eleven do go to Galilee, and Jesus appears as promised. Jesus says he has been given all authority, and then he authorizes his disciples to make disciples of all nations, which is said to involve baptizing in the trinitarian name and teaching converts to obey all that Jesus commanded. But Jesus does far more than just authorize and empower his "learners." He promises to be with them (Immanuel) as the divine power, presence, and Wisdom of God until the close of the age. Never again will they be bereft of him. Thus, the Gospel closes with a presentation of Jesus as God's Wisdom, his wise presence, who dwells within the People of God and guards and guides them. As God's people we are called to live and call others to live according to the counterorder wisdom of Jesus the sage. The Gospel for learners is also the Gospel for teachers. Ultimately, there is only one teacher, one sage, one Wisdom—Jesus himself.

Why did Jesus tell the disciples that he would be with them to the end of the age? In what ways is Jesus Christ with us now? Consider how Jesus is present with you today and how his presence impacts your understanding of the with-God life.

Testifying About Jesus

Then Peter began to speak to them: "I truly understand that God shows no partiality, but in every nation anyone who fears him and does what is right is acceptable to him. You know the message he sent to the people of Israel, preaching peace by Jesus Christ—he is Lord of all. That message spread throughout Judea, beginning in Galilee after the baptism that John announced: how God anointed Jesus of Nazareth with the Holy Spirit and with power; how he went about doing good and healing all who were oppressed by the devil, for God was with him. We are witnesses to all that he did both in Judea and in Jerusalem. They put him to death by hanging him on a tree; but God raised him on the third day and allowed him to appear, not to all the people but to us who were chosen by God as witnesses, and who ate and drank with him after he rose from the dead. He commanded us to preach to the people and to testify that he is the one ordained by God as judge of the living and the dead. All the prophets testify about him that everyone who believes in him receives forgiveness of sins through his name."

Acts 10:34–43

THE CENTRAL THEME of the book of Acts is the forward thrust of God's activity in history. Here, in more profound depth and detail than in any other book in the New Testament, Luke offers a historical interpretation of our life with God. It is here that we see God's aim of forming an all-inclusive community of loving persons with God himself at its very center. With the advent of this new order, the Church is established. Those gifted in evangelism are sent out to spread the good news of the kingdom of God into new regions and to establish new fellowship. In the process of declaring God's love to all humanity, the Church becomes a blessing without equal.

How has the Church been a blessing in helping you understand life with God? What might be done to help the Church be a blessing to the world?

You Will Live

If the Spirit of him who raised Jesus from the dead dwells in you, he who raised Christ from the dead will give life to your mortal bodies also through his Spirit that dwells in you. So then, brothers and sisters, we are debtors, not to the flesh, to live according to the flesh—for if you live according to the flesh, you will die; but if by the Spirit you put to death the deeds of the body, you will live. For all who are led by the Spirit of God are children of God.

Romans 8:11–14

RESURRECTION IS THE biggest thing about Jesus. It is also the biggest thing about us. The very same Spirit who raised Jesus from the tomb raises us from a dead life. Paul works every variation he can come up with to get us to understand, and to get it deep into our imaginations, that the same resurrection miracle that brought Jesus alive brings us alive. Resurrection is the most unnoticed and underappreciated miracle that takes place in our common lives. But, of course, that's the way it also was with Jesus, hardly noticed at the time, and certainly by nobody in authority or of "importance."

Take this prayer with you into your day as you reflect on the miracle of Jesus' resurrection:

Lord Jesus Christ, you said that you are
the Way, the Truth, and the Life;
let us never stray from you, who are the Way;
nor distrust you, who are the Truth;
nor rest in any other but you, who are the Life,
beyond whom there is nothing to be desired,
either in heaven or on earth.
We ask it for your name's sake.

—Erasmus

⟿ Learning from Jesus

Power Made Perfect in Weakness

A thorn was given me in the flesh, a messenger of Satan to torment me,
to keep me from being too elated. Three times I appealed to the Lord
about this, that it would leave me, but he said to me, "My grace is suf-
ficient for you, for power is made perfect in weakness." So, I will boast
all the more gladly of my weaknesses, so that the power of Christ may
dwell in me. Therefore I am content with weaknesses, insults, hardships, persecutions, and calamities for the sake of Christ; for whenever
I am weak, then I am strong.

2 Corinthians 12:7b–10

PAUL IS SO consistently counterintuitive! His insistence on the inver-
sion of power and weakness is central to his teaching. Human glory is
revealed in what the world misconstrues as weakness, such as failing to
take advantage of one's opponents or standing aside so that one's own
will does not impede true obedience to God. Paul is especially proud
that the "thorn in the flesh" has not deterred his ministry, which has
thrived in spite of it. Overcoming adversity enables one to glorify God
all the more. The Christian life is one of strength and endurance in
the face of suffering. We learn by the power of the Holy Spirit to walk
cheerfully on the earth. And when we do, God strengthens our resolve
and empowers us to engage life without compromise. In so doing, we
participate in God's plan for transforming the world and ourselves.

Teach us, Lord,
to serve you as you deserve,
to give and not to count the cost,
to fight and not to heed the wounds,
to toil and not to seek for rest,
to labor and not to seek for any reward,
save that of knowing that we do your will.

—St. Ignatius of Loyola

The Gifts God Gives

The gifts [God] gave were that some would be apostles, some prophets, some evangelists, some pastors and teachers, to equip the saints for the work of ministry, for building up the body of Christ, until all of us come to the unity of the faith and of the knowledge of the Son of God, to maturity, to the measure of the full stature of Christ.

Ephesians 4:11–13

THIS IS ONE of several lists of spiritual gifts found in the Letters. The colossal gift of the risen Christ is the equipping of the saints for the work of ministry. Christians show themselves to be who they are when they do "the work of ministry." We do not need to cast about for a purpose in life. It is given to us as a gift!

All of us have certain strengths in the spiritual life and also areas where we are less strong. Our spiritual strengths are God-given and are something we should recognize and celebrate. We do not have to shoehorn ourselves into a ministry role for which we are not meant. Our strengths combine with those of our brothers and sisters to form the whole Body of Christ, the Church. Yet that doesn't mean we should neglect any areas of spiritual weakness. Those of us who find study difficult do not have to become teachers, but neither should we give up on study. As professor and author Dallas Willard writes, "The disciplines we need to practice are precisely the ones we are not good at."[1] Take a look at the disciplines listed in the table of contents in this book. Which do you think are strengths of yours? And which do you think are areas in which you need a little more work? Jot down your thoughts, and as you work through the book, consider giving some special attention to those sections about the disciplines you feel less comfortable with.

Be Strong in the Lord

Finally, be strong in the Lord and in the strength of his power. Put on the whole armor of God, so that you may be able to stand against the wiles of the devil. For our struggle is not against enemies of blood and flesh, but against the rulers, against the authorities, against the cosmic powers of this present darkness, against the spiritual forces of evil in the heavenly places. Therefore take up the whole armor of God, so that you may be able to withstand on that evil day, and having done everything, to stand firm. Stand therefore, and fasten the belt of truth around your waist, and put on the breastplate of righteousness. As shoes for your feet put on whatever will make you ready to proclaim the gospel of peace. With all of these, take the shield of faith, with which you will be able to quench all the flaming arrows of the evil one. Take the helmet of salvation, and the sword of the Spirit, which is the word of God.

Ephesians 6:10–17

THE SPIRITUAL LIFE begins, is sustained, and ends by the power of God. This passage signifies two very important dynamics of the spiritual life: the malevolent intent of our adversary and the necessity of a radical rearrangement of the world's settled order. There is a greater power afoot in the universe than Rome with its military prowess—the truth, righteousness, peace, faith, salvation, and word of God!

> *Christ be with me, Christ within me,*
> *Christ behind me, Christ before me,*
> *Christ beside me, Christ to win me,*
> *Christ to comfort and restore me.*
> *Christ beneath me, Christ above me,*
> *Christ in quiet, Christ in danger,*
> *Christ in hearts of all that love me,*
> *Christ in mouth of friend and stranger.*

—From the breastplate of St. Patrick

Christ: Lord and Reconciler

[Christ] is the image of the invisible God, the firstborn of all creation; for in him all things in heaven and on earth were created, things visible and invisible, whether thrones or dominions or rulers or powers—all things have been created through him and for him. He himself is before all things, and in him all things hold together. He is the head of the body, the church; he is the beginning, the firstborn from the dead, so that he might come to have first place in everything. For in him all the fullness of God was pleased to dwell, and through him God was pleased to reconcile to himself all things, whether on earth or in heaven, by making peace through the blood of his cross.

And you who were once estranged and hostile in mind, doing evil deeds, he has now reconciled in his fleshly body through death, so as to present you holy and blameless and irreproachable before him—provided that you continue securely established and steadfast in the faith, without shifting from the hope promised by the gospel that you heard, which has been proclaimed to every creature under heaven.

Colossians 1:15–23a

CHRIST IS LORD over all creation and the reconciler between God and his creation. Our lives are built upon this truth, shaped in every way by it, so that now through Christ's reconciliation we may be given back to God as persons who are now blameless, holy, and irreproachable. Once we were hostile toward God and acting wrongly. Now, through Christ's death, we are a new people, acting rightly. Thus, we are to remain steadfast in this new reality and not shift from the hope that it promises.

Thanks be to thee, my Lord Jesus Christ, for all the benefits thou hast won for me, for all the pain and insults thou hast borne for me. O most merciful Redeemer, Friend and Brother, may I know thee more clearly, love thee more dearly, and follow thee more nearly, day by day.

—St. Richard of Chichester

~ *Learning from Jesus*

The Lord God Will Be Our Light

Then the angel showed me the river of the water of life, bright as crystal, flowing from the throne of God and of the Lamb through the middle of the street of the city. On either side of the street is the tree of life with its twelve kinds of fruit, producing its fruit each month; and the leaves of the tree are for the healing of the nations. Nothing accursed will be found there any more. But the throne of God and of the Lamb will be in it, and his servants will worship him; they will see his face, and his name will be on their foreheads. And there will be no more night; they need no light of lamp or sun, for the Lord God will be their light, and they will reign forever and ever.

Revelation 22:1–5

WE HAVE COME full circle. God walked with Adam and Eve in the garden; now the creation of an all-inclusive community of loving persons with God himself at the very center as its prime Sustainer and most glorious inhabitant is completed.

Father God, as I reflect on all the ways you have been with your people throughout the Bible, in history, and in my own life, I find myself so grateful for your constant presence—your guidance, companionship, and love. I know that so often I overlook, ignore, or misunderstand your presence and work in the world, so I eagerly anticipate those days in eternity in which I will see not through a glass darkly, but clearly, face to face, where I will live in this glorious community of which you are the center. Thank you once again for creating me, for wishing to be in relationship with me. Teach me to honor you by recognizing and treating all people as your glorious creations. In your name I pray. Amen.

For more verses on the with-God life and ideas on how to practice the with-God life, see the Responding exercises and Spiritual Disciplines Index in *The Life with God Bible*.

Prayer

Interactive conversation with God about what we and God are thinking and doing together

Prayer is how we come to God and participate in our growing love relationship with him. The mid-twentieth-century minister and writer George Buttrick refers to prayer as "friendship with God." Author Richard Foster tells us in *Prayer: Finding the Heart's True Home* that prayer is the key to the heart of God, the one place we truly belong. Yet for many of us, prayer is a constant source of guilt or confusion. We fear we don't pray enough or we don't pray the right way. For some of us prayer might feel more like a punishment or an onerous task than a friendship. But the example of those in the Bible, especially Jesus, makes it clear: we are to talk to God often, in solitude when possible.

Foster offers some encouragement as we set about talking with God: we should not panic about doing it right, having pure motives, or asking for the right things. As Foster writes, "We will never have pure enough motives, or be good enough, or know enough in order to pray rightly. We simply must set all these things aside and begin praying. In fact, it is in the very act of prayer itself—the intimate, ongoing interaction with God—that these matters are cared for in due time."[1]

One thing is certain. If we set forward on this journey of prayer, we will change and so will the world around us. God uses prayer as the primary way to transform us, to make us more like Christ. When we pray we find our thoughts and our will becoming more and more like God's. And we are better able to pray for the right things, to join God in his kingdom work in the world.

We do not know how to pray as we ought, but that very Spirit intercedes with sighs too deep for words.

—*Romans 8:26*

Prayer

Simple Prayer

Rejoice always, pray without ceasing, give thanks in all circumstances;
for this is the will of God in Christ Jesus for you.

1 Thessalonians 5:16–18

WHAT DOES IT really mean to pray without ceasing? Is it even possible? A good starting place is what Richard Foster calls "simple prayer."
Simple prayer is bringing ourselves and all of our needs and circumstances to God in prayer, even if our concerns feel petty and selfish and
ordinary. It means telling God how frustrated we are when we cannot
find a parking space or when our co-worker interrupts us yet again in
a meeting. It means sharing our joys and small pleasures with God in
thanks. We just share all, the good and the bad. When we look at the
pages of the Bible, we see that this is the way most of the people in it
pray. They complain and celebrate, gloat and weep.

For the next ten days, try to engage in simple prayer, sharing with
God all the events in your life and your feelings about them—your
hopes, desires, frustrations, and anger. Do this at least once a day. Do
not try to present yourself as better or more holy than you feel you are;
do not worry that you are being too self-centered or that you are sharing with God what you know to be sin. Just share. The following prayer
is a good place to start and perhaps to return to periodically during the
next few days:

I am, O God, a jumbled mass of motives.

*One moment I am adoring you, and the next I am shaking my fist at
you.*

I vacillate between mounting hope, and deepening despair.

I am full of faith, and full of doubt.

I want the best for others, and am jealous when they get it.

*Even so, God, I will not run from your presence. Nor will I pretend to
be what I am not. Thank you for accepting me with all my contradictions.
Amen.*

—Richard J. Foster, *Prayers from the Heart*[2]

Spiritual Practice

How to Pray

[Jesus] was praying in a certain place, and after he had finished, one of his disciples said to him, "Lord, teach us to pray, as John taught his disciples." He said to him, "When you pray, say:
Father, hallowed be your name.
Your kingdom come.
Give us each day our daily bread.
And forgive us our sins,
for we ourselves forgive everyone indebted to us.
And do not bring us to the time of trial."

Luke 11:1–4

THE PATTERN FOR prayer that Jesus gives his disciples is short on our wants and big on God's wants. Half of what Jesus tells us to do in prayer is to worship God, keep him holy, and ask that his kingdom and his will take shape, not ours. God the Father looms large. It is important for us to recognize the source of our spiritual and physical sustenance and to ground our days in asking for and receiving forgiveness as well as calling for freedom from evil and all that pulls us toward wrong. It is a very bare-bones sort of prayer compared to many of the ways we pray today. There is nothing here about material wealth or perfect health or things that get me more of me. Instead, it is about there being more of God.

As you try your simple prayer today, begin and end your prayer time with the Lord's Prayer. How does it feel different from your personal, simple prayer?

"The Our Father contains all possible petitions; we cannot conceive of any prayer not already contained in it. It is to prayer what Christ is to humanity. It is impossible to say it once through, giving the fullest possible attention to each word, without a change, infinitesimal perhaps but real, taking place in the soul."

—Simone Weil, "Concerning the Our Father"[3]

~ *Simple Prayer*

Making Prayer a Habit

Soon Daniel distinguished himself above all the other presidents and satraps because an excellent spirit was in him, and the king planned to appoint him over the whole kingdom. So the presidents and the satraps tried to find grounds for complaint against Daniel in connection with the kingdom. But they could find no grounds for complaint or any corruption, because he was faithful, and no negligence or corruption could be found in him. The men said, "We shall not find any ground for complaint against this Daniel unless we find it in connection with the law of his God."

So the presidents and the satraps conspired and came to the king and said to him, "The king should establish an ordinance and enforce an interdict, that whoever prays to anyone, divine or human, for forty days, except to you, O king, shall be thrown into a den of lions." Therefore King Darius signed the document and interdict.

Although Daniel knew that the document had been signed, he continued to go to his house, which had windows in its upper room open toward Jerusalem, and to get down on his knees three times a day to pray to his God and praise him, just as he had previously. The conspirators came and found Daniel praying and seeking mercy before his God.

Daniel 6:3–6a, 7b, 9–11

DANIEL'S ENEMIES ATTACK him precisely at the point of his reliability—his prayer practice. Daniel's prayer life is exemplified in a few brief phrases. It is private (in his house), yet public (with windows open). He prays several times a day. Though in exile and under watch, he continues to praise God. Most important, Daniel is steadfast in prayer, doing "as he had done previously."

Consider praying a simple prayer on your knees three times today at predetermined times. What do you learn from planning your prayer times in this way? How does it differ from more spontaneous prayer?

All Times, All Prayer

Pray in the Spirit at all times in every prayer and supplication. To that end keep alert and always persevere in supplication for all the saints.

Ephesians 6:18

To THRIVE IN the land of spiritual formation we must grow deep in the soil of prayer. The expansive life of prayer is underscored by the fourfold repetition of "all" in the Greek of this verse—"all times," "all prayer," "all perseverance," and "all the saints." This kind of expansiveness far surpasses the inclinations of any individual believer's heart and points to a Word-centered, communally framed prayer life.

What does it mean to you to "pray in the Spirit"? Today as you are offering your simple prayer, make a special effort to pray in the Spirit, to let the Spirit guide your prayer rather than your individual needs and wants. What did you learn about the Spirit? About yourself? If you find yourself discouraged or needing more encouragement to pray, spend a few minutes reflecting on this quote:

"Praying with frequency gives us the readiness to pray again as needed from moment to moment. The more we pray, the more we think to pray, and as we see the results of prayer—the responses of our Father to our requests—our confidence in God's power spills over into other areas of our life."

—Dallas Willard, *The Spirit of the Disciplines*[4]

~ *Simple Prayer*

Praying in the Spirit

We know that the whole creation has been groaning in labor pains until now; and not only the creation, but we ourselves, who have the first fruits of the Spirit, groan inwardly while we wait for adoption, the redemption of our bodies. For in hope we were saved. Now hope that is seen is not hope. For who hopes for what is seen? But if we hope for what we do not see, we wait for it with patience.

Likewise the Spirit helps us in our weakness; for we do not know how to pray as we ought, but that very Spirit intercedes with sighs too deep for words. And God, who searches the heart, knows what is the mind of the Spirit, because the Spirit intercedes for the saints according to the will of God.

Romans 8:22–27

WHEN WE PRAY, we are never "on our own." The Spirit at all times is praying in and for us. The primary energy and influence in our spiritual formation is not our will or knowledge, not our determination or stamina, but the ever-present and active Spirit. Prayer involves far more than God's listening to us; the greater part of prayer, as in so much else, is the active intercessory Presence of the Spirit of God in our lives.

Reflect on this prayer for a few minutes and how it corresponds to your own experience so far of simple prayer and trying to "pray in the Spirit."

You have made me so rich, oh God, please let me share out Your beauty with open hands. My life has become an uninterrupted dialogue with You, oh God, one great dialogue. Sometimes when I stand in some corner of the camp, my feet planted on Your earth, my eyes raised toward Your Heaven, tears sometimes run down my face, tears of deep emotion and gratitude. At night, too, when I lie in bed and rest in You, oh God, tears of gratitude run down my face, and that is my prayer.

—Etty Hillesum, "Prayer from Auschwitz"[5]

Taking All Our Needs to God

Hear, O our God, for we are despised; turn their taunt back on their own heads, and give them over as plunder in a land of captivity. Do not cover their guilt, and do not let their sin be blotted out from your sight; for they have hurled insults in the face of the builders.

Nehemiah 4:4–5

NEHEMIAH'S WORDS ABOUT those who mocked the wall he and his fellow Jews were building around Jerusalem sound harsh, but notice that the man of action did not trade taunts with his opponents. Nehemiah simply prayed. Nehemiah's prayers are simple and direct petitions, usually with heavy allusions to earlier writings of the Old Testament. Time and again, Nehemiah's actions are preceded by prayer. Prayer, for Nehemiah, was not merely an exercise in piety, but a means for the strengthening and reshaping of his own heart. Prayers such as this one sometimes appear rather crude and spiritually primitive, but they represent the honest feelings and thoughts of a man still growing in his relationship with God. It is reassuring to know that God listens to the prayers of his children even when they are marred by human weakness. Still, the prayer of Nehemiah may be questioned. Clearly, it was not a prayer of Jesus, who instructed all his disciples to love their enemies (Matt 5:44). But all authentic prayer is a scraping of the heart whereby the dregs of the soul are offered up to God. Nehemiah's prayer reveals his heart, which God welcomes even if God does not always approve of its sentiments.

As you continue with your simple prayer practice, ask yourself whether you are sharing your struggles and failures with God. Rest assured that God can handle your emotions that feel sinful as well as those that feel "good."

> *Help me, O Lord, to reveal to you the ugliness in my soul, for you already know it. Help me turn to you with my feelings of anger and frustration, for you always hear me. Thank you, Lord, for your patience with me. Amen.*

Lamenting to God

Do not be silent, O God of my praise. / For wicked and deceitful mouths are opened against me, / speaking against me with lying tongues. / They beset me with words of hate, / and attack me without cause. / In return for my love they accuse me, / even while I make prayer for them. / "When he is tried, let him be found guilty; / let his prayer be counted as sin. / May his days be few; / may another seize his position. / May his children be orphans, / and his wife a widow." / May that be the reward of my accusers from the LORD, / of those who speak evil against my life. / But you, O LORD my Lord, / act on my behalf for your name's sake; / because your steadfast love is good, deliver me.

Psalm 109:1–4, 7–9, 20–21

PUZZLED AND DISTRAUGHT, the psalmist catalogs the crimes of those who want to kill him. Appealing to God's steadfast love and care for the needy, the psalmist wants God to turn the evil back toward his oppressors. Lament psalms such as this one shout that evil is real, is awful, and is undercutting God's loving purposes for the world. It urges God to act to overturn it, to even things up. As is typical of the lament, the psalmist leaves justice in God's hands rather than acting vengefully on his own—a valuable word for us today. Psalms like this one may serve as a mirror for our own struggles with resentment, anger, and despair in our encounters with real evil and real enemies. After all, knowing we should love and pray for our enemies is different from doing it. We may also use these songs to ponder how God's love mysteriously satisfies God's justice without the mathematics of payback and how that love will ultimately prevail to mend the world and bring God's purposes to full fruit.

But all shall be well, and all shall be well, and all manner of things shall be well.

—Julian of Norwich

Returning to God

For surely I know the plans I have for you, says the LORD, plans for your welfare and not for harm, to give you a future with hope. Then when you call upon me and come and pray to me, I will hear you. When you search for me, you will find me; if you seek me with all your heart, I will let you find me, says the LORD, and I will restore your fortunes and gather you from all the nations and all the places where I have driven you, says the LORD, and I will bring you back to the place from which I sent you into exile.

Jeremiah 29:11–14

WE DO NOT know a great deal about the faith community of Jeremiah's time, but we do know that it was going through a tough, painful time. Cities were laid waste, national hopes were dashed, and the faith of the people was in crisis as they were carted off into Babylonian captivity. Yet in this passage Jeremiah assures the people that there is hope. God will hear and answer their prayers if they honestly take responsibility for their situation, repent—that is, *change*—and return to the love and service of the God who loved and created them. Jeremiah provides us with a wonderful invitation to a passionate, honest relationship with the God who has called our faith community to be a community not only of love and hope, but also of truth.

Sometimes as we come to God in prayer, we find ourselves overwhelmed by our own mistakes, our pettiness, and our lack of faith and hope. Today ask God for forgiveness for those times you have trusted in yourself rather than God and for the courage to keep returning.

Lord God, like exiled Israel, I also ignore you and seek false gods— those of money, of power, of prestige. It is hard to hear that I have created my own times of trouble, but what blessed comfort it is to know that your plans for me are good, that there is hope. Lord, help me to seek you in my daily life, even when the results are not immediately apparent. Amen.

Praying for Enemies

"But I say to you that listen, Love your enemies, do good to those who
hate you, bless those who curse you, pray for those who abuse you."

Luke 6:27–28

IT IS ONE thing to love a friend, a stranger, or the virtually anonymous
mass of humanity and another to love and forgive an enemy who hates
and hurts us. When Jesus tells us to love, bless, and pray for our enemies
and turn the other cheek, he's emphasizing he doesn't want us to be
people who thrive on aggression and retaliation, who return blow for
blow, curse for curse, grudge for grudge, eye for eye, tooth for tooth. He
wants us to break the cycle of hostility. Protecting a woman or man or
child who is being abused is one thing. But getting to the point of praying for the abusers, having mercy on them, visiting them in prison, or
bringing them a gift to express your love and forgiveness is something
else. This is where Jesus is telling us to go. This is loving an enemy. This is
turning the other cheek. This is Christianity. It is not an easy thing to do.
But following Christ has never been an easy thing to do.

Spend a few minutes thinking about this quote, then name one person
who has abused you and ask Jesus to give you his forgiveness for that
person.

"Whose name should come first [in prayer]? Perhaps the name of
our enemies. The injunction of Jesus is plain: 'Pray for them which de-
spitefully use you.' He told us that worship is vain if we are embittered;
that we should be wise to leave our gifts before the altar, go to make
peace with our neighbor, and then worship. Only then can we truly
worship. So the first intercession is, 'Bless So-and-so, whom I foolishly
regard as an enemy. Bless So-and-so whom I have wronged. Keep them
in Thy favor. Banish my bitterness.'"

—George Buttrick, "A Simple Regimen of Private Prayer"[6]

Out to the Mountain to Pray

Now during those days [Jesus] went out to the mountain to pray; and he spent the night in prayer to God. And when day came, he called his disciples and chose twelve of them, whom he also named apostles.

Luke 6:12–13

LUKE TAKES GREAT pains to make Christ's life of prayer an example to us. Other Gospel writers mention Jesus' calling of the twelve apostles, but they don't tell us Jesus prayed all night about it. They relate his challenge to the disciples, "Who do the crowds say that I am?" (9:18), but not that he was praying before he put the question. Only Luke takes care to point this out. This is also true when he introduces the Lord's Prayer. Matthew drops it into the Sermon on the Mount without preamble. But Luke characteristically brings out the omnipresence of Jesus' life of prayer beforehand: "[Jesus] was praying in a certain place, and after he had finished, one of his disciples said to him, 'Lord, teach us to pray . . .'" (11:1). Matthew and Mark mention Jesus at Gethsemane, but they do not give us the great prayer of forgiveness Jesus utters from the cross (23:34). As his disciples, we must seek to weave prayer as closely into the fabric of our lives as Jesus did.

After these days of practicing simple prayer, do you find that prayer is becoming more a part of your life? Would you say that you are starting to "become prayer"?

"The purpose of living is not to learn to make prayer, but to become prayer; to live in and for God according to the divine call, wholly surrendered to the Spirit's activity in the soul for the glory of God."

—Father Gilbert Shaw[7]

Asking God

Then Jesus told them a parable about their need to pray always and not to lose heart. He said, "In a certain city there was a judge who neither feared God nor had respect for people. In that city there was a widow who kept coming to him and saying, 'Grant me justice against my opponent.' For a while he refused; but later he said to himself, 'Though I have no fear of God and no respect for anyone, yet because this widow keeps bothering me, I will grant her justice, so that she may not wear me out by continually coming.'" And the Lord said, "Listen to what the unjust judge says. And will not God grant justice to his chosen ones who cry to him day and night? Will he delay long in helping them? I tell you, he will quickly grant justice to them."

Luke 18:1–8a

AN IMPORTANT PART of our prayer lives is asking God for things, often called petitionary prayer. God knows our hearts already, but asks us to bring our needs, both large and small, as part of our relationship. We are also to petition God on behalf of others. Yet, as author Agnes Sanford writes, "Many Christians are afraid to [come before God with specific requests.]... How strange it is that people who fear to do this do not hesitate to pray for the most difficult objectives of all, such as the peace of the world or the salvation of their souls!"[8]

If you have hesitated to bring specific requests before God, set aside time within the next ten days to ask God for some of your needs. Make a list and be as specific as possible. As Sanford advises, start small.

Or maybe you have repeatedly asked God for a specific thing, and your prayer seems unanswered. This can be hard to understand, for Jesus assures us, "Whatever you ask for in prayer, believe that you have received it, and it will be yours" (Mark 11:24). If you struggle with an unanswered petition, set aside time within the next ten days to talk with God about it. Ask God to show you whether this request is one for which you should continue praying or whether it should be set aside.

Spiritual Practice

Praying for Everyone

First of all, then, I urge that supplications, prayers, intercessions, and thanksgivings be made for everyone, for kings and all who are in high positions, so that we may lead a quiet and peaceable life in all godliness and dignity. This is right and is acceptable in the sight of God our Savior, who desires everyone to be saved and to come to the knowledge of the truth. For

there is one God;

there is also one mediator between God and humankind

Christ Jesus, himself human,

who gave himself as a ransom for all.

—this was attested at the right time. For this I was appointed a herald and an apostle (I am telling the truth, I am not lying), a teacher of the Gentiles in faith and truth.

I desire then, that in every place the men should pray, lifting up holy hands without anger or argument.

1 Timothy 2:1–8

PRAYER IS THE serious business of the Church, the first and best business it renders for the world. The community's prayers are not limited to the confines of the community, but stretch forth even to those who are not part of or who may even be in opposition to the community. We are to be the sort of people who can pray for our enemies.

As you think about your petitionary prayer, meditate for a few moments on this quote:

"Christ has no body now on earth but yours, no hands but yours, no feet but yours; yours are the eyes through which he looks with compassion on the world, yours are the feet with which he is to go about doing good, and yours are the hands with which he is to bless us now."

—St. Teresa of Avila

Our Eyes Are On You

Jehoshaphat stood in the assembly of Judah and Jerusalem, in the house of the LORD, before the new court, and said, "O LORD, God of our ancestors, are you not God in heaven? Do you not rule over all the kingdoms of the nations? In your hand are power and might, so that no one is able to withstand you. Did you not, O our God, drive out the inhabitants of this land before your people Israel, and give it forever to the descendants of your friend Abraham? They have lived in it, and in it have built you a sanctuary for your name, saying, 'If disaster comes upon us, the sword, judgment, or pestilence, or famine, we will stand before this house, and before you, for your name is in this house, and cry to you in our distress, and you will hear and save.' See now, the people of Ammon, Moab, and Mount Seir, whom you would not let Israel invade when they came from the land of Egypt, and whom they avoided and did not destroy—they reward us by coming to drive us out of your possession that you have given us to inherit. O our God, will you not execute judgment upon them? For we are powerless against this great multitude that is coming against us. We do not know what to do, but our eyes are on you."

2 Chronicles 20:5–12

JEHOSHAPHAT'S PRAYER, IN which he enumerates Yahweh's past help in the conquest of the land and the people's faithfulness in building the Temple before asking for God to intercede one more time, is one of the finest model petitionary prayers in all of Scripture for the formation of the People of God. Its conclusion strikes exactly the right posture: "We do not know what to do, but our eyes are on you."

Meditate on Jehoshaphat's prayer and the prayer below before you bring your petition before God today:

O Lord, never let us think that we can stand by ourselves, and not need you. Amen.

—John Donne

Praying Earnestly

[Hannah] was deeply distressed and prayed to the LORD, and wept bitterly. She made this vow: "O Lord of hosts, if only you will look on the misery of your servant, and remember me, and not forget your servant, but will give to your servant a male child, then I will set him before you as a nazirite until the day of his death. He shall drink neither wine nor intoxicants, and no razor shall touch his head."

As she continued praying before the LORD, Eli observed her mouth. Hannah was praying silently; only her lips moved, but her voice was not heard; therefore Eli thought she was drunk. So Eli said to her, "How long will you make a drunken spectacle of yourself? Put away your wine." But Hannah answered, "No, my lord, I am a woman deeply troubled; I have drunk neither wine nor strong drink, but I have been pouring out my soul before the LORD." Then Eli answered, "Go in peace; the God of Israel grant the petition you have made to him."

In due time Hannah conceived and bore a son. She named him Samuel, for she said, "I have asked him of the LORD."

1 Samuel 1:10–15, 17, 20

IN HER PRAYERS, Hannah loses all restraint, and her fervency leads an observer to imagine she is intoxicated. Such a model of prayer is in stark contrast to the ways in which many believers regularly approach God, with tentativeness and formality. The experience of worship, prayer, and the unburdening transaction that occurs in the making of her vow to the Lord leaves Hannah a new person.

Have you ever made a request like Hannah's? What was the result?

"It is important when we have a need to go to God in prayer. I know, whenever I have prayed earnestly, that I have been heard and have obtained more than I prayed for. God sometimes delays, but He always comes."

—Martin Luther, "What a Great Gift We Have in Prayer"[9]

— *Asking God*

Petitioning God

In those days Hezekiah became sick and was at the point of death. The prophet Isaiah son of Amoz came to him and said to him, "Thus says the LORD: Set your house in order, for you shall die; you shall not recover." Then Hezekiah turned his face to the wall, and prayed to the LORD: "Remember now, O LORD, I implore you, how I have walked before you in faithfulness with a whole heart, and have done what is good in your sight." And Hezekiah wept bitterly.

Then the word of the LORD came to Isaiah: "Go and say to Hezekiah, Thus says the LORD, the God of your ancestor David: I have heard your prayer, I have seen your tears; I will add fifteen years to your life. I will deliver you and this city out of the hand of the king of Assyria, and defend this city."

Isaiah 38:1–6

NOTE THE PASTORAL tone in which the sick king of honest faith prays passionately to God. He appeals to God on the basis of his faithfulness and obedience. The text confirms that God is the Lord of all healing in personal matters, even as Isaiah has attested that God is the Lord of the future in public political matters. The public and the personal are always kept together in Isaiah, as indeed they are in the person of Hezekiah, who is both a powerful king and a man of faith. His prayer attests that candid petition is an appropriate appeal to the God of all healings.

Would you call Hezekiah's prayer selfish because he prayed to prolong his life? What is the difference between a selfish prayer and a prayer that complies with God's way?

Dear Father God, I feel like I ask for so many things. But you bid me ask. And behind all my asking is the deeper longing for you, Lord. I do want you above all things. I can survive if you say No to the things, but please, Father, I must have you or I die. Amen.

—Richard J. Foster, *Prayers from the Heart*[10]

Complaining to God

You will be in the right, O LORD, / when I lay charges against you; / but let me put my case to you. / Why does the way of the guilty prosper? / Why do all who are treacherous survive? / You plant them, and they take root; / they grow and bring forth fruit; / you are near in their mouths / yet far from their hearts. / But you, O LORD, know me; / You see me and test me—my heart is with you. / Pull them out like sheep for the slaughter, / and set them apart for the day of slaughter. / How long will the land mourn, / and the grass of every field wither? / For the wickedness of those who live in it / the animals and the birds are swept away, / and because people said, "He is blind to our ways."

Jeremiah 12:1–4

HERE WE ARE given an extraordinary glimpse into the soul of the prophet Jeremiah. This passage is one of his personal laments, in which he complains about the ill treatment he has received because he dared to speak for God. A plot has been hatched against his life. Jeremiah preached to the people the word that he had been given, "yet they did not obey or incline their ear" (11:8). The prophet is depressed. So Jeremiah becomes a prosecuting attorney, building a case against God. It is important for contemporary servants of God to hear Jeremiah complain to God. God does not punish Jeremiah for his accusations. Rather, God receives the complaint, and the prophet and his God go on together. Anger, even anger directed against God, is not unthinkable in a prophet.

Jeremiah's question for God was why good things happen to bad people. Today, in addition to any other petitions you might have, take time to make a list of your most central God questions, your most troublesome gaps in understanding. Pray with your most pressing question at the forefront of your mind. Did you learn from the asking?

Negotiating with God

The LORD said, "Shall I hide from Abraham what I am about to do? No, for I have chosen him." Then the LORD said, "How great is the outcry against Sodom and Gomorrah and how very grave their sin!"

Then Abraham came near and said, "Will you indeed sweep away the righteous with the wicked? Suppose there are fifty righteous within the city; will you then sweep away the place and not forgive it for the fifty righteous who are in it? Far be it from you to do such a thing, to slay the righteous with the wicked, so that the righteous fare as the wicked! Far be that from you! Shall not the Judge of all the earth do what is just?" And the LORD said, "If I find at Sodom fifty righteous in the city, I will forgive the whole place for their sake." Then [Abraham] said, "Oh do not let the Lord be angry if I speak just once more. Suppose ten are found there." [The LORD] answered, "For the sake of ten I will not destroy it."

Genesis 18:17a, 19a, 20, 23–26, 32

IN THIS FASCINATING text God reflects theologically, behind Abraham's back, about the future of Sodom and Gomorrah. Abraham intervenes, and God is ultimately swayed by Abraham's intercession and influenced by his righteousness. Here Abraham takes God to the mat in intense negotiation, reminding us that the One who calls us into relationship is a conversation partner in word and deed.

"[Our prayer] objective must of course be in accordance with God's will. . . . A wise seeker after God had better study the laws of God and adapt his prayers to those laws. There is no great mystery concerning the will of God, in so far as it applies to our small selves. God's will is written into His nature, and the nature of God is love. Therefore, when we pray in accordance with the law of love, we are praying in accordance with the will of God."

—Agnes Sanford, *The Healing Light*[11]

Reconciling Ourselves to God's Will

They went to a place called Gethsemane; and [Jesus] said to his disciples, "Sit here while I pray." He took with him Peter and James and John, and began to be distressed and agitated. And he said to them, "I am deeply grieved, even to death; remain here, and keep awake." And going a little farther, he threw himself on the ground and prayed that, if it were possible, the hour might pass from him. He said, "Abba, Father, for you all things are possible; remove this cup from me; yet, not what I want, but what you want." He came and found them sleeping; and he said to Peter, "Simon, are you asleep? Could you not keep awake one hour? Keep awake and pray that you may not come into the time of trial; the spirit indeed is willing, but the flesh is weak." And again he went away and prayed, saying the same words.

Mark 14:32–39

IT IS CLEAR from this passage that Jesus shared our humanity and sympathizes with our weaknesses. Jesus knows what he should do, but he desperately hopes there is another way to do it. He is looking for a way out of the agony and darkness. Many consider his request an important affirmation of the humanness of the divine Son of God. But it is just as much an affirmation that our spirituality can express weakness and pain and fear and reluctance. Jesus ends his prayer by giving us a model for all our prayers: "Yet not what I want, but what you want." Jesus does not fall into our sin of expecting God to give us what we want, but is obedient to God even to the point of death (Heb 4:15). This prayer comes from a lifetime of spiritual formation.

> *Today, O Lord, I yield myself to you.*
> *May your will be my delight today.*
> *May your way have perfect sway in me.*
> *May your love be the pattern of my living.*
> —Richard J. Foster, *Prayers from the Heart*[12]

Prayer-Based Community

When they had entered the city, they went to the room upstairs where they were staying, Peter and John, and James, and Andrew, Philip and Thomas, Bartholomew and Matthew, James son of Alphaeus, and Simon the Zealot, and Judas son of James. All these were constantly devoting themselves to prayer, together with certain women, including Mary the mother of Jesus, as well as his brothers.

Acts 1:13–14

NOT LONG AFTER Jesus' ascension we find the disciples forming new communities of faith based on prayer and worship. Prayer is the center-piece of communal life. It is also the most prominent individual disci-pline. Repeatedly, we find Peter and John, then Barnabas, and eventually Paul waiting for God in prayer and then exploding into action as God's spirit propels them into the world. Vigorous petition, profound interces-sion, and pleas for guidance pour forth from the hearts of these early dis-ciples. And heaven answers: "When they had prayed, the place in which they were gathered together was shaken; and they were all filled with the Holy Spirit and spoke the word of God with boldness" (Acts 4:31).

What do you think it would feel like to be so connected to God that your petitions are his, that you have "become Word," as this quote calls it?

"Prayer is the superabundance of the heart. It is brim-full and run-ning over with love and praise, as once it was with Mary, when the Word took root in her body. So too, our heart breaks out into a Mag-nificat. Now the Word has achieved its 'glorious course' (2 Thess. 3:1): it has gone out from God and been sown in the good soil of the heart. Having now been *chewed over* and assimilated, it is regenerated in the heart, to the praise of God. It has taken root in us and is now bearing its fruit: we in our turn utter the Word and send it back to God. We have become Word; we are prayer."

—Andre Louf, *Teach Us to Pray* [13]

Prayers in Eternity

Then I saw between the throne and the four living creatures and among the elders a Lamb standing as if it had been slaughtered. He went and took the scroll from the right hand of the one who was seated on the throne. When he had taken the scroll, the four living creatures and the twenty-four elders fell before the Lamb, each holding a harp and golden bowls full of incense, which are the prayers of the saints.

Another angel with a golden censer came and stood at the altar; he was given a great quantity of incense to offer with the prayers of the saints on the golden altar that is before the throne. And the smoke of the incense, with the prayers of the saints, rose before God from the hand of the angel.

Revelation 5:6a, 7–8; 8:3–4

OUR PRAYERS ARE honored beyond anything we imagine here on earth. They break through the time barrier to join the eternal worship. Angels bring them before God with reverence and tenderness. The prayers of the faithful are placed upon the altar. At long last those noiseless cries for justice are about to be answered.

Try to enter your time of prayer today with a feeling of gratitude and assurance that your prayers and petitions are heard, that they matter, even if you do not receive the results or answers you want.

O, most merciful God, incline your loving ears to our prayers, and illuminate the hearts of those called by you, with the grace of the Holy Spirit, that they may be enabled worthily to minister to your mysteries, and to love you with an everlasting love, and to attain everlasting joys; through Jesus Christ our Lord. Amen.

—Charlemagne

For more verses on prayer and ideas on how to practice the discipline of prayer, see the Responding exercises and Spiritual Disciplines Index in *The Life with God Bible*.

Study

The intentional process of engaging the mind with the written and spoken Word of God and the world God has created in such a way that the mind takes on an order conforming to the order upon which it concentrates

When God made his covenant with the Israelites, he established the books of the Law, which laid out in detail the way God's people were to live. From that point forward, study became an important part of life with God. Now in addition to the Law, we have the other books of the Old Testament and the revelation in Jesus Christ. Scripture is an expansive gift that shows how God has been with us throughout history.

Accordingly, one of the best ways we can learn more about and grow closer to God is to study the written word. Scripture is the foundation of all of the disciplines. We know Jesus studied the Torah. Luke 2 tells us that Jesus went to the Temple as a young boy and spent time with the teachers there, asking questions. Indeed, he knew the Torah backwards and forwards, quoting from it time and time again. We too are well served by studying and, yes, even memorizing large pieces of Scripture. For our purposes, study refers to an analytical process of learning as opposed to the more devotional practice of meditation. It is appropriate for the study to come first. Before we get to the devotional stage, in which we meditate upon what a certain passage means to us specifically, we must first seek to understand the passage. But this is not to say that study has no effect on us. Indeed, the opposite is true. What we study, what we concentrate on, becomes ingrained in us. Study transforms us from the inside out.

Great are the works of the LORD,
  studied by all who delight in them.

—*Psalm 111:2*

Study

Learning from Scripture

All scripture is inspired by God and is useful for teaching, for reproof, for correction, and for training in righteousness, so that everyone who belongs to God may be proficient, equipped for every good work.

2 Timothy 3:16–17

MOST OF US don't need to be convinced of the value of the Bible in our walk with God, yet most of us also know that we do not study it nearly enough. Richard Foster writes that what Christians today most lack is the study of long passages of Scripture. So for the next ten days choose one long passage, perhaps a longer psalm such as 119, several chapters of one of the Gospels, or an entire Letter. Read your selected passage each day, beginning by asking the Holy Spirit to illuminate it for you, to show you its meaning.

You might want to do something different each time. For the first few days, focus on *repetition* in reading the passage. Try reading it aloud or writing it out longhand. Then move to *concentration*. Seek to memorize parts of the passage by putting a couple of verses on a sticky note and sticking it to your bathroom mirror, your desk or cubicle wall at work, or above the kitchen sink. Next, consider the *interpretation*. You might want to read what a commentary has to say about the passage or study the footnotes in your Bible. Finally, end with *reflection*. Think about the passage and what you have learned. Throughout, try to enter into the reading each day with an open mind, ready to let God show you whatever is helpful.

As you study, remember: "The proper outcome of studying the Bible is growth in the supernatural power of love, the love of God and of all people. We could call this the 1 Corinthians 13 Test: 'If I . . . understand all mysteries and all knowledge, and if I have all faith, so as to remove mountains, but do not have love, I am nothing' (v 2). And so the test of whether we have really gotten the point of the Bible would then be the quality of the love we show."[1]

Directions for Living

When [the king] has taken the throne of his kingdom, he shall have a copy of this law written for him in the presence of the levitical priests. It shall remain with him and he shall read in it all the days of his life, so that he may learn to fear the LORD his God, diligently observing all the words of this law and these statutes, neither exalting himself above other members of the community nor turning aside from the commandment, either to the right or to the left, so that he and his descendants may reign long over his kingdom in Israel.

Deuteronomy 17:18–20

THE BOOKS OF the Law established the stipulations of the covenant God made with Israel, in which he would be their God and they were to be his people. Composed of more than six hundred commandments, these laws defined the unique relationship between Israel and Yahweh. Carried across the pages of Scripture, these laws and the obedience they evoked provided Israel, now the People of God, with clear directions for living: keeping God's laws, exhibiting God's love, expressing God's righteousness. In this passage we see that even, and perhaps especially, the king was to read daily and to diligently observe the laws. Even a king must know his proper place before God. He must fear the Lord, demonstrating that he knows he is a creature and has power only at God's discretion. We would do well to seek the same understanding.

Begin the study of your selected Scripture passage with this prayer:

Father God, you have provided Scripture as "a lamp to my feet and a light to my path" (Ps 119:105). Help me to make the most of this precious gift. Give me the gift of understanding and the discipline to return to your word again and again, for my flesh is so weak and easily distracted or frustrated when the task grows difficult. I ask that you kindle in me a desire for learning more of you, so that I may come to your word with the joy and delight of the psalmists. In your name I pray. Amen.

Obeying God's Law

Obey the LORD your God by observing his commandments and decrees that are written in this book of the law, because you turn to the LORD your God with all your heart and with all your soul.

Surely, this commandment that I am commanding you today is not too hard for you, nor is it too far away. No, the word is very near to you; it is in your mouth and in your heart for you to observe.

Deuteronomy 30:10b–11, 14

IN DEUTERONOMY, MOSES warns the second wilderness generation that they must obey God's will as expressed in the law. If they do obey, blessings will abound, but judgment will be the consequence of disobedience. The question of the relationship of God's people to Old Testament law today is a complicated one and one on which people differ. The New Testament tells us that Jesus came to establish the new covenant with his followers (Luke 22:20). As a matter of fact, Jesus tells us that he did not come to abolish the law, but to fulfill it (Matt 5:17–20). It is clear that some laws are no longer relevant (sacrifices, distinctions between clean and unclean food, etc.) while others still are to be observed (the injunction against murder). It is best to reflect on individual laws on a case-by-case basis to know their significance for today. What is obvious, however, is that people today are no more able to perfectly keep God's law than they were during the period of the Old Testament. Indeed, according to the New Testament, there is only one person who has fully heeded Moses's call to obedience, and that is Jesus Christ.

Lord God, I pray for wisdom and discernment when I read your law and your word today. Without the Holy Spirit I am hopelessly confused and humbled, for I know that every day I do what is wrong in your eyes. Although I have no hope of being perfectly obedient, I ask that you show me through your word how to be renewed, formed daily into a person who is more like Christ. In your name I pray. Amen.

One Teacher

Then Jesus said to the crowds and to his disciples, "The scribes and the Pharisees sit on Moses's seat; therefore, do whatever they teach you and follow it; but do not do as they do, for they do not practice what they teach. They tie up heavy burdens, hard to bear, and lay them on the shoulders of others; but they themselves are unwilling to lift a finger to move them. They love to have people call them rabbi. But you are not to be called rabbi, for you have one teacher, and you are all students."

Matthew 23:1–4, 6a, 7b–8

THIS DISCOURSE IS given in the Temple, and Jesus offers the divine wisdom. The scribes and Pharisees he criticizes were the professors of their time. They studied Scripture in minute detail and memorized huge chunks of it. Yet all of their study and memorization didn't keep them from doing things contrary to what they were studying. Jesus' disciples are commanded not to accept the title rabbi, father, or teacher, for there is only one final and authoritative teacher—not Moses or Solomon, but the Christ. Thus, Jesus' followers must always remain learners.

"We can often use the Bible in ways that stifle spiritual life or even destroy the soul. This happened to any number of people who walked with Jesus. . . . For many, their very study of the Scriptures prevented them from recognizing who he was and putting their confidence in him (John 5:39–47). And later, Peter speaks in very grim terms of people who can 'twist' Scripture 'to their own destruction' (2 Pet 3:16). . . .

"If we want to receive from the Bible the life 'with God' that is portrayed *in* the Bible, we must be prepared to have our dearest and most fundamental assumptions about ourselves and our associations called into question. We must read humbly and in a constant attitude of repentance. Only in this way can we gain a thorough and practical grasp of the spiritual riches that God has made available to all humanity."

—Richard J. Foster and others, eds., *The Life with God Bible*[2]

⌐ Learning from Scripture

Knowledge of God

We have not ceased praying for you and asking that you may be filled with the knowledge of God's will in all spiritual wisdom and understanding, so that you may lead lives worthy of the Lord, fully pleasing to him, as you bear fruit in every good work and as you grow in the knowledge of God.

Colossians 1:9b–10

THE TRUTH OF faith is not "library" knowledge, a kind of abstract and impractical knowledge. Rather, it is knowledge of the God who acts purposely in history to bring people to live lives fully pleasing to God through the person and ministry of Jesus Christ. Christians are expected to grow in this knowledge and conform their lives to it. In this way it is the anchor and source of the kind of living that God empowers within and among us.

Wrong knowledge of God—getting God "wrong," being "hostile in mind" (1:21)—leads to broken and misshapen lives. So often today an antitheological bent is allowed to take over our spirituality. It is enough, apparently, to feel or experience something that we take to be the presence of God. Paul is wiser. He understands that theology—knowledge of God—and experience belong together, for without a true knowledge of God our piety will go astray. We will have no basis for interpreting our piety and our spiritual experience. We will be in danger of being taken captive by "plausible arguments" (2:4) that will lead us into error. Thus Paul insists that we are to grow "in the knowledge of God." In this sense, every Christian is a theologian.

Think about these questions before or after you work on concentrating on, or memorizing, your selected passage: How has wrong knowledge of God negatively impacted your life or the life of someone around you? Which do you tend to rely more heavily upon—experience or theology? What can you do to become more balanced?

Setting Our Hearts to Study

Ezra went up from Babylonia. He was a scribe skilled in the law of Moses that the LORD the God of Israel had given; and the king granted him all that he asked, for the hand of the LORD his God was upon him.

On the first day of the fifth month he came to Jerusalem, for the gracious hand of his God was upon him. For Ezra had set his heart to study the law of the LORD, and to do it, and to teach the statutes and ordinances in Israel.

Ezra 7:6, 9b–10

EZRA ARRIVED IN Jerusalem determined to accomplish three things. First, he desired to study the law. Rabbinical teachings suggest that among the duties of prayer, good works, and study, the most important of these is study. Study forms the basis of the other two. Second, Ezra committed himself to practice what he had learned. Third, he was called to teach others what he had learned. Ezra's whole-life commitment to Scripture knit Ezra's life closely with God, so that many times Ezra acknowledged that "the gracious hand of his God was upon him." Ezra's study of God's law and his commitment to the law in his own life formed his heart like God's. As we see in Ezra's life, committed study of Scripture can bring about much more than merely head knowledge. It can bring God himself into all the recesses of our being, for "the word of God is living and active" (Heb 4:12).

Take inspiration from this quote as you concentrate on your passage:

"The Bible is the loving heart of God made visible and plain. And receiving this message of exquisite love is the great privilege of all who long for life with God. *Reading, studying, memorizing, and meditating upon Scripture has always been the foundation of the Christian disciplines.* . . . God has so superintended the writing of Scripture that it serves as a most reliable guide for our own spiritual formation."

—Richard J. Foster and others, eds., *The Life with God Bible*[3]

⁓ Learning from Scripture

Saturated with Scripture

[Nehemiah] said, "O Lord God of heaven, the great and awesome God who keeps covenant and steadfast love with those who love him and keep his commandments; let your ear be attentive and your eyes open to hear the prayer of your servant that I now pray before you day and night for your servants, the people of Israel, confessing the sins of the people of Israel, which we have sinned against you. Both I and my family have sinned. We have offended you deeply, failing to keep the commandments, the statutes, and the ordinances that you commanded your servant Moses. Remember the word that you commanded your servant Moses, 'If you are unfaithful, I will scatter you among the peoples; but if you return to me and keep my commandments and do them, though your outcasts are under the farthest skies, I will gather them from there and bring them to the place at which I have chosen to establish my name.' They are your servants and your people, whom you redeemed by your great power and your strong hand. O Lord, let your ear be attentive to the prayer of your servant, and to the prayer of your servants who delight in revering your name. Give success to your servant today, and grant him mercy in the sight of this man!"

Nehemiah 1:5–11a

THIS PRAYER, WHICH Nehemiah offered after learning that the people of Jerusalem were in great trouble, reflects his thorough knowledge of Scripture. Almost every phrase in the prayer is derived from the sacred text (see Deut 7:9, 21; 10:17; 1 Kings 8:52; Ps 130:2; Deut 34:5; 4:27; 30:1–4; 9:29). Nehemiah was so saturated with Scripture that the words of Scripture had become the thoughts of Nehemiah. In the prayer life of Jesus, as well as the Church, the Bible has often served as a resource for addressing God.

Father God, give me the strength, the discipline, and the desire to study your word as Nehemiah did, to become so saturated in Scripture that its words come to my mouth and heart unbidden. In your name I pray. Amen.

The People of the Book

And Ezra opened the book in the sight of all the people, for he was standing above all the people; and when he opened it, all the people stood up. The Levites helped the people to understand the law, while the people remained in their places. So they read from the book, from the law of God, with interpretation. They gave the sense, so that the people understood the reading.

And Nehemiah, who was the governor, and Ezra the priest and scribe, and the Levites, who taught the people said to all the people, "This day is holy to the LORD your God; do not mourn or weep." For all the people wept when they heard the words of the law. Then he said to them, "Go your way, eat the fat and drink sweet wine and send portions of them to those for whom nothing is prepared, for this day is holy to our LORD; and do not be grieved, for the joy of the LORD is your strength."

Nehemiah 8:5, 7b–10

FROM THIS POINT on Israel would be known as the "People of the Book." The community would revolve around the study of Torah and the interpretation and application of its laws. There is nothing simplistic about Scripture. The understanding of God's Word demands our whole attention, and even then there is ongoing need for the traditions of the Church, and the Holy Spirit. And although the hearing of Scripture can be a disturbing event, the ultimate result for obedient and careful listeners is joy. Joy is not to be equated with momentary happiness; rather, biblical joy is a deep sense of peace that all is well with one's soul. The psalmist knew this deep peace when he wrote, "May those who sow in tears, reap with shouts of joy" (Ps 126:5).

Who in your life helps you with understanding as the Levites helped the people? Consider asking one of the people who comes to mind to help you interpret and understand the Bible passage you are studying.

⌐ Learning from Scripture

Eating God's Word

[The LORD] said to me, O mortal, eat what is offered to you; eat this scroll, and go, speak to the house of Israel. So I opened my mouth, and he gave me the scroll to eat. He said to me, Mortal, eat this scroll that I give you and fill your stomach with it. Then I ate it; and in my mouth it was as sweet as honey.

Ezekiel 3:1–3

IN THIS PASSAGE the prophet Ezekiel eats—literally and figuratively—a message of "lamentation and mourning and woe" (2:10). Ezekiel internalizes the word of God until it becomes a part of his being. This word of ache and loss nourishes Ezekiel's body and soul. The bitter news tastes surprisingly sweet, a reminder of the sweetness of the law (Ps 19:10) and of another scroll that is eaten by John (Rev 10:10). As Ezekiel eats the word, we glimpse the purpose of the disciplines of the spiritual life. Through prayer and study, worship and service, we regularly digest God's word into the core of our being, where it feeds and transforms us.

Continue the interpretation of your selected passage as you reflect on this quote:

"As I spent time chewing over the endless assurances and promises to be found in the Bible, so my faith in the living God grew stronger and held me safe in his hands. God's word to us, especially his word spoken by his Spirit through the Bible, is the very ingredient that feeds our faith. If we feed our souls regularly on God's word, several times each day, we should become robust spiritually just as we feed on ordinary food several times each day, and become robust physically. Nothing is more important than hearing and obeying the word of God."

—David Watson, *Fear No Evil: A Personal Struggle with Cancer*[4]

Treasuring God's Word

How can young people keep their way pure? / By guarding it according to your word. / With my whole heart I seek you; / do not let me stray from your commandments. / I treasure your word in my heart, / so that I may not sin against you. / Blessed are you, O Lord; / teach me your statutes. / With my lips I declare / all the ordinances of your mouth. / I delight in the way of your decrees / as much as in all riches. / I will meditate on your precepts, / and fix my eyes on your ways. / I will delight in your statutes; / I will not forget your word.

Psalm 119:9–16

THIS PSALM EXPLORES the wonders of God's provision through the law (Torah; see Ps 19) and the delight of living under its guidance. The psalm deserves rumination, thoughtful brooding. Psalm 119 is a wide-ranging A–Z reflection on living gladly under God's rule. It includes praise and thanksgiving, frequent admiration of God's wisdom and generosity in giving the Torah, pleas for deliverance and renewal, and much more. People who have been taught that the Israelites suffered under or were burdened by Torah may be surprised at the psalm's joy-fulness. It brims over with how precious Torah is and with eagerness to be shaped toward the life it portrays.

Let the joyous spirit of this psalm and this quote bubble up within you as you reflect on your passage this last day.

"I believe the Bible is the best gift God has ever given to man. All the good from The Savior of the world is communicated to us through this Book."

—Abraham Lincoln[5]

Discerning Our Teachers

Do not be conformed to this world, but be transformed by the renewing of your minds, so that you may discern what is the will of God—what is good and acceptable and perfect.

Romans 12:2

As Dallas Willard observes in *The Divine Conspiracy,* we are all somebody's disciples.[6] At different times in our lives we are the students of our parents, our playmates, our teachers, and our peers. These apprenticeships are necessary, so that we can learn about the world and our place in it, how to act and talk and treat one another. Whether we mean to or not, we also apprentice ourselves to books, magazines, TV shows, and movies. When we spend a lot of time with particular people, books, or TV shows, their habits, ideas, and behavior patterns start to become ingrained in us. That is why it matters who and what we surround ourselves with. God wants to renew us from the inside out, transforming our minds, so that we become ever more like God as revealed in Jesus Christ. But if we are spending time with things or people not of God, we will find ourselves changing in ways we may not intend.

Within the next ten days, take a block of time to consider the central influences in your life. Jot down a time line of your life, dividing it into stages (such as childhood, adolescence, young adulthood, marriage, parenthood, etc.) or organizing it by another system of your choice (such as places you have lived or jobs you have had). Think about the teachers and influences that were most important at each time. Focus particularly on the present. Ask yourself who your teachers are and what they are teaching you. Scripture tells us that we can know who has been inwardly transformed by God by the fruit they produce. Ask God to show you if there are people or influences you should minimize in your life. Then ask God about what new ways you can learn. Is God calling you toward more frequent study of Scripture? Are there particular people or books God is urging you to learn from? Finally, ask yourself who is learning from you and what you are teaching them.

Delighting in the Law of the Lord

Happy are those
    who do not follow the advice of the wicked,
or take the path that sinners tread,
    or sit in the seat of scoffers;
but their delight is in the law of the LORD,
    and on his law they meditate day and night.
They are like trees
    planted by streams of water,
which yield their fruit in its season,
    and their leaves do not wither.
In all that they do, they prosper.

Psalm 1:1–3

THE OPENING VERSES of the book of Psalms point directly to a central issue in spiritual formation: What do you give your attention to? What do you immerse yourself in? What do you take pleasure in? Where do you take your life cues from? The verbs suggest habits: following, walking, sitting, meditating. Do we loiter with and turn our ears to rebels and scoffers, or do we go beyond mere duty and eagerly attend to God's guidance and teaching?

Reflect on this quote as you prepare for your time of discernment:

"It is one of the major transitions in life to recognize who has taught us, mastered us, and then to evaluate the results in us of their teaching. This is a harrowing task, and sometimes we just can't face it. But it can also open the door to choose other masters, possibly better masters, and one Master above all."

—Dallas Willard, *The Divine Conspiracy*[7]

True Teachers

Who is wise and understanding among you? Show by your good life that your works are done with gentleness born of wisdom. But if you have bitter envy and selfish ambition in your hearts, do not be boastful and false to the truth. Such wisdom does not come down from above, but is earthly, unspiritual, devilish. For where there is envy and selfish ambition, there will also be disorder and wickedness of every kind. But the wisdom from above is first pure, then peaceable, gentle, willing to yield, full of mercy and good fruits, without a trace of partiality or hypocrisy. And a harvest of righteousness is sown in peace for those who make peace.

James 3:13–18

TRUE TEACHERS IMPART godly wisdom that informs our faith and forms our character. James advises about how to discern between so-called wisdoms. There is an earthly wisdom that is "unspiritual, devilish" and leads to "disorder and wickedness," because it seeks a selfish human end; and there is a heavenly wisdom that makes one pure, peaceable, gentle, willing to yield, merciful, and fruitful and brings about godly results.

The image here of "sowing peace" suggests that righteousness becomes visible in persons who work for peace and live by peaceful rules. Self-promoting leaders work against righteousness, lacking what the first verse mentions as a "good life" and the "gentleness born of wisdom [from above]." Just as true faith shows itself in good works, true wisdom shows itself in unselfish, godly conduct.

Father God, thank you for those people in my life through whom you have taught and shepherded me—my parents, my teachers, my pastors, my friends, my partners in ministry. I also thank you for those times you have taught others through me. What a privilege to be engaged in your work this way. In your name I pray. Amen.

False Prophets

But false prophets also arose among the people, just as there will be false teachers among you, who will secretly bring in destructive opinions. They will even deny the Master who brought them—bringing swift destruction on themselves. Even so, many will follow their licentious ways, and because of these teachers the way of truth will be maligned. And in their greed they will exploit you with deceptive words. Their condemnation, pronounced against them long ago, has not been idle, and their destruction is not asleep.

You therefore, beloved, since you are forewarned, beware that you are not carried away with the error of the lawless and lose your own stability. But grow in the grace and the knowledge of our Lord and Savior Jesus Christ. To him be the glory both now and to the day of eternity. Amen.

2 Peter 2:1–3; 3:17–18

PETER REMINDS HIS readers that the environment in which we live and those with whom we choose to associate will continually press against us and inevitably shape us, for good or for ill. Peter is particularly concerned that the skewed biblical interpretation and lifestyle of the false teachers, if heard and seen enough by his readers, will eventually erode their ability to distinguish truth from error and will increasingly be viewed as acceptable in the eyes of the Church and of God. Repeat a bad idea or praise a sinful behavior often enough, and the entire cultural and moral landscape will eventually shift. Thus, Peter's strong exhortation to maintain "stability" in the midst of spiritual and moral chaos.

As you prepare for or begin the process of discerning your teachers, ask God for his wisdom and guidance.

Grant me, Lord, to know what I ought to know, to love what I ought to love, to praise what delights you most, to value what is precious in your sight, and to hate what is offensive to you. Amen.

—Thomas à Kempis

Observing One Another

Now you have observed my teaching, my conduct, my aim in life, my faith, my patience, my love, my steadfastness.

2 Timothy 3:10

THE CHRISTIAN FAITH is contagious. If we are to endure as Christians, it must be through apprenticeship—observing more experienced and well-formed Christians, following their moves, taking up their way of life, inculcating their virtues. Through such observation and imitation, we take up the practices of the faith and come to embody those practices for ourselves. The Church must look for ample opportunities for its members to be observed by and to observe one another as we mature in the faith.

But a caution is also necessary. Since we are all to learn from observing each other, we need to be cautious and humble about what we may be teaching with our words and deeds. Teaching is so much easier than learning. It is also more dangerous. In the act of teaching, especially when we know what we are saying is right, we inevitably sense that we embody what we teach. The admiration and appreciation of others reinforce the feeling. Meanwhile, a huge gap gradually widens between what we say and the way we live. It happens a lot in life, but nowhere with more deadly consequences than among those who teach about God and his ways with us. The truth is that there are no "masters" in the spiritual life. Mature and wise teachers, yes. But fundamentally we are all beginners receiving and giving on our knees before God and with open hands before one another. In this business no one "lords it over" another.

Pay special attention today to whose examples and virtues you are imitating, and also to those who may be observing and imitating you.

Remember Jesus Christ

Remember Jesus Christ, raised from the dead, a descendant of David—that is my gospel, for which I suffer hardship, even to the point of being chained like a criminal. But the word of God is not chained. Therefore I endure everything for the sake of the elect, so that they may also obtain the salvation that is in Christ Jesus, with eternal glory. The saying is sure:

> If we have died with him, we will also live with him; / if we endure,
> we will also reign with him; / if we deny him, he will also deny us; / if
> we are faithless, he remains faithful— / for he cannot deny himself.

Remind them of this, and warn them before God that they are to avoid wrangling over words, which does no good but only ruins those who are listening.

2 Timothy 2:8–14

THE CHRISTIAN FAITH is distinctly traditionalist. Much of our worship on Sunday is consumed with the loving reiteration and joyful celebration of tradition—remembering Jesus Christ. Here you are, studying a two-thousand-year-old letter. That's the way we Christians continue as Christians. Our remembering of the tradition is our revolutionary act of defiance against the lures of the present age, one of our most significant practices of the faith. Through such remembering, we are freed from the merely contemporary. In our reading and studying the Word of God, that Word speaks anew, lives among us. The Word of God is not, thank God, chained!

Second Timothy is clear that we have a distinct, demanding body of doctrine that needs to be taught, a message that requires reiteration every Sunday if we, as the Church, are to be who we are called to be. Does your worship, your church life, your study have enough biblical content ("Jesus Christ, raised from the dead") to sustain you? What about those who have taught you?

~ *Discerning Our Teachers*

Learning in Community

But Peter, standing with the eleven, raised his voice and addressed them, "Men of Judea and all who live in Jerusalem, let this be known to you, and listen to what I say. Indeed, these are not drunk, as you suppose, for it is only nine o'clock in the morning. No, this is what was spoken through the prophet Joel:

'In the last days it will be, God declares,
that I will pour out my Spirit upon all flesh,
and your sons and your daughters shall prophesy,
and your young men shall see visions,
and your old men shall dream dreams.
Even upon my slaves, both men and women
in those days, I will pour out my Spirit;
and they shall prophesy.'"

Acts 2:14–18

PETER IS THE representative disciple and spokesman for the early Church. His sermon, given right after the Pentecost experience in which all of Jesus' followers spoke in tongues, explains that what is happening fulfills Joel 2:28–32. It summarizes the Church's proclamation that (1) the Old Testament predicts Jesus; (2) Jesus is the Messiah who is exalted by God (see Acts 2:22–32); and (3) God sends the empowering Holy Spirit (Acts 2:33). This passage demonstrates how the early Church studied Scripture, the Septuagint (the Old Testament in Greek), to understand events. Prayerful consideration of God's word was crucial.

As you continue thinking about your teachers, today consider the role of the community in shaping your knowledge of God. How has preaching, group Bible study, church fellowship, or another group positively or negatively helped you in your study and understanding of God's word? If you have never taken part in such a group or are not currently attending one, consider joining or even starting a study group.

Learning from Creation

The heavens are telling the glory of God;
>   and the firmament proclaims his handiwork.
Day to day pours forth speech,
>   and night to night declares knowledge.
There is no speech, nor are there words;
>   their voice is not heard;
yet their voice goes out through all the earth,
>   and their words to the end of the world.

> *Psalm 19:1–4*

THE TERMS "NATURAL revelation" or "general revelation" aptly point to how the world itself pours out on us wordless speech about God. In our wordy, busy lives we can learn a lot by listening more closely to creation's voices.

What has the creation taught you about God?

> *Praised be You, my Lord, with all your creatures,*
> > *especially Sir Brother Sun,*
> > *Who is the day and through whom You give us light.*
> *And he is beautiful and radiant with great splendor;*
> > *and bears a likeness of You, Most High One.*
> *Praised be You, my Lord, through Sister Moon and the stars,*
> > *in heaven You formed them clear and precious and beautiful . . .*
> *Praised be You, my Lord, through Sister Water,*
> > *which is very useful and humble and precious and chaste . . .*
> *Praised be You, my Lord, through our Sister Mother Earth,*
> > *who sustains and governs us,*
> > *and who produces varied fruits with colored flowers and herbs.*

> —St. Francis of Assisi, *Francis and Clare:*
> *The Complete Writings* [8]

Studying God's Ways

Make me understand the way of your precepts, / and I will
meditate on your wondrous works. / My soul melts away for
sorrow; / strengthen me according to your word. / Put false ways
far from me; / and graciously teach me your law. / I have chosen
the way of faithfulness; / I set your ordinances before me. / I cling
to your decrees, O LORD; / let me not be put to shame. / I run the
way of your commandments, / for you enlarge my understanding.

Psalm 119:27–32

IN THESE WAYS and others throughout this song ("Open my eyes,"
119:18; "Turn my heart," 119:36), the psalmist asks God to teach him.
This points to a dynamic, continuing relationship between God and the
singer, not to a bookishness that serves erudition and keeping rules. It appeals to practical, ongoing guidance and transformation. The study that
transforms us moves with patient, focused attention and listens deeply,
ready to respond. For example, in studying psalms that are hymns we
can list all of the reasons why people are called to praise or the variety of
ways people are invited to praise. Study that shapes us, however, must be
willing to join in praise and to ponder the reasons why.

How can you ask God to teach you? Minister and theologian A.W.
Tozer asserts that one way is to learn more about who God is:

"What is God like? What kind of God is He? How may we expect
Him to act toward us and toward all created things? Such questions are
not merely academic. They touch the far-in reaches of the human spirit,
and their answers affect life and character and destiny. When asked in
reverence and their answers sought in humility, these are questions that
cannot but be pleasing to our Father which art in heaven."

A. W. Tozer, *The Knowledge of the Holy*[9]

Transformed into the Image of Jesus Christ

And all of us, with unveiled faces, seeing the glory of the Lord as though reflected in a mirror, are being transformed into the same image from one degree of glory to another; for this comes from the Lord, the Spirit.

2 Corinthians 3:18

WHEN WE REST in the splendor of God revealed by Christ, we find ourselves changed by it. Gradually, by degrees, Paul says, we incline toward the divine glory and it begins to overtake us. This is by the power of the Spirit, which prepared us for such growth beginning at baptism. We are transformed into his likeness, becoming splendid and glorious, to the glory of God.

At last we arrive at the point of all this study—to be changed, overtaken by God as revealed in Christ. Perhaps this prayer will be helpful in deliberately turning your attention to this process:

Lord God, with all the mistakes I make on a daily basis, sometimes I feel so far from becoming Christlike. Grant me patience with the gradual process of transformation and help me to place myself in your hands without hesitation, that you may mold me into your likeness. In your name I pray. Amen.

For more verses on study and ideas on how to practice the discipline of study, see the Responding exercises and Spiritual Disciplines Index in *The Life with God Bible.*

Confession

Sharing our deepest weaknesses and failures with God and trusted others, so that we may enter into God's grace and mercy and experience his ready forgiveness and healing

When Jesus died on the cross, he took in all the sins of the world past and present. We are freed from sin if we but confess and ask for forgiveness. Confession requires us to be honest. Perhaps we are ashamed of our sin, so we hide our sin from others. Or perhaps we are unwilling to turn from our sin, so we hide it even from ourselves, denying that our thoughts or actions are wrong. In either case, sin can do untold damage to our souls, if we do not have the courage to shine God's healing light upon it.

Confession can be a private matter between an individual and God; nothing more is required for forgiveness. As 1 Timothy 2:5 tells us, "For there is one God; there is also one mediator between God and humankind, Christ Jesus, himself human." But we can also confess to others, to a trusted friend or pastor, as James 5:16 instructs: "Confess your sins to one another, and pray for one another."

Confession has three distinct parts: "an examination of conscience, sorrow, and a determination to avoid sin."[1] First, we invite God to show us those areas where we need forgiveness and healing, focusing if possible on specific sins rather than more general confessions. Next, we feel sorrow, in the sense that we deeply regret our sin and the grief it has caused God and others. Finally, we resolve to turn away from our sin. We ask God for the strength and courage to love and desire God's way and to hate anything that keeps us from it.

If we confess our sins, he who is faithful and just will forgive us our sins and cleanse us from all unrighteousness.

—*1 John 1:9*

Confession

Confessing Our Sins

If we say that we have no sin, we deceive ourselves, and the truth is not in us. If we confess our sins, he who is faithful and just will forgive us our sins and cleanse us from all unrighteousness. If we say that we have not sinned, we make him a liar, and his word is not in us.

My little children, I am writing these things to you so that you may not sin. But if anyone does sin, we have an advocate with the Father, Jesus Christ the righteous.

1 John 1:8–2:1

EACH DAY FOR the next ten days, take time in prayer to make confession. This practice may be something you already do regularly. If so, think of it as paying special attention to this part of your prayer life. Perhaps you will want to focus on a particular sin each day, or perhaps you would rather simply ask forgiveness for the sins that you have committed that day. In prayer, go through the three steps of examination of conscience, sorrow, and determination to avoid sin in the future.

Some of us may need to ask God to reach into the deepest recesses of our soul and show us our sin more clearly, so that we can confess it. But others of us may feel so burdened and weighed down by a sin, even one that we have confessed more than once, that we doubt whether we have been released or can be forgiven. Especially in those cases, we may want to confess our sin to others. In John 20:23 Jesus gives his disciples the power to forgive one another's sins: "If you forgive the sins of any, they are forgiven them." Yet this sharing of sins with others can be very hard. As Richard Foster writes, "Confession is a difficult Discipline for us because we all too often view the believing community as a fellowship of saints before we see it as a fellowship of sinners. We feel that everyone else has advanced so far into holiness that we are isolated and alone in our sin."[2]

Throughout the next ten days, give prayerful consideration to whether you need to find someone to whom to confess your sins.

Spiritual Practice

Sincere Repentance

Return, O Israel, to the LORD your God,
> for you have stumbled because of your iniquity.
Take words with you
> and return to the LORD;
say to him,
> "Take away all guilt;
accept that which is good,
> and we will offer
> the fruit of our lips."

Hosea 14:1–2

ALTHOUGH REPENTANCE IS about doing something (the Hebrew verb is "to turn/return") rather than just saying something, it often begins with the speaking of words. Yet the very wrongs for which repentance is needed can keep us from finding the right words. The grace of this passage, however, is that the divine command to "take words" is immediately followed by the divine provision of the very words that are to be taken. The divine grace that responds to our confession of sin is already at work in eliciting it.

Our words, the "fruit of our lips," are all we need to confess and receive forgiveness. Where once animal sacrifice was required, now we can confess personally to God with nothing more to offer than our repentance. What a blessing! Take time today to respond to God's grace with a sincere confession of your heart.

I Am Sorry for My Sin

O LORD, do not rebuke me in your anger,
   or discipline me in your wrath.
For your arrows have sunk into me,
   and your hand has come down on me.
There is no soundness in my flesh
   because of your indignation;
there is no health in my bones
   because of my sin.
For my iniquities have gone over my head;
   they weigh like a burden too heavy for me.
For I am ready to fall,
   and my pain is ever with me.
I confess my iniquity;
   I am sorry for my sin.

Psalm 38:1–4, 17–18

THIS SONG OF repentance sets up the singer's confession with a long, detailed list of aches and pains. Unlike Job, who in his distress rightly defends his integrity, this psalmist takes his illness as a sign of God's judgment. In the last verse, he finally gets to it: "I am sorry for my sin." This simple, unqualified confession models what it means to accept full responsibility without excuses or blaming. "I did it, I'm sorry" is all we need.

Have you ever felt so burdened by a sin that it made you physically ill? Sometimes the simplest of heartfelt confessions is all we need. Take time today to tell God, "I'm sorry."

The People Were Baptized, Confessing Their Sins

John the baptizer appeared in the wilderness, proclaiming a baptism of repentance for the forgiveness of sins. And people from the whole Judean countryside and all the people of Jerusalem were going out to him, and were baptized by him in the river Jordan, confessing their sins. Now John was clothed with camel's hair, with a leather belt around his waist, and he ate locusts and wild honey. He proclaimed, "The one who is more powerful than I is coming after me; I am not worthy to stoop down and untie the thong of his sandals. I have baptized you with water; but he will baptize you with the Holy Spirit."

Mark 1:4–8

JOHN THE BAPTIST'S dress and diet remind us of Elijah and other prophets. His baptism prepares people for baptism into Jesus. Repentance prepares us to receive the good news Jesus brings. A change of heart and mind that allows us to let go of old ways of life, old burdens and wrongs, and to know we are forgiven and loved makes us more ready to hear and believe that Jesus can bring us new life!

It is not only when we become Christians that we need to confess. Regular confession is a discipline that we all need to practice. Try an experiment today. As soon as you find yourself in a sin, take a moment and confess it to God. What does this type of confession teach you?

Confessing Our Sins

Forgive the Sin of Your People Israel

Then Solomon stood before the altar of the LORD in the presence of all the assembly of Israel, and spread out his hands to heaven. He said, "O LORD, God of Israel, there is no God like you in heaven above or on earth beneath, keeping covenant and steadfast love for your servants who walk before you with all their heart. Hear the plea of your servant and of your people Israel when they pray toward this place; O hear in heaven your dwelling place; heed and forgive.

"If someone sins against a neighbor and is given an oath to swear, and comes and swears before your altar in this house, then hear in heaven, and act, and judge your servants, condemning the guilty by bringing their conduct on their own head, and vindicating the righteous by rewarding them according to their righteousness.

"When your people Israel, having sinned against you, are defeated before an enemy but turn again to you, confess your name, pray and plead with you in this house, then hear in heaven, forgive the sin of your people Israel, and bring them again to the land that you gave to their ancestors."

1 Kings 8:22–23, 30–34

SOLOMON BRINGS TOGETHER the leaders and people of Israel to dedicate the Temple as the only house of God in the land. In this prayer he makes it clear that the Temple will be the place where they can come to confess and make things right with God. In fact, he anticipates the kinds of sins they will need to confess. In anticipating the sins of the people and asking God to honor their repentance, Solomon's prayer of dedication is as much for the gathered people as for God.

How does confessing your sins in church, assembled with the rest of the congregation and with a pastor at the front, feel different than when you are praying alone or confessing to a friend or small group? Why do you think that is?

We Have Sinned and Done Wrong

In the first year of [Darius's] reign, I, Daniel, perceived in the books the number of years that, according to the word of the LORD to the prophet Jeremiah, must be fulfilled for the devastation of Jerusalem, namely, seventy years.

Then I turned to the Lord God, to seek an answer by prayer and supplication with fasting and sackcloth and ashes. I prayed to the LORD my God and made confession, saying,

"Ah, Lord, great and awesome God, keeping covenant and steadfast love with those who love you and keep your commandments, we have sinned and done wrong, acted wickedly and rebelled, turning aside from your commandments and ordinances. We have not listened to your servants the prophets, who spoke in your name to our kings, our princes, and our ancestors, and to all the people of the land."

Daniel 9:2–6

DANIEL 9 CONCERNS a crisis of timing and delayed expectations. Around 587 BCE Jeremiah announced that Israel's exile would last seventy years. But, at the time of the writing of Daniel, nearly five hundred years have passed! Daniel seeks an answer through confession and prayer based not on human righteousness, but on God's "great mercies" (9:18). Through the angel Gabriel, God announces not seventy years of exile, but "seventy weeks of years" (9:24, RSV), or 490 years in all. In other words, the time of exile is over.

In this prayer Daniel confesses his own sin and also the sin of the People of God, one of the many biblical examples of confession by proxy. Although it can never take the place of confession of our individual and specific sins, we should not overlook corporate confession in our own practice. During your next prayer time, contemplate the sins of your family, your church, your nation; confess these too and ask God's forgiveness even for those sins in which you have been unwittingly complicit.

Teach Me to Do Your Will

Hear my prayer, O LORD;
> give ear to my supplications in your faithfulness;
> answer me in your righteousness.
Do not enter into judgment with your servant,
> for no one living is righteous before you.
Teach me to do your will,
> for you are my God.
Let your good spirit lead me
> on a level path.

Psalm 143:1–2, 10

THE PHRASE "NO one living is righteous before you" brings this psalm into the group of penitential psalms, although most of the psalm pleads for God to deliver the singer from his enemies. The Psalms show paradox. In a variety of ways they recognize people as truly righteous, but here such righteousness is overwhelmed by the sense of God's holiness. Spiritual maturity holds the two at once—genuine faithfulness, on the one hand, and a vision of God's unmatched holiness, on the other.

No matter how righteous and faithful we are or think we are, no one is completely righteous before God. So we do as the psalm instructs: after we confess and show sorrow, we ask God to help us in our commitment to do right. Today as you make your confession, repeat the last stanzas of the psalm, asking God to ignite your desire for holy living.

Lord God, reading your word only reminds me of how far I am from being righteous. I make the wrong choices; I put myself and my desires before the needs of others and before what you want for my life. I am deeply sorry for my mistakes, Lord. Please forgive me and continue teaching me to do your will. Amen.

Observing All the Commandments

The rest of the people, the priests, the Levites, the gatekeepers, the singers, the temple servants, and all who have separated themselves from the peoples of the lands to adhere to the law of God, their wives, their sons, their daughters, all who have knowledge and understanding, join with their kin, their nobles, and enter into a curse and an oath to walk in God's law, which was given by Moses the servant of God, and to observe and do all the commandments of the LORD our Lord and his ordinances and his statutes.

Nehemiah 10:28–29

THIS OATH COMES at the end of a long prayer of confession. The prayer ends rather abruptly without even so much as an "Amen." But the "Amen" was supplied by the people, who put their very lives on the line. They vowed to "observe and do all the commandments of the LORD." Yes, God's forgiveness is an act of grace, but it takes effort on our part to live out the disciplines of faith. True repentance is always linked with a changed life. The word for "repentance" in both Testaments implies the idea of a "return" to God or to the ways of God. Repentance results in a commitment to put one's entire life under God's authority. The "doing" of the commandments is our signature of faith, our "Amen" to God's grace.

When you make your confession today, make a commitment to put your life under God's authority. Reflect on this quote and think of your commitment as a way to consider the seriousness of your sin:

"If penance is viewed as a way of earning forgiveness, it is dangerous indeed. But if it is seen as an opportunity to pause a moment to consider the seriousness of our sin, then it has genuine merit. Today we take our offenses to the love of God far too lightly. If we had only a tinge of the sense of revulsion that God feels toward sin, we would be moved to holier living."

—Richard J. Foster, *Celebration of Discipline*[3]

~ *Confessing Our Sins*

Confession and Restitution

The LORD spoke to Moses, saying: Speak to the Israelites: When a man or a woman wrongs another, breaking faith with the LORD, that person incurs guilt and shall confess the sin that has been committed. The person shall make full restitution for the wrong, adding one-fifth to it, and giving it to the one who was wronged. If the injured party has no next of kin to whom restitution may be made for the wrong, the restitution for wrong shall go to the LORD for the priest, in addition to the ram of atonement for which atonement is made for the guilty party.

Numbers 5:5–8

WITH THESE SPECIFIC instructions for making restitution for a wrong someone has confessed, we see that restitution can itself be a discipline. The Spiritual Disciplines transform those who are enslaved by their ingrained habits through new, holy habits. This is the process we see in Numbers. God wanted the Israelites to leave their habits of slavery behind and attain holy habits with which to enter their new lives. Confession and restitution were two of these holy habits.

Prayerfully consider whether restitution is required for any of the sins you have confessed.

"Not all sin calls for restitution. But it is unthinkable that I should sincerely confess to my brother or sister that I have stolen a purse or harmed a reputation and then blithely go my way without trying to make some restoration for the loss. In general, our own innate integrity, a force within our personality, *requires* such restitution. This often is not a pleasant experience, but it actually strengthens us in our will to do the right thing."

—Dallas Willard, *The Spirit of the Disciplines*[4]

The Joy of Forgiveness

Happy are those whose transgression is forgiven,
    whose sin is covered.
Happy are those to whom the LORD imputes no iniquity,
    and in whose spirit there is no deceit.
While I kept silence, my body wasted away
    through my groaning all day long.
For day and night your hand was heavy upon me;
    my strength was dried up as by the heat of summer.
Then I acknowledged my sin to you,
    and I did not hide my iniquity;
I said, "I will confess my transgressions to the LORD,"
    and you forgave the guilt of my sin.

Psalm 32:1–5

THIS SONG OF repentance is in the spirit of thanksgiving, and the singer basks in the delight of having been forgiven. The ill effects of living in the silence of denial and deceit stand in sharp contrast to the joy of forgiveness for those who can honestly confess their sin. The steady use of the Spiritual Discipline of confession helps us overcome the many and subtle ways we are tempted to fool ourselves and others.

As you have focused on confession these last several days, have you experienced the joy of being forgiven?

"To confess your sins to God is not to tell God anything God doesn't already know. Until you confess them, however, they are the abyss between you. When you confess them, they become the Golden Gate Bridge."

—Frederick Buechner, *Beyond Words*[5]

Revealing Our Secrets

"Nothing is covered up that will not be uncovered, and nothing secret that will not become known. Therefore whatever you have said in the dark will be heard in the light, and what you have whispered behind closed doors will be proclaimed from the housetops."

Luke 12:2–3

OUR NEXT PRACTICE will be to ask for forgiveness for sins from our past. In *Celebration of Discipline* Richard Foster writes of how he addressed a growing conviction that something in his past was impeding his relationship with God:

> I devised a plan. I divided my life into three periods: childhood, adolescence, adulthood. On the first day I came before God in prayer and meditation, pencil and paper in hand. Inviting him to reveal to me anything during my childhood that needed either forgiveness or healing or both, I waited in absolute silence for about ten minutes. Anything about my childhood that surfaced to my conscious mind, I wrote down. I made no attempts to analyze the items or put any value judgment on them. My assurance was that God would reveal anything that needed his healing touch. Having finished, I put the pencil and paper down for the day. The next day I went through the same exercise for my adolescent years, and the third day for my adult years.[6]

Then he took his paper to a friend who had agreed to serve as a confessor, read the paper aloud, and received an assurance of forgiveness and prayers. After the experience, Foster writes, he was able to explore new and uncharted areas of the Spirit.

As you might have guessed, your practice is to try a similar experiment sometime within the next ten days. Perhaps you would like to organize your life in different categories that make more sense to you. Or you might not feel ready to take your list to another person. Do what you can to explore and confess any sins hidden in your past.

Spiritual Practice

Being Open and Honest

So they went out of Egypt and came to their father Jacob in the land of Canaan. And they told him, "Joseph is still alive! He is even ruler over all the land of Egypt." He was stunned; he could not believe them. But when they told him all the words of Joseph that he had said to them, and when he saw the wagons that Joseph had sent to carry him, the spirit of their father Jacob revived. Israel said, "Enough! My son Joseph is still alive. I must go and see him before I die."

Genesis 45:25–28

THESE BROTHERS WHO tell their father that Joseph is still alive are the same ones who sold him into slavery and then lied to their father, deceiving him into thinking that Joseph had been eaten by a wild animal. The Bible does not record if Joseph's brothers ever told their father, Jacob, that they were responsible for selling him into slavery.

How do you think the relationship of the sons with their father would have been affected if they had openly confessed what they had done? Has there ever been a situation in your family that would have improved, had family members been open and honest with each other? What can you do to restore those relationships?

When You Realize Your Guilt

When any of you sin in that you have heard a public adjuration to testify and—though able to testify as one who has seen or learned of the matter—do not speak up, you are subject to punishment. Or when any of you touch any unclean thing—whether the carcass of an unclean beast or the carcass of unclean livestock or the carcass of an unclean swarming thing—and are unaware of it, you have become unclean, and are guilty. Or when you touch human uncleanness—any uncleanness by which one can become unclean—and are unaware of it, when you come to know it, you shall be guilty. Or when any of you utter aloud a rash oath for a bad or a good purpose, whatever people utter in an oath, and are unaware of it, when you come to know it, you shall in any of these be guilty. When you realize your guilt in any of these, you shall confess the sin that you have committed.

Leviticus 5:1–5

THE ISRAELITES WERE commanded to confess their sin when they were guilty of refusing to testify when they could have, touching unclean things, touching an unclean human, or uttering a rash oath even when they were unaware of doing anything wrong.

Recall a time when you did something and only later became aware that it was wrong. Take a moment now to confess it to God.

Father God, I know your law is what is best for me. Help me to see the right path before I take the wrong one; tune my inner ear so I can more clearly hear your guiding voice. Please forgive me for those times when I have blindly charged down the wrong paths. Amen.

Our Ancestors Have Not Kept Your Law

Then those of Israelite descent separated themselves from all foreigners, and stood and confessed their sins and the iniquities of their ancestors. They stood up in their place and read from the book of the law of the LORD their God for a fourth part of the day, and for another fourth they made confession and worshiped the LORD their God. And Ezra said: "You are the LORD, you alone. You have been just in all that has come upon us, for you have dealt faithfully and we have acted wickedly; our kings, our officials, our priests, and our ancestors have not kept your law or heeded the commandments and the warnings that you gave them. Even in their own kingdom, and in the great goodness you bestowed on them, and in the large and rich land that you set before them, they did not serve you and did not turn from their wicked works. Here we are, slaves to this day—slaves in the land that you gave to our ancestors to enjoy its fruit and its good gifts. Its rich yield goes to the kings whom you have set over us because of our sins; they have power also over our bodies and over our livestock at their pleasure, and we are in great distress."

Nehemiah 9:2–3, 6a, 33–37

IN THIS LONG confession, Ezra explains how the people of Israel got to the sorry state they are currently in. In Hebrew, Ezra's prayer ends with the phrase "in great distress we are." The words are an obvious cry for help to the God whose character is extolled in the early part of the prayer. Given Israel's miserable record of failing God time and time again, Ezra recognizes that the Jews are hardly deserving of God's favor. Yet once again the Israelites plead for God to have mercy on them. The Israelites' history with God gives them hope that once again he will intervene on their behalf. The good news of Jesus Christ is God's gracious reply not only to the failures of Israel, but to the sin of the world.

Take time today to think about and confess any sins in your life that have repeated themselves throughout the generations.

I Was Born Guilty

Have mercy on me, O God,
    according to your steadfast love,
according to your abundant mercy
    blot out my transgressions.
Wash me thoroughly from my iniquity,
    and cleanse me from my sin.
For I know my transgressions,
    and my sin is ever before me.
Against you, you alone, have I sinned,
    and done what is evil in your sight,
so that you are justified in your sentence
    and blameless when you pass judgment.
Indeed, I was born guilty,
    a sinner when my mother conceived me.

Psalm 51:1–5

PSALM 51 IS a song of repentance with a moving appeal to God's steadfast love and mercy. The singer offers a radical sense of how sinful he is, admitting full blameworthiness. Surely to be understood as hyperbole, his claim is that he was even a wicked zygote. How deeply do we feel the power of sin?

Recognizing that we always have and always will sin can lead to despair and an inability to let go of past sins for which we have already repented. The next time you feel haunted by a past sin, pray this prayer and think of your sin not just as a failing, but as a reminder of God's saving grace:

Hold not our sins up against us, but hold us up against our sins, so that the thought of thee when it wakens in our soul . . . should not remind us of what we have committed, but of what Thou didst forgive, not of how we went astray but of how Thou didst save us.

—Søren Kierkegaard, *The Living Thoughts of Kierkegaard*[7]

Concealed Sin

When one will not listen to the law,
    even one's prayers are an abomination.
No one who conceals transgressions will prosper,
    but one who confesses and forsakes them will obtain mercy.

Proverbs 28:9, 13

HAVE YOU EVER had a prayer block? A reluctance to pray stemming from a deep-down fear that something you're doing is wrong and that God will tell you so? Attempting to conceal a sin from God is the worst kind of folly, yet we sometimes fear confession because, once we admit to a sin, the next step is to forsake it.

Prayerfully consider a chronic sin, one that you have confessed before but have trouble forsaking. Write the sin or draw a symbol of it on a piece of paper. In a fireplace or wherever you can do so safely, light the paper on fire. Confess the sin as you watch the paper darken, shrink, and turn into ash. Ask God to bring his refining fire into your life.

⤙ Revealing Our Secrets

Our Sins Weigh upon Us

Now you, mortal, say to the house of Israel, Thus you have said: "Our transgressions and sins weigh upon us, and we waste away because of them; how then can we live?" Say to them, As I live, says the LORD GOD, I have no pleasure in the death of the wicked, but that the wicked turn back from their ways and live; turn back, turn back from your evil ways; for why will you die, O house of Israel? Again, though I say to the wicked, "You shall surely die," yet if they turn from their sin and do what is lawful and right—if the wicked restore the pledge, give back what they have taken by robbery, and walk in the statutes of life, committing no iniquity—they shall surely live, they shall not die. None of the sins that they have committed shall be remembered against them; they have done what is lawful and right, they shall surely live.

Ezekiel 33:10–11, 14–16

FOR THE FIRST time the exilic community tells the truth about its situation. Its prayer of confession is a longing acknowledgment that the weight of past sin is so great that the community is dying. Denial now turns to despair. Ezekiel preaches a recurrent sermon (see also Ezek 18) that offers a way into the future through a sharp turn to the ways and doings of God. The People of God are at their lowest ebb and, yet, on the verge of renewal.

Sometimes confessing privately to God can leave us feeling weighed down, not sure we have confessed properly or that we deserve forgiveness. Today consider asking a trusted friend or pastor to hear your confession.

"A man who confesses his sins in the presence of a brother knows that he is no longer alone with himself; he experiences the presence of God in the reality of the other person. As long as I am by myself in the confession of my sins everything remains in the dark, but in the presence of a brother the sin has to be brought into the light."

—Dietrich Bonhoeffer, *Life Together* [8]

Healing and Forgiveness

When [Jesus] returned to Capernaum after some days, it was reported that he was at home. So many gathered around that there was no longer room for them, not even in front of the door; and he was speaking the word to them. Then some people came, bringing to him a paralyzed man, carried by four of them. And when they could not bring him to Jesus because of the crowd, they removed the roof above him; and after having dug through it, they let down the mat on which the paralytic lay. When Jesus saw their faith, he said to the paralytic, "Son, your sins are forgiven." Now some of the scribes were sitting there, questioning in their hearts, "Why does this fellow speak in this way? It is blasphemy! Who can forgive sins but God alone?" At once Jesus perceived in his spirit that they were discussing these questions among themselves; and he said to them, "Why do you raise such questions in your heart? Which is easier, to say to the paralytic, 'Your sins are forgiven,' or to say, 'Stand up and take your mat and walk'? But so that you may know that the Son of Man has authority on earth to forgive sins"—he said to the paralytic—"I say to you, stand up, take your mat and go to your home." And he stood up, and immediately took the mat and went out before all of them.

Mark 2:1–12a

GOD HAS CALLED us not only to individual spiritual formation, but to be formed into communities of faith too. We pray for one another and work for the healing and wholeness of others, just as this paralytic's four friends help him receive the healing he needs. Jesus connects healing and forgiveness, recognizing that guilt or self-hatred can paralyze our spirit as much as a physical illness or injury can paralyze our limbs.

Dear Lord, only you have the power to heal me and relieve my burdens. With nothing to offer but faith, I come to you with my sin and shame. Please forgive me, heal me, and help me to trust, follow, and obey. I want to be holy, as you are. In your name I pray. Amen.

Forgive and Console Him

But if anyone has caused pain, he has caused it not to me, but to some extent—not to exaggerate it—to all of you. This punishment by the majority is enough for such a person; so now instead you should forgive and console him, so that he may not be overwhelmed by excessive sorrow. So I urge you to reaffirm your love for him. I wrote for this reason: to test you and to know whether you are obedient in everything. Anyone whom you forgive, I also forgive. What I have forgiven, if I have forgiven anything, has been for your sake in the presence of Christ. And we do this so that we may not be outwitted by Satan; for we are not ignorant of his designs.

2 Corinthians 2:5–11

PAUL IS ADMONISHING the Corinthians to rehabilitate a sinner in their midst. The community's disapproval of him has gone on long enough. There comes a time when shaming eats the soul, and Paul wisely does not want discouragement to set in. Communities must tend to comforting those who have fallen, lest they despair. Trying to discern when punishment is helpful and when forgiveness and love are what are needed is a delicate matter. Those bound together by baptism in the Body of Christ are called to this ministry for one another.

Part of the discipline of confession involves hearing and forgiving others when they have repented, even if their sin has harmed us personally. We see the same message in Colossians 3:13: "Bear with one another and, if anyone has a complaint against another, forgive each other; just as the Lord has forgiven you, so you also must forgive." Is there anyone in your life who has confessed and asked you for forgiveness, but whom you have not been able to forgive? Ask God to give you forgiveness.

I Wait for the Lord

Out of the depths I cry to you, O LORD, / Lord, hear my voice! /
Let your ears be attentive / to the voice of my supplications! / If
you, O LORD, should mark iniquities, / Lord, who could stand? /
But there is forgiveness with you, / so that you may be revered. /
I wait for the LORD, my soul waits, / and in his word I hope; /
my soul waits for the Lord / more than those who watch for the
morning, / more than those who watch for the morning. / O Israel,
hope in the LORD! / For with the LORD there is steadfast love, /
and with him is great power to redeem. / It is he who will redeem
Israel / from all its iniquities.

Psalm 130:1–8

THIS SONG OF repentance appeals to God's "steadfast love." The first
few verses note clearly an understanding of the enormity of sin—if God
were an accountant, we would all be doomed. The wonder of God's
grace was just as vivid then as now. Then the interplay between waiting and hoping comes through in eagerness to receive the generosity of
God's grace. The psalm reminds us to neither trivialize sin nor under-
estimate God's love.

Reflect on what you have learned about yourself and about God
throughout these days of practicing confession. Has your burden
become lighter?

Forgive us our debts as we forgive our debtors, so that we may have a
clear and joyful conscience before you, and never again fear, nor be fright-
ened. Amen.

—Martin Luther, *Luther's Prayers*[9]

For more verses on confession and ideas on how to practice the discipline of confession,
see the Responding exercises and Spiritual Disciplines Index in *The Life with God Bible*.

Worship

Expressing in words, music, rituals, and silent adoration the greatness, beauty, and goodness of God, by means of which we enter the supranatural reality of the shekinah, *or glory, of God*

In Exodus, God makes clear that we are to worship the Lord and only the Lord, a message Jesus reiterates when the devil asks Jesus to worship him during the temptation in the wilderness: "Worship the Lord your God, and serve only him" (Luke 4:8b). In worship we seek to enter into God's presence. We can and do worship in many ways—in song, in prayer, in silence, on our knees, seated at our desks, or standing in a forest. As Richard Foster writes, we cannot guarantee true worship by form and ritual or the lack thereof.[1] Ritual can be important and helpful, but it is our hearts that matter. True worship is about our attitude.

In worship we reflect on all that God is and does and offer our praise and gratitude. To worship is to, as much as is possible, see God in full glory and worthiness. That is why so often worship is preceded by study. We seek to understand who God is and remember all that God has done, and then all we can do is marvel and adore. We can only enter into worship of God if we view God as worthy, if we understand our proper place in our relationship with God.

Indeed, the pages of Scripture testify to the fact that so often God's people revert to worshiping idols, to giving their allegiance and adoration to what they can see or taste or touch. We too are guilty of idol worship. We worship money, sex, power, even other people, but everything other than God will ultimately disappoint. Only God is worthy.

Worship the LORD in holy splendor;
tremble before him, all the earth.

—Psalm 96:9

Worship

Everyday Worship

"But the hour is coming, and is now here, when the true worshipers will worship the Father in spirit and truth, for the Father seeks such as these to worship him."

John 4:23

GOD THE FATHER is seeking worshipers. Most often we respond to this call by worshiping God during the hour or two we spend in church. At least we try. We know that worship should not be limited to Sunday mornings, but often we find ourselves doing just that. Yet what we are meant to do is spend each day in praise and adoration, in a never ceasing conversation with our Lord. When we pour worship out over our daily lives, we grow ever more sensitive to God's voice and presence. Richard Foster writes that he spent an entire year trying to live in constant awareness of and openness to Jesus as his teacher. He found that it greatly enhanced his experience of communal worship. He found himself thinking, "After all, [Jesus] had graciously spoken to me in dozens of little ways throughout the week; he will certainly speak to me here as well."[2] Foster also discovered that his efforts greatly increased his ability to distinguish God's voice from the cacophony of other sounds of daily living.

To try to integrate worship more fully into your everyday life, make an effort during each of the next ten days to worship in some way. This practice could take many forms: singing a praise song during your morning commute, remembering to thank God for something good that happens, finding a few minutes in a quiet place to sit in silent adoration, gathering a couple of friends to praise and worship together. On Sunday consider attending a church that you know has a style of worship different from your own to see what you learn from experiencing another way of entering God's presence.

Spiritual Practice

Sing to the Lord

O sing to the LORD a new song;
   sing to the LORD, all the earth.
Sing to the LORD, bless his name;
   tell of his salvation from day to day.
Declare his glory among the nations,
   his marvelous works among all the peoples.
For great is the LORD, and greatly to be praised;
   he is to be revered above all gods.

Psalm 96:1–4

ALONG WITH PRAYER, praise is the pulse beat of the Psalms. The praise or adulation often looks like proclamation, but poetic proclamation is our natural response when we have entered into surpassing magnificence—the Person and the Creation of the Lord God, the Almighty. We simply *must* bear witness to it, proclaim it, shout it from the rooftops as an essential part of engaging, enjoying, and being faithful to it.

Meditate for a few minutes on this quote as you begin your time of worship today:

"To worship is to quicken the conscience by the holiness of God, to feed the mind with the truth of God, to purge the imagination by the beauty of God, to open the heart to the love of God, to devote the will to the purpose of God."

—William Temple[3]

Admiring Who God Is

The LORD is king; let the peoples tremble!
  He sits enthroned upon the cherubim; let the earth quake!
The LORD is great in Zion;
  he is exalted over all the peoples.
Let them praise your great and awesome name.
  Holy is he!
Mighty King, lover of justice,
  you have established equity;
you have executed justice
  and righteousness in Jacob.
Extol the LORD our God;
  worship at his footstool.
  Holy is he!

Psalm 99:1–5

THIS ENTHRONEMENT PSALM repeatedly calls the People of God to worship, to tremble, to be overwhelmed by the God who is with us, but is set apart from us. Other songs celebrating God as King point to acts of creation and deliverance. This one focuses more on God's character as one who is just, who answers those who call for help, who forgives and establishes justice all at once, who is holy. One way to "worship at his footstool" is to admire who God is.

According to Augustine, "A Christian should be an alleluia from head to foot." What does this quote mean to you? How well does this description fit you?

Worshiping God Through Song

These are the men whom David put in charge of the service of song in the house of the Lord, after the ark came to rest there. They ministered with song before the tabernacle of the tent of meeting, until Solomon had built the house of the Lord in Jerusalem; and they performed their service in due order.

1 Chronicles 6:31–32

THE SINGERS PLAY a very important role in the worship described by the Chronicler; they are here given a levitical pedigree. David found great joy in worshiping God through song and promoted music as a ministry, a practice that continues today through traditional hymns and modern praise bands.

Today seek to worship God through song. As you prepare to worship, challenge yourself to let go of feeling self-conscious in your worship and really rejoice, even if it feels as though you are making a fool of yourself. Reflect on these words:

"To worship God *means* to serve God. Basically there are two ways to do it. One way is to do things for God that God needs to have done— run errands for God, carry messages for God, fight on God's side, feed God's lambs, and so on. The other way is to do things for God that you need to do—sing songs for God, create beautiful things for God, give things up for God, tell God what's on your mind and in your heart, in general rejoice and make a fool of yourself for God the way lovers have always made fools of themselves for the one they love."

—Frederick Buechner, *Beyond Words*[4]

~ *Everyday Worship*

How We Worship

The LORD said to Moses and Aaron in the land of Egypt: Tell the whole congregation of Israel that on the tenth of this month they are to take a lamb for each family, a lamb for each household. Then the whole assembled congregation of Israel shall slaughter it at twilight. They shall take some of the blood and put it on the two doorposts and the lintel of the houses in which they eat it. This is how you shall eat it: your loins girded, your sandals on your feet, and your staff in your hand; and you shall eat it hurriedly. It is the passover of the LORD. For I will pass through the land of Egypt that night, and I will strike down every firstborn in the land of Egypt, both human beings and animals; on all the gods of Egypt I will execute judgments: I am the LORD. The blood shall be a sign for you on the houses where you live: when I see the blood, I will pass over you, and no plague shall destroy you when I strike the land of Egypt.

This day shall be a day of remembrance for you. You shall celebrate it as a festival to the LORD; throughout your generations you shall observe it as a perpetual ordinance.

Exodus 12:1, 3, 6b–7, 11–14

EVEN IN TIMES of great danger and haste there is a place for ritual in the spiritual life. God is careful to give very specific instructions on how families should celebrate the first Passover. God is a God of symbols, who impregnates common objects with divine significance. The precision with which God creates the Passover meal will be a precision he brings to the law and to the construction of the tabernacle. *Why* is important, and *what*, but also *how:* how we speak, how we pray, how we act, how we worship. This matters to God, and it ought to matter to us. It plays a role in what we retain and what kind of persons we become.

Today pay attention to the "how" of your worship. What kind are you most comfortable with? Do you find that having a certain order or ritual to your individual worship of God is helpful? Why or why not?

Remembering God's Deliverance

Now, the fifteenth day of the seventh month, when you have gathered in the produce of the land, you shall keep the festival of the LORD, lasting seven days; a complete rest on the first day, and a complete rest on the eighth day. On the first day you shall take the fruit of majestic trees, branches of palm trees, boughs of leafy trees, and willow of the brook; and you shall rejoice before the LORD your God for seven days. You shall keep it as a festival to the LORD seven days in the year; you shall keep it in the seventh month as a statute forever throughout your generations. You shall live in booths for seven days; all that are citizens in Israel shall live in booths, so that your generations may know that I made the people of Israel live in booths when I brought them out of the land of Egypt: I am the LORD your God.

Leviticus 23:39–43

THE WORSHIP EXPERIENCE of festivals emphasized memory, in this case memory of the exodus experience. That experience was one of deliverance and guidance. The purpose of worship is to remember that experience, to live it, to rehearse and reenact it, and so to bring it into the present. The people then can see that God is still the one who delivers and guides and can remember to structure their lives on that basis and move into the future with hope. This kind of memory is extremely important to our spiritual life. As we might expect, the spiritual journey includes high points and low points—it does not move at a steady rate of growth. Remembering God's work in the past has a sustaining and renewing effect during times of spiritual drought. Memory and worship are thus keys to a long life of spiritual formation.

Try starting your worship practice today by remembering and thanking God for some of the things he has done for his people through the ages and in your own life. How does this practice affect your worship?

Worshiping Jesus

Immediately [Jesus] made the disciples get into the boat and go on ahead to the other side, while he dismissed the crowds. . . . And early in the morning he came walking toward them on the sea. But when the disciples saw him walking on the sea, they were terrified, saying, "It is a ghost!" And they cried out in fear. But immediately Jesus spoke to them and said, "Take heart, it is I; do not be afraid."

Peter answered him, "Lord, if it is you, command me to come to you on the water." He said, "Come." So Peter got out of the boat, started walking on the water, and came toward Jesus. But when he noticed the strong wind, he became frightened, and beginning to sink, he cried out, "Lord, save me!" Jesus immediately reached out his hand and caught him, saying, "You of little faith, why did you doubt?" When they got into the boat, the wind ceased. And those in the boat worshiped him, saying, "Truly you are the Son of God."

Matthew 14:22, 25–33

JESUS INITIALLY IS mistaken for a ghost, since Jews at that time viewed bodies of water as the dwelling place of spirits and demons. Only Peter attempts to step out in faith and walk toward Jesus, until the elements of wind and wave frighten him. It is a story of walking by faith, rather than in fear. Peter is called "you of little faith," but in the end all those in the boat, including Peter, worship Jesus as the divine son of God.

Today pay special attention to remembering and thanking God for Jesus.

"When we worship, we fill our minds and hearts with wonder at [Jesus]—the detailed actions and words of his earthly life, his trial and death on the cross, his resurrection reality, and his work as ascended intercessor. Here, in the words of Albertus Magnus (died 1280), we find 'God through God himself; that is, we pass by the Manhood into the Godhood, by the wounds of humanity into the depths of his divinity.'"

—Dallas Willard, *The Spirit of the Disciplines*[5]

Worship in Times of Suffering

One day when his sons and daughters were eating and drinking wine in the eldest brother's house, a messenger came to Job and said, "The oxen were plowing and the donkeys were feeding beside them, and the Sabeans fell on them and carried them off, and killed the servants with the edge of the sword; I alone have escaped to tell you." While he was still speaking, another came and said, "The fire of God fell from heaven and burned up the sheep and the servants, and consumed them; I alone have escaped to tell you." While he was still speaking, another came and said, "Your sons and daughters were eating and drinking wine in their eldest brother's house, and suddenly a great wind came across the desert, struck the four corners of the house, and it fell on the young people, and they are dead; I alone have escaped to tell you."

Then Job arose, tore his robe, shaved his head, and fell on the ground and worshiped. He said, "Naked I came from my mother's womb, and naked shall I return there; the LORD gave, and the LORD has taken away; blessed be the name of the LORD."

Job 1:13, 16, 18–21

JOB'S ACTIONS SHOW just how deeply rooted his piety is. There is a solemnity in them, and we can visualize him shaving his head, tearing his robe, falling on his face, and quietly worshiping God. The power of good ritual bears us through many a time of distress. We come to see with Job that suffering helps us to know God in bad times as well as good. Only in this way do we gain a clearer vision of God and know that he is with us even when we cannot hear or see him. In suffering we learn the ways God is truly present even when he seems far, far away.

As you worship today, remember God's work in your life during times of suffering. If you find yourself in a dark time now, reflect on the meaning of this passage for your present circumstances and try to worship as best you can.

⌒ Everyday Worship

Trusting That God Is with Us

My God, my God, why have you forsaken me?
   Why are you so far from helping me,
   from the words of my groaning?
O my God, I cry by day, but you do not answer;
   and by night, but find no rest.
Yet you are holy,
   enthroned on the praises of Israel.
In you our ancestors trusted;
   they trusted, and you delivered them.
To you they cried, and were saved;
   in you they trusted, and were not put to shame.

Psalm 22:1–5

THE PSALMS MOVE between two poles; on one side is the desperate condition of human beings when left to stand on their own and, on the other, the unlimited greatness and goodness of God. From that movement there emerges, strangely but beautifully, the greatness of humanity under God and within God's life and cosmic plan. This is the result of God's salvation or deliverance, which in psalm after psalm is remembered, praised, and anticipated. "God-with-us" is the essence of deliverance regardless of the specific circumstance.

As you worship God today, begin with this prayer and reflect on how God is with you:

Dear Lord, sometimes I come to you confused by life. Things have not gone as I planned or hoped, and I don't know why. I struggle; I weep. I don't understand. Yet even in my sadness and confusion, I know that you are holy and that all I have to do is trust you. You know what is good for me. You are always on the side of your people and will deliver me as you did them. I thank you for being You. I praise your holy name. Amen.

Worship That Is Dependent on God

Then the Lord said [to Moses], "I have observed the misery of my people who are in Egypt; I have heard their cry on account of their taskmasters. Indeed, I have known their sufferings, and I have come down to deliver them from the Egyptians."

Moses told Aaron all the words of the Lord with which he had sent him, and all the signs with which he had charged him. Then Moses and Aaron went and assembled all the elders of the Israelites. Aaron spoke all the words that the Lord had spoken to Moses, and performed the signs in the sight of the people. The people believed; and when they heard that the Lord had given heed to the Israelites and that he had seen their misery, they bowed down and worshiped.

Exodus 3:7–8a; 4:28–31

WHEN MOSES AND Aaron first come to the Hebrews, the people believe and worship God. But it does not last. "They would not listen to Moses, because of their broken spirit and their cruel slavery" (6:9). Again and again—when they are still in Egypt, when they are in the desert, when they are at the foot of Mt. Sinai—they complain and rebel and refuse to trust God. We are no different. One month our faith is strong, another it is weak. We have had a golden calf or two, often right after a period of profound spiritual blessing. Grace is essential for followers of God. We can never make it on our best intentions. Yet even in our frailty, it is better if we seek worship that will last—worship that is wholly dependent on God and absolutely nothing else.

End your time of worship today with this prayer:

Loving Father, our eternal friend: May we never forget or dishonor you this day; but in all places and in all activities remember your presence and cherish your love; for Jesus Christ's sake. Amen.

—Charles Vaughan

Worshiping with Our Hearts

The Lord said: / Because these people draw near with their mouths / and honor me with their lips, / while their hearts are far from me, / and their worship of me is a human commandment learned by rote; / so I will again do / amazing things with this people, / shocking and amazing. / The wisdom of their wise shall perish, / and the discernment of the discerning shall be hidden.

Isaiah 29:13–14

Spiritual Practice

THE WORDS OF this passage hit home. Each of us has sat in church with our mind far from God or prayed a familiar prayer with our lips and not our heart. There is beauty in familiarity, but it can also lead to boredom or, worse, contempt. It is easy to get into a rut and not bother to interrupt our routine with the real work of worship. Others of us may even have given up entering into the presence of God or don't really believe such experiences are possible or even helpful.

Hopefully, the work you have done during the previous ten days in seeking to worship God in your daily life will have helped you to better distinguish God's voice and presence and appreciate just why such seeking is so necessary. So this week, when you attend your worship service, go with every expectation of meeting and worshiping God to your best ability.

Start by arriving at the service ten or so minutes early so that you can sit and prepare yourself. Open your heart to God; give thanks for the many gifts given to God's people, particularly the gift of Jesus. Pray for the worship leaders, that they may feel God's hand upon them and speak and lead boldly. Then pick one or two people in the congregation to particularly pray for, that each may experience God's presence. Think about what it means to be in God's house of worship. Focus on singing the songs directly to God and listening for God in the Scripture readings and the words preached. When you return home, you might want to write down your thoughts and feelings about worship and how approaching worship this way did or did not change your experience of it.

God-Directed Worship

These are the statues and ordinances that you must diligently observe in the land that the Lord, the God of your ancestors, has given you to occupy all the days that you live on the earth.

You must demolish completely all the places where the nations who you are about to dispossess served their gods, on the mountain heights, on the hills, and under every leafy tree. Break down their altars, smash their pillars, burn their sacred poles with fire, and hew down the idols of their gods, and thus blot out their name from their places. You shall not worship the Lord your God in such ways. But you shall seek the place that the Lord your God will choose out of all your tribes as his habitation to put his name there. You shall go there, bringing there your burnt offerings and your sacrifices, your tithes and your donations, your votive gifts, your freewill offerings, and the firstlings of your herds and flocks. And you shall eat there in the presence of the Lord your God, you and your households together, rejoicing in all the undertakings in which the Lord your God has blessed you.

Deuteronomy 12:1–7

THESE INSTRUCTIONS RECOGNIZE that places of false worship are dangerous, since they might tempt the Israelites to serve the wrong god. They are to destroy them. Although few of us today would be tempted to worship a false god as such, many things tempt our hearts to put them first and God second. We must root out the desire to worship these things and focus on the true God.

The Lord also directs the Israelites to seek out the place the Lord will choose. The principle, which should still be honored today, is that God defines the conditions of our worship of him.

What might be a place of false worship in your life? In what ways have you felt God directing your worship over the last several days?

Worshiping with Our Hearts

Building the House of the Lord

So Solomon built the house [of the LORD], and finished it. He lined the walls of the house on the inside with boards of cedar; from the floor of the house to the rafters of the ceiling, he covered them on the inside with wood; and he covered the floor of the house with boards of cypress. He built twenty cubits of the rear of the house with boards of cedar from the floor to the rafters, and he built this within as an inner sanctuary, as the most holy place. Solomon overlaid the inside of the house with pure gold, then he drew chains of gold across, in front of the inner sanctuary, and overlaid it with gold. Next he overlaid the whole house with gold, in order that the whole house might be perfect; even the whole altar that belonged to the inner sanctuary he overlaid with gold.

1 Kings 6:14–16, 21–22

A RESPLENDENT TEMPLE, unsurpassed in beauty, is erected under Solomon's direction. Indeed, the exacting ritual of building the Temple is in itself an act of worship. The Temple, now the center of worship and celebration for the people of Israel, provides a visible anchor for their faith and an enduring physical space for the disciplines of spiritual formation that had developed since the establishment of the tent of meeting at Shiloh. The permanent building provides the continuity needed to develop songs and liturgies that enhance the Israelites' worship experience. Imagine walking up several flights of steps to bring sacrifices to the priests, who then kill the animals and place them upon the huge altar, while trumpets blare and choirs sing. The rituals we participate in while worshiping in the great cathedrals of the world might be comparable. There is something in this type of worship that lifts our spirits and gives us a glimpse into what our worship of God can and should be.

The opulence described here may seem over the top, but to Solomon and his people, the perfection of the Temple was nothing more than what God deserved. When have your surroundings most enhanced your worship?

Worshiping False Gods

King Solomon loved many foreign women along with the daughter of Pharaoh: Moabite, Ammonite, Edomite, Sidonian, and Hittite women, from the nations concerning which the Lord had said to the Israelites, "You shall not enter into marriage with them, neither shall they with you; for they will surely incline your heart to follow their gods"; Solomon clung to these in love. Among his wives were seven hundred princesses and three hundred concubines; and his wives turned away his heart. For when Solomon was old, his wives turned away his heart after other gods, and his heart was not true to the Lord his God, as was the heart of his father David.

1 Kings 11:1–4

NOT LONG AFTER Solomon built the Temple, he built "high places" so that his wives could worship other gods (11:7–8). The worship of other gods was still the People of God's most consistent failure. In spite of the warning that the Israelites would be cut off from the land and cast from God's sight if they served and worshiped other gods, in the abundance and relative peace of this golden age of national unity, the human capacity for idolatry and neglect of the source of all blessing stubbornly shined through. We struggle with the very same problems in our own day. We may not worship statues of gold shaped like animals or ourselves, but we most certainly find many other things besides God to rely upon—our 401(k), profession, education, marriage, physical appearance, and the like. For the sake of our spirit, we need to bring them all to God as a sacrifice of praise, much as the faithful did in Solomon's great Temple.

Father God, help me to remember that I can serve only one master, that when I worship money or sex or power, then I cannot worship you. Purge my heart of all loyalties that interfere with my worship of you, dear Lord. In your name I pray. Amen.

⌒ *Worshiping with Our Hearts*

Preparing for Worship

"In the first year of his reign, King Cyrus issued a decree: Concerning the house of God at Jerusalem, let the house be rebuilt, the place where sacrifices are offered and burnt offerings are brought; its height shall be sixty cubits and its width sixty cubits, with three courses of hewn stone and one course of timber; let the cost be paid from the royal treasury. Moreover, let the gold and silver vessels of the house of God, which Nebuchadnezzar took out of the temple in Jerusalem and brought to Babylon, be restored and brought back to the temple in Jerusalem, each to its place; you shall put them in the house of God."

Ezra 6:3–5

THROUGH DISOBEDIENCE AND worship of false gods, the beautiful Temple was destroyed and the people of God exiled. Here the people have finally returned to Jerusalem and been allowed to rebuild the Temple. As the returned Jews reinstituted worship practice in Jerusalem, there was a great concern to do things right. Meticulous care was taken to ensure that the "house of God" was properly built and furnished. God's work is not haphazard, a kind of fly-by-the-seat-of-your-pants effort. The planning and coordinating of worship services, hours of sermon study by the pastor, and thoughtful prayers by the worshipers do not quench the stirrings of the Spirit. On the contrary, deliberate and intentional preparation for entering into God's presence rids the mind and heart of trivial and worldly distractions.

Reflect on this quote as you prepare yourself for worship this week:

"If Christians worshiped only when they felt like it, there would be precious little worship. . . . Worship is an *act* that develops feelings for God, not a *feeling* for God that is expressed in an act of worship. When we obey the command to praise God in worship, our deep, essential need to be in relationship with God is nurtured."

—Eugene Peterson, *A Long Obedience in the Same Direction*[6]

Worshiping in Community

Now in the church at Antioch there were prophets and teachers: Barnabas, Simeon who was called Niger, Lucius of Cyrene, Manaen a member of the court of Herod the ruler, and Saul. While they were worshiping the Lord and fasting, the Holy Spirit said, "Set apart for me Barnabas and Saul for the work to which I have called them." Then after fasting and praying they laid their hands on them and sent them off.

Acts 13:1–3

THIS PASSAGE MARKS the great turn of the Church to missions. During periods of "worshiping and fasting" an impression grows that Barnabas and Saul have a special work to do. And the group response to this impression is fasting, prayer, and the laying on of hands. In worship, these valiant disciples move beyond the narrow experiences of personal faith into the reality of God's presence in community. Later, it will lead to the full manifestation of God across time and history, and into eternity. Here, worship demonstrates the way in which God leads the first Christians beyond their narrow ethnic religion to embrace a universal call to all the peoples of the earth.

How does worshiping with the community differ from worshiping alone? Do you experience the feelings described in this quote?

"A quickening Presence pervades us, breaking down some part of the special privacy and isolation of our individual lives and blending our spirits within a superindividual Life and Power. An objective, dynamic Presence enfolds us all, nourishes our souls, speaks glad, unutterable comfort with us, and quickens us in depths that had before been slumbering."

—Thomas R. Kelly, *The Eternal Promise*[7]

~ *Worshiping with Our Hearts*

Worshiping God, Not Spiritual Experiences

For to which of the angels did God ever say, / "You are my Son; / today I have begotten you"? / Or again, / "I will be his Father, / and he will be my Son"? / And again, when he brings the firstborn into the world, he says, / "Let all God's angels worship him." / Of the angels he says, / "He makes his angels winds, / and his servants flames of fire." / But of the Son he says, / "Your throne, O God, is forever and ever, / and the righteous scepter is the scepter of your kingdom. / You have loved righteousness and hated wickedness; / therefore God, your God, has anointed you / with the oil of gladness beyond your companions."

Hebrews 1:5–9

AS THE SON of God, Jesus is vastly superior to angels, indeed is worshiped by them. A salvo of scriptural quotations demonstrates that spiritual creatures and spiritual experience are subordinate to Jesus Christ, the Son of God, and cannot be substituted for him. Making spiritual experience one's primary objective is like being in love with marriage instead of one's spouse. A good marriage results from loving and serving one's spouse; a healthy spiritual life results from glorifying Christ. Being in love with spiritual experience is not the same as loving and serving Christ and can even eclipse Christ.

As we seek to practice the discipline of worship, or indeed any discipline, we must always be aware of the danger of worshiping the discipline instead of Christ. Have you found yourself worshiping for worship's sake rather than for God's? Ask God to help you keep your focus on God alone.

Practicing God's Presence

There was also a prophet, Anna the daughter of Phanuel, of the tribe of Asher. She was of a great age, having lived with her husband seven years after her marriage, then as a widow to the age of eighty-four. She never left the temple but worshiped there with fasting and prayer night and day. At that moment, she came, and began to praise God and to speak about the child to all who were looking for the redemption of Jerusalem.

Luke 2:36–38

WE MAY NOT be able to identify with Anna's call to prophecy or her living situation, yet her commitment to the Spiritual Disciplines of prayer, fasting, and worship—a life focused in mind, body, and activity on engaging with God—is a commitment we all can pursue. Brother Lawrence, a seventeenth-century monk, informs us in his writings that we can pray and worship both in times of focused quiet and spiritual activity and in times of work and routine daily life. Brother Lawrence served in the monastery's kitchen, performing mundane work familiar to most of us, yet he developed a way of focusing on God's presence throughout all of his days. In his timeless work *Practicing the Presence of God,* he reveals his focused perspective: "Applying my mind to these thoughts in the morning and then spending the rest of the day, even in the midst of all my work, in the presence of God, I considered that he was always with me, that he was even within me."

The discipline of worship is a powerful tool that allows us to practice God's presence throughout all facets of our being, to live daily and hourly as a dwelling place of God. As Anna rejoiced in the coming of Jesus, our Immanuel, we too can experience the thrill of Jesus, "God with us," in increasing measure as we make worship central in our lives.

Have your worship experiences helped you get a sense of continual worship? If so, how? As you worship today, imagine what it would feel like always to be communicating with God in this way.

~ *Worshiping with Our Hearts*

Coming Close to the Glory of God

And above the dome over their heads there was something like a throne, in appearance like sapphire; and seated above the likeness of a throne was something that seemed like a human form. Upward from what appeared like the loins I saw something like gleaming amber, something that looked like fire enclosed all around; and downward from what looked like the loins I saw something that looked like fire, and there was a splendor all around. Like the bow in a cloud on a rainy day, such was the appearance of the splendor all around. This was the appearance of the likeness of the glory of the LORD.

When I saw it, I fell on my face.

Ezekiel 1:26–28a

THE GLORY OF the Lord is the shining, potent, almost material presence of God. Coming close to the glory of God causes Ezekiel to fall on his face before such high-voltage energy. Like Ezekiel, A.W. Tozer felt the only response to God was simply to fall on one's face. Tozer would spend four to five hours at a time lying face down on the floor, saying nothing. Being with God in such intensity overpowered both men in awe and fear.

Have you experienced "holy expectancy" in worship?

"A striking feature of worship in the Bible is that people gathered in what we could only call a 'holy expectancy.' They believed they would actually hear the Kol Yahweh, the voice of God. . . . They were coming into the awful, glorious, gracious presence of the living God. They gathered with anticipation, knowing that Christ was present among them and would teach them and touch them with his living power. . . . When more than one or two come into public worship with a holy expectancy, it can change the atmosphere of a room. People who enter harried and distracted are drawn quickly into a sense of the silent Presence. Hearts and minds are lifted upward. The air becomes charged with expectancy."

—Richard J. Foster, *Celebration of Discipline*[8]

Praise Without Ceasing

Day and night without ceasing they sing,
"Holy, holy, holy,
the Lord God the Almighty,
     who was and is and is to come."
And whenever the living creatures give glory and honor and thanks
to the one who is seated on the throne, who lives forever and ever, the
twenty-four elders fall before the one who is seated on the throne and
worship the one who lives forever and ever; they cast their crowns
before the throne, singing,
     "You are worthy, our Lord and God,
          to receive glory and honor and power,
     for you created all things,
          and by your will they existed and were created."

Revelation 4:8b–11

WHEN WE WORSHIP, we join with all the company of heaven in the
praise that continually echoes throughout the cosmos. Their hymn hal-
lows God as Creator of all realities.

End your worship time with this prayer, which comes from a popular
hymn:

*Now thank we all our God / with heart and hands and voices, / Who
wondrous things has done, / in whom his world rejoices; / Who, from our
mothers' arms, / has blessed us on our way / With countless gifts of love, /
and still is ours today.*

—Martin Rinckart, "Now Thank We All Our God"

For more verses on worship and ideas on how to practice the discipline of worship, see
the Responding exercises and Spiritual Disciplines Index in *The Life with God Bible*.

Service

Loving, thoughtful, active promotion of the good of others and the causes of God in our world, through which we experience the many little deaths of going beyond ourselves

Service is one of the most frequently mentioned disciplines in the Bible. From the very beginning God's people pledged themselves as God's servants and were directed in the law to serve and care for others. Being a servant of God and of others was a way of living—a declaration of obedience, not an occasional volunteer activity.

In the New Testament, Jesus made it clear that he was God's servant, but also the servant of others. These two were inextricably linked. Again and again, he spoke of turning the cultural order upside down: "Whoever wants to be first must be last of all and servant of all" (Mark 9:35b). In Luke 22:25–26, he said, "The kings of the Gentiles lord it over them; and those in authority over them are called benefactors. But not so with you; rather the greatest among you must become like the youngest, and the leader like one who serves." Jesus underscored his point by humbling himself to wash the feet of the disciples (John 13:1–20), making it clear that this servanthood was much more than symbolic.

Then after Jesus' ultimate act of submission and servanthood on the cross, Paul took up the theme of servanthood, referring to himself time and again as a servant of the gospel (Eph 3:7; Col 1:23). We can follow in Jesus' footsteps and serve God and others purely as an act of love, but service is also an excellent way to train ourselves in humility and submission to God's will.

Like good stewards of the manifold grace of God, serve one another with whatever gift each of you has received.

—*1 Peter 4:10*

Service

Serving God in Every Task

Slaves, obey your earthly masters in everything, not only while being watched and in order to please them, but wholeheartedly, fearing the Lord. Whatever your task, put yourselves into it, as done for the Lord and not for your masters, since you know that from the Lord you will receive the inheritance as your reward; you serve the Lord Christ.

Colossians 3:22–24

MANY OF US view service as an occasional commitment that comprises a small part of our day or week or month, but here Paul tells us to view every task as service not only to those around us, but to the Lord. Service is less a task or series of tasks than an attitude of obedience. Paul's words in this passage are directed specifically at slaves, so our first reaction may be that these words are not directly applicable to us. But we are all slaves to God. Throughout the Old Testament and the New, the words often translated "servant," *ebed* in Hebrew and *doulos* in Greek, both literally mean "slave." In the Old Testament the People of God owed "slave service" to God in Temple worship.[1] Being God's servant evokes a master/slave relationship, a relationship of obedience in which we submit to God. In the New Testament both Jesus and Paul teach that Jesus' followers owe this same kind of service to one another, not because others are our masters, but because Christ is. By serving others, we serve him.

This week try to put Paul's words into action. Put yourself wholeheartedly into every task. Do everything you do, especially the lowest and most menial of tasks, with an attitude that you are serving the Lord. Whenever possible, look for additional ways to serve or to lighten another's burden. If you can perform your service without notice, all the better.

Spiritual Practice

Serving and Carrying

This is the service of the clans of the Gershonites, in serving and bearing burdens: They shall carry the curtains of the tabernacle, and the tent of meeting with its covering, and the outer covering of fine leather that is on top of it, and the screen for the entrance of the tent of meeting, and the hangings of the court, and the screen for the entrance of the gate of the court that is around the tabernacle and the altar, and their cords, and all the equipment in their service; and they shall do all that needs to be done with regard to them.

As for the Merarites, this is what they are charged to carry, as the whole of their service in the tent of meeting: the frames of the tabernacle, with its bars, pillars, and bases, and the pillars of the court all around with their bases, pegs, and cords, with all their equipment and all their related service.

According to the commandments of the LORD through Moses they were appointed to their several tasks of serving or carrying; thus they were enrolled by him, as the LORD commanded Moses.

Numbers 4:24–26, 29a, 31–32a, 49

AS THE ISRAELITES were moving from place to place in the wilderness, specific levitical clans were enrolled to break down the tabernacle, carry it to the new site, and reassemble it. Scripture refers to these tasks as "serving" or "carrying." To be part of God's community is to participate in it. God gave the Israelites work to do, because he was interested in the spiritual transformation and maturity of each individual. Just as God appointed the duties of the priests, he assigns work to each of us. Offering service to God is an important aspect of our continued growth in character. Doing our best to serve in our God-given ministries and constantly pursuing spiritual maturity is pleasing to God.

Today make an effort to help others by serving and carrying; for example, serve coffee to a colleague or carry someone's groceries.

Serving God in Every Task

Consecrated for God's Service

You shall bring the Levites before the tent of meeting, and assemble the whole congregation of the Israelites. When you bring the Levites before the LORD, the Israelites shall lay their hands on the Levites, and Aaron shall present the Levites before the LORD as an elevation offering from the Israelites, that they may do the service of the LORD.

Numbers 8:9–11

THIS PASSAGE DESCRIBES the consecration of the priests for God's service. Consecrated means "declared or set apart as sacred, dedicated to God." Today we are set apart for God when we are baptized, but many of us forget to live our lives that way. We must be concerned to first present ourselves before the Lord, not before people. As we learn to live our lives knowing we are standing before the living God, we will grow in simplicity and transparency.

How does it make you feel to think that you are set apart for God's service? Does it imbue you with a sense of purpose?

O Lord,
the author of all good things in your holy church:
Work mightily in your servants,
that they might be profitable to other people,
and vessels of your mercy and grace.
Control us, and so govern our thoughts and deeds,
that we may serve you in righteousness and holiness;
and sanctify us unto that eternal life,
which we, with all your creatures,
groaning together, wait for and expect;
through Jesus Christ our Lord. Amen.

—Philip Melanchthon

Do Not Neglect Them

As for the Levites resident in your towns, do not neglect them, because they have no allotment or inheritance with you. Every third year you shall bring out the full tithe of your produce for that year, and store it within your towns; the Levites, because they have no allotment or inheritance with you, as well as the resident aliens, the orphans, and the widows in your towns, may come and eat their fill so that the LORD your God may bless you in all that you undertake.

Deuteronomy 14:27–29

DEUTERONOMY IS A covenant renewal, reaffirming the relationship between the Great King, Yahweh, and his servant people, Israel. Here we see that the people are to bring tribute to their King. This tithe, or a tenth of the yield (or its monetary equivalent), was to be used in the worship of God, and every third year the tithe was to be used for the support of those who were not able to work the fields themselves (Levites, whom God set aside for special service to him, widows, orphans, and resident aliens).

Today think about a way you can serve those who are not able to work or support themselves. This service could be anything from dropping off some goods at a soup kitchen to visiting or making a meal for someone who has been laid off, is sick, or has recently had a baby. Make arrangements to put your plan into action sometime this week.

~ *Serving God in Every Task*

My Servant Caleb

The LORD said to Moses, "Send men to spy out the land of Canaan, which I am giving to the Israelites." At the end of forty days they returned from spying out the land. And they told him, "We came to the land to which you sent us; it flows with milk and honey. Yet the people who live in the land are strong, and the towns are fortified and very large."

Then all the congregation raised a loud cry and the people wept.

And Joshua son of Nun and Caleb son of Jephunneh, who were among those who had spied out the land, tore their clothes and said to all the congregation of the Israelites, "The land that we went through as spies is an exceedingly good land. If the LORD is pleased with us, he will bring us into this land and give it to us, a land that flows with milk and honey. Only, do not rebel against the LORD." But the whole congregation threatened to stone them.

Then the LORD said, "None of the people who have seen my glory and the signs I did in Egypt and in the wilderness, and yet have tested me these ten times and have not obeyed my voice, shall see the land that I swore to give to their ancestors; none of those who despised me shall see it. But my servant Caleb, because he has a different spirit and has followed me wholeheartedly, I will bring him into the land into which he went, and his descendants shall possess it."

Numbers 13:1a, 25, 27a, 28a; 14:1a, 6–9a, 10, 20a, 22–24

PART OF SERVING God is always trying to do God's will even when those around us make it difficult. Joshua and Caleb were a unique minority: they had a clear idea of who God was and who they were. The spiritual life requires that we learn to see things as God does.

God calls Caleb his "servant" and describes him as having a "different spirit." What qualities do servants have? Jot down a few of the qualities that come to mind and ask God for the grace to receive those qualities.

A Willing Heart

And they came, everyone whose heart was stirred, and everyone whose spirit was willing, and brought the LORD's offering to be used for the tent of meeting, and for all its service, and for the sacred vestments. So they came, both men and women; all who were of a willing heart brought brooches and earrings and signet rings and pendants, all sorts of gold objects, everyone bringing an offering of gold to the LORD. And everyone who possessed blue or purple or crimson yarn or fine linen or goats' hair or tanned rams' skins or fine leather, brought them. Everyone who could make an offering of silver or bronze brought it as the LORD's offering; and everyone who possessed acacia wood of any use in the work, brought it. All the skillful women spun with their hands and brought what they had spun. All the Israelite men and women whose hearts made them willing to bring anything for the work that the LORD had commanded by Moses to be done, brought it as a freewill offering to the LORD. Moses then called Bezalel and Oholiab and every skillful one to whom the LORD had given skill, everyone whose heart was stirred to come to do the work.

Exodus 35:21–25a, 29; 36:2

BEZALEL IS FILLED with the Holy Spirit to work on the tabernacle. The people who contribute to its construction do it of their own free will. A community built the tabernacle, not an elite handful; a community creates a house for God. All the people contribute, not just the leaders. Everyone who has a heart for it is part of it. It is a spirituality of the many, not the few, that makes it possible for God to have a home among his people.

Would your heart be "stirred" and your spirit "willing" to serve God by giving your gold jewelry and silver flatware, or something else of yours that is financially or sentimentally valuable, to your place of worship to be melted down to make a Communion set? What other possession or skill might you bring before God as a freewill offering?

~ *Serving God in Every Task*

Service in the Home

A capable wife who can find? / She is far more precious than jewels. / The heart of her husband trusts in her, / and he will have no lack of gain. / She does him good, and not harm, / all the days of her life. / She seeks wool and flax, / and works with willing hands. / She is like the ships of the merchant, / she brings her food from far away. / She rises while it is still night / and provides food for her household / and tasks for her servant-girls.

Proverbs 31:10–15

THE IDEAL WIFE described here provides us with a fine role model for the virtuous life. Here the virtue of wife and husband are intertwined. This teaching concerns a harmonious marriage and a strong family. This virtuous wife is a woman who lives in response to the grace of God, but who has her own struggles and challenges. She is no plaster saint. First of all, she is in a trusting relationship with her husband and family. Her husband has faith in her, and his confidence is justified. This woman has personal gifts and skills. Notice this faithful woman is running a rather large household. She is a good manager. She gets up early and uses her time well. She also delegates; she plans things for others in the household to do. This famous passage describes the ordinary happiness to be gained through virtuous living. The woman's children call her "happy" (31:28). Her husband thinks she is outstanding. But "charm" and "beauty" are not her watchwords. Likewise, the virtuous person has an inner beauty that comes from serving God and others.

So often we view service as something we perform for strangers, something that occurs outside the home, but some of our best opportunities to serve come every day among those we love. Today take an opportunity to serve someone with whom you live or help out at a friend's home. Wash the dishes or do another chore normally done by someone else.

As for Me and My Household

And Joshua said, "Now therefore revere the LORD, and serve him in sincerity and in faithfulness; put away the gods that your ancestors served beyond the River and in Egypt, and serve the LORD. Now if you are unwilling to serve the LORD, choose this day whom you will serve, whether the gods your ancestors served in the region beyond the River or the gods of the Amorites in whose land you are living; but as for me and my household, we will serve the LORD."

Joshua 24:2a, 14–15

IN THIS OFTEN quoted verse Joshua declares his intention to serve the Lord and tells the people to choose whom they will serve—the God who had chosen, liberated, and provided for them or the false gods of their ancestors on the other side of the Euphrates before God called Abraham. This choice is the one left for us as well; we must "choose this day whom we will serve." If we choose false gods, we lapse back into what we too had once been but for the grace of God.

Meditate on the phrase, "As for me and my household, we will serve the LORD." What does it mean for a family to "serve the Lord"? Is it more difficult today than it was in Joshua's time? Why or why not?

Two Servants

Ruth the Moabite said to Naomi, "Let me go to the field and glean among the ears of grain, behind someone in whose sight I might find favor." As it happened, she came to the part of the field belonging to Boaz. Then Boaz said to his servant who was in charge of the reapers, "To whom does this young woman belong?" The servant who was in charge of the reapers answered, "She is the Moabite who came back with Naomi from the country of Moab. She said, 'Please, let me glean and gather among the sheaves behind the reapers.' So she came, and she has been on her feet from early this morning until now, without resting even for a moment."

Then Boaz said to Ruth, "Now listen, my daughter, do not go to glean in another field or leave this one, but keep close to my young women." Then she fell prostrate, with her face to the ground, and said to him, "Why have I found favor in your sight, that you should take notice of me, when I am a foreigner?" But Boaz answered her, "All that you have done for your mother-in-law since the death of your husband has been fully told me. May the LORD reward you for your deeds."

Ruth 2:2a, 3b, 5–8, 10–11a, 12a

RUTH'S WORDS AND posture ("face to the ground") in response to the generosity of Boaz are indicators of the social distance between the Israelite man and the Moabite woman. Ruth identifies herself as a "foreigner," an outsider to Israelite culture and religion who was commonly denied covenant privileges extended to the other socially disadvantaged classes like widows, orphans, and aliens. The kindness of Boaz, like God's justice, shows no partiality. Boaz helps us understand the "second great commandment": loving our neighbor as we love ourselves (Matt 22:39).

Boaz served from a position of power by helping with the resources at his disposal; Ruth served by doing whatever she could with a joyful and willing spirit. What insights have you gained about each model of serving?

In Every Good Work

So then, brothers and sisters, stand firm and hold fast to the traditions that you were taught by us, either by word of mouth or by our letter. Now may our Lord Jesus Christ himself and God our Father, who loved us and through grace gave us eternal comfort and good hope, comfort your hearts and strengthen them in every good work and word.

2 Thessalonians 2:15–17

PAUL ASSURES HIS friends, "May our Lord Jesus Christ himself . . . strengthen [you] in every good work and word." With this confidence in God's faithfulness ringing in their ears, Paul calls them to be at work here and now and stay faithfully at their posts.

Think back on your practice of the discipline of service. Did you feel strengthened by Jesus in your good works and words?

Behold, Lord,
an empty vessel that needs to be filled.
My Lord, fill it.
I am weak in the faith;
strengthen me.
I am cold in love;
warm me and make me fervent
that my love may go out to my neighbor.

—Martin Luther

Not to Be Served, but to Serve

But Jesus called them to him and said, "You know that the rulers of the Gentiles lord it over them, and their great ones are tyrants over them. It will not be so among you; but whoever wishes to be great among you must be your servant, and whoever wishes to be first among you must be your slave; just as the Son of Man came not to be served but to serve, and to give his life a ransom for many."

Matthew 20:25–28

AS YOU CONTINUE in practicing the discipline of service, sometime within the next ten days try to find a way to serve that will turn the tables in the way Jesus describes. Perhaps you will want to wash the feet, literally or metaphorically, of someone from church or your family, or perhaps you will want to try to take on the daily tasks of someone in your life who often serves you. Most of us find ourselves in a position of power or leadership to at least one person in our lives, and to try to serve someone who serves us can be powerful, humbling, and illuminating. As Dallas Willard writes, "The discipline of service is even more important for Christians who find themselves in positions of influence, power, and leadership. To live as a servant while fulfilling socially important roles is one of the greatest challenges any disciple ever faces."[2]

Willard continues:

> Service to others in the spirit of Jesus allows us the freedom of a humility that carries no burdens of "appearance." It lets us be what we are—simply a particularly lively piece of clay who, as servant of God, happens to be here now with the ability to do this good and needful thing for that other bit of clay there. The experience of active love freed up and flowing by faith through us on such occasions will safeguard us from innumerable pitfalls of the spiritual life.[3]

Reflect on these words as you give careful and prayerful thought to finding the gesture that is right for you.

Spiritual Practice

I Devoted Myself to the Work

Moreover from the time that I [Nehemiah] was appointed to be their governor in the land of Judah, from the twentieth year to the thirty-second year of King Artaxerxes, twelve years, neither I nor my brothers ate the food allowance of the governor. The former governors who were before me laid heavy burdens on the people, and took food and wine from them, besides forty shekels of silver. Even their servants lorded it over the people. But I did not do so, because of the fear of God. Indeed, I devoted myself to the work on this wall, and acquired no land; and all my servants were gathered there for the work. Moreover there were at my table one hundred fifty people, Jews and officials, besides those who came to us from the nations around us. Now that which was prepared for one day was one ox and six choice sheep; also fowls were prepared for me, and every ten days skins of wine in abundance; yet with all this I did not demand the food allowance of the governor, because of the heavy burden of labor on the people. Remember for my good, O my God, all that I have done for this people.

Nehemiah 5:14–19

REJECTING THE EXAMPLES of his predecessors, Nehemiah devotes himself to the building of the wall rather than the building of his earthly wealth and influence, knowing that was the best way to serve his people. Nehemiah's sense of justice was derived from both his relationship with God and his concern for his fellow humans. Nehemiah, the man of action, practiced what he preached. He refused to profit at the expense of the less fortunate. In the New Testament the picture is clear that Jesus too was both radically obedient to God and selfless in his love for others. Theology and ethics are inseparable.

Today focus on asking God for ways to serve, writing down everything that comes to mind. Afterwards select the ideas you would like to pursue now, saving the others for another time.

Do Not Withhold Good

Do not withhold good from those to whom it is due,
    when it is in your power to do it.
Do not say to your neighbor, "Go, and come again,
    tomorrow I will give it"—when you have it with you.
Do not plan harm against your neighbor
    who lives trustingly beside you.
Do not quarrel with anyone without cause,
    when no harm has been done to you.
Do not envy the violent
    and do not choose any of their ways.

Proverbs 3:27–31

CONFIDENTLY SERVING GOD requires serving one's neighbor, being at peace with those who are good, and not being envious of the wicked, because the Lord's friendship is entirely on the side of the just and against evildoers.

We have all hurried by a friend or a stranger in need, telling ourselves that we would help if only we had more time, more money, more courage. "Next time," we say to ourselves, knowing full well that there might not be an opportunity tomorrow. Ask forgiveness for any sins of omission that you have committed, and ask God for the will to put your own desires aside in order to serve in the present.

~ *Not to Be Served, but to Serve*

Wash One Another's Feet

[Jesus] got up from the table, took off his outer robe, and tied a towel around himself. Then he poured water into a basin and began to wash the disciples' feet and to wipe them with the towel that was tied around him. He came to Simon Peter, who said to him, "Lord, are you going to wash my feet?" Jesus answered, "You do not know now what I am doing, but later you will understand." Peter said to him, "You will never wash my feet." Jesus answered, "Unless I wash you, you have no share with me." Simon Peter said to him, "Lord, not my feet only but also my hands and my head!" Jesus said to him, "One who has bathed does not need to wash, except for the feet, but is entirely clean. And you are clean."

After he had washed their feet, had put on his robe, and had returned to the table, he said to them, "Do you know what I have done to you? You call me Teacher and Lord—and you are right, for that is what I am. So if I, your Lord and Teacher, have washed your feet, you also ought to wash one another's feet. For I have set you an example, that you also should do as I have done to you. Very truly, I tell you, servants are not greater than their master, nor are messengers greater than the one who sent them. If you know these things, you are blessed if you do them."

John 13:4–10a, 12–17

JESUS' LAST SUPPER begins with profound lessons in humility and baptism. Notice the incredible extent of Jesus' love, the ignorance of human responses, and the immensity of Christ's servanthood.

What does Jesus' gesture teach you about greatness?

"The disciples were keenly aware that someone needed to wash the others' feet. The problem was that the only people who washed feet were the least. So there they sat, feet caked with dirt. . . . Then Jesus took a towel and a basin and redefined greatness."

—Richard J. Foster, *Celebration of Discipline*[4]

~ Not to Be Served, but to Serve

Servants of the Lord

Praise the LORD!
Praise, O servants of the LORD;
    praise the name of the LORD.
Blessed be the name of the LORD
    from this time on and forevermore.
From the rising of the sun to its setting
    the name of the LORD is to be praised.
The LORD is high above all nations,
    and his glory above the heavens.
Who is like the LORD our God,
    who is seated on high,
who looks far down
    on the heavens and the earth?
He raises the poor from the dust,
    and lifts the needy from the ash heap,
to make them sit with princes,
    with the princes of his people.

Psalm 113:1–8

THE LORD WHO is high above the heavens looks far down to see and care for the folk most people don't notice at all—the poor and the needy in ash heaps and garbage dumps. It should open the eyes of "servants of the Lord."

Meditate on this quotation as you think about how being a servant of God enables us to do Jesus' work of bringing his love and healing to the hungry, thirsty, strangers, needy, ill, and imprisoned (see Matt 25):

"By obedience to the ways of God we come to know the heart of God. By entering the heart of God we are enabled to be of help to people. Wholeness reigns in us, which means effective service for others."

—Richard J. Foster, *The Challenge of the Disciplined Life*[5]

Serving Others' Needs

Now during those days, when the disciples were increasing in number, the Hellenists complained against the Hebrews because their widows were being neglected in the daily distribution of food. And the twelve called together the whole community of the disciples and said, "It is not right that we should neglect the word of God in order to wait on tables. Therefore, friends, select from among yourselves seven men of good standing, full of the Spirit and of wisdom, whom we may appoint to this task, while we, for our part, will devote ourselves to prayer and to serving the word." What they said pleased the whole community, and they chose Stephen, a man full of faith and the Holy Spirit, together with Philip, Prochorus, Nicanor, Timon, Parmenas, and Nicolaus, a proselyte of Antioch. They had these men stand before the apostles, who prayed and laid their hands on them.

Acts 6:1–6

WHEN POOR JEWS became Christian, they lost Jewish public support. Increasing numbers of Christians meant more needy people, which necessitated greater church organization. The culturally Greek Jews (Hellenists) felt the culturally Semitic Jews (Hebrews) were not providing equally for their widows. Christian leaders called the whole community together to seek a solution. This shows how God used administrative means to solve a spiritual problem. Structural change resulted. Requirements for ministry and a "job description" were clarified. The new ministry was for those of good reputation, full of the Spirit, and wise. Ministry was now divided between "praying and serving the word" (worship and preaching) and "waiting on tables" (benevolent work).

The early disciples chosen to make even distributions of food to the widows in their fellowship had to be reputable, Spirit-filled, and wise. Why are these qualities important in people who are enlisted to serve the needs of others? In your church are those who do benevolent work respected as much as those who "pray and serve the word"? Why or why not?

~ Not to Be Served, but to Serve

A Servant Heart

When Uriah came to him, David asked how Joab and the people fared, and how the war was going. Then David said to Uriah, "Go down to your house, and wash your feet." Uriah went out of the king's house, and there followed him a present from the king. But Uriah slept at the entrance of the king's house with all the servants of his lord, and did not go down to his house. When they told David, "Uriah did not go down to his house," David said to Uriah, "You have just come from a journey. Why did you not go down to your house?" Uriah said to David, "The ark and Israel and Judah remain in booths; and my lord Joab and the servants of my lord are camping in the open field; shall I then go to my house, to eat and to drink, and to lie with my wife? As you live, and as your soul lives, I will not do such a thing."

2 Samuel 11:7–11

HERE DAVID IS trying his best to get Uriah to return home to his wife to try to cover up the fact that David himself has made Uriah's wife, Bathsheba, pregnant. But when given the opportunity to "go down to his [own] house"—shorthand for being reunited with his wife and having conjugal relations—Uriah chose instead to stay with David's other servants. In ironic contrast to the king who refuses to go where he is supposed to (to battle) and instead goes where he wants (to Bathsheba), Uriah refuses to go where he wants (to Bathsheba) as a silent demand to be allowed by the king to return to the place where both he and the king should be (in battle). In Uriah's response to David, we get a peek into a heart that makes Uriah intent on fulfilling his duties as a soldier and a servant of the king regardless of the cost.

Who do you know with a heart like Uriah's? As the opportunity arises, thank those persons for their service.

A Servant of the Gospel

And you who were once estranged and hostile in mind, doing evil deeds, [Christ] has now reconciled in his fleshly body through death, so as to present you holy and blameless and irreproachable before him—provided that you continue securely established and steadfast in the faith, without shifting from the hope promised by the gospel that you heard, which has been proclaimed to every creature under heaven. I, Paul, became a servant of this gospel.

I am now rejoicing in my sufferings for your sake, and in my flesh I am completing what is lacking in Christ's afflictions for the sake of his body, that is, the church. I became its servant according to God's commission that was given me for you, to make the word of God fully known.

Colossians 1:21–25

THE PAULINE TRADITION makes much of the apostle's suffering and weakness, on the one hand, and even more of God's or Christ's strength, on the other. The gospel is not about Paul, but about Jesus Christ. Paul, "a servant of this gospel," labors tirelessly for the spreading of the word of God (1:29). Serving his Lord, he shares also in his Lord's burden. In effect, he shares in his Lord's cross. In general, we might say that through the selfless sacrifice of believers, the reality and power of the cross of Christ extend through history in a real way.

Paul rejoices in his suffering. There is something counterintuitive about this. What Paul means is that, in his suffering as a result of his ministry, he has entered more fully into communion with the Lord of the cross. He shares in the life and death of Christ, and thus also in his resurrection. This, for Paul, is the living out of his baptism.

What does Paul mean when he states he is a servant of the gospel? Can we be servants of the gospel without serving other people? Why or why not?

∼ Not to Be Served, but to Serve

Serving the Saints

Let all that you do be done in love.

Now, brothers and sisters, you know that members of the household
of Stephanas were the first converts in Achaia, and they have devoted
themselves to the service of the saints. I urge you to put yourselves at
the service of such people, and of everyone who works and toils with
them.

1 Corinthians 16:14–16

IN THESE FINAL instructions to the Christians at Corinth, Paul
first charges them to let all that they do "be done in love" and then
put themselves "at the service" of such people as the household of
Stephanas. Loving service to the saints seems to be the norm, not the
exception.

In *Celebration of Discipline* Richard Foster makes a distinction between
self-righteous service and true service. Self-righteous service flows out
of human effort and goals; true service flows out of God and love.[6] As
you work on "serving the saints," examine your motives. Is your service
based on getting praise and accolades from others or done because you
love the people you are serving? Or are your motives mixed?

~ Not to Be Served, but to Serve

A Light to the Nations

[God] says, / "It is too light a thing that you should be my servant /
to raise up the tribes of Jacob / and to restore the survivors of Israel; /
I will give you as a light to the nations, / that my salvation may
reach to the end of the earth.' / Thus says the LORD, / the Redeemer
of Israel and his Holy One, / to one deeply despised, abhorred by
the nations, / the slave of rulers, / "Kings shall see and stand up, /
princes, and they shall prostrate themselves, / because the LORD
who is faithful, / the Holy One of Israel, who has chosen you."

Isaiah 49:6–7

THE POET SPEAKS of Yahweh's "servant," almost certainly referring to
Israel. In the initial lines there is the curious sense that servant Israel
has a mission and ministry to Israel, perhaps a faithful subcommunity
of Israel with a mission to the larger one. Be that as it may, this poetic
articulation looks beyond the rescue of Israel and indicates that Israel
has a much larger service to perform: to be "a light to the nations." The
God of Israel is indeed the God of all the nations. The mandate given
to Israel here is also included in the initial mandate given to Abraham
in Genesis 12:3. Israel does not exist for its own sake. Israel exists as an
instrument whereby God's governance of all the nations of the world
will produce the happy outcome of rescue, salvation, and well-being.
The missionary impetus of this vision is immensely important for the
self-understanding of Israel. Of course, this claim is transposed in the
Christian reading of the text to the missionary impetus of the Church.

The note above says that being a light to the nations means that "Israel does
not exist for its own sake." What does this mean for Christians? What insight does this give you into the importance of your practice of service?

For more verses on service and ideas on how to practice the discipline of service, see the
Responding exercises and Spiritual Disciplines Index in *The Life with God Bible.*

Secrecy

Consciously refraining from having our good deeds and qualities generally known, which in turn rightly disciplines our longing for recognition

We often long to talk about the good deeds that we do, wanting others to think well of us. The danger of this inclination is that approval will become our motivation. When we fast or pray or give in secret, as Jesus advises us in Matthew 6, we can know we are doing so for the right reasons, looking to God for approval rather than to our fellow humans. God knows all that we are and all that we do; his heavenly reward for any good that we do will far outweigh any earthly approbation (Matt 6:1). Deliberately avoiding earthly recognition, fame, and attention helps to cultivate within us humility and true love for others. It also gives us the opportunity to meditate on the nature of our God, who the Bible tells us is also "hidden" (Isa 45:15) and "in secret" (Matt 6).

That is not to say that our good qualities will never be recognized by others, just that we leave it to God to point them out. We see Jesus avoiding crowds and performing miracles in private, but the crowds invariably find him and spread the word about him. Jesus told us that a city set on a hill cannot be hid, and that we are to be the light of the world, not hidden under a bushel (Matt 5:14–16). Practicing the discipline of secrecy simply relinquishes to God the power to reveal our light. This submission is only appropriate, because everything in us that is good comes from God.

Whenever you pray, go into your room and shut the door and pray to your Father who is in secret; and your Father who sees in secret will reward you.

—Matthew 6:6

Secrecy

Keeping Our Works Private

Then [Jesus] returned from the region of Tyre, and went by way of Sidon towards the Sea of Galilee, in the region of the Decapolis. They brought to him a deaf man who had an impediment in his speech; and they begged him to lay his hand on him. He took him aside in private, away from the crowd, and put his fingers into his ears, and he spat and touched his tongue. Then looking up to heaven, he sighed and said to him, "Eph-phatha," that is, "Be opened." And immediately his ears were opened, his tongue was released, and he spoke plainly. Then Jesus ordered them to tell no one; but the more he ordered them, the more zealously they proclaimed it. They were astounded beyond measure, saying, "He has done everything well; he even makes the deaf to hear and the mute to speak."

Mark 7:31–37

HERE WE SEE how Jesus practiced the discipline of secrecy and its results. He took the deaf man to a private place to heal him and ordered those who seem to have followed them to tell no one, "but the more he ordered them, the more zealously they proclaimed it." There can hardly be a better example of what Dallas Willard refers to as letting God be our public relations department. For the next ten days make an effort to practice several different Spiritual Disciplines, such as prayer, service, giving, or fasting, keeping all such practices as private as possible, even from your spouse, other family members, or your housemate. Pray where no one can see you, for example, and, most important, try to refrain from mentioning any such actions to others. Guard your speech carefully, working to curb any impulse to brag or to present yourself in a more favorable light. Focus on talking with God about any spiritual practices you are engaging in and the results you are seeing. You may find that others point out good things you have done or positive qualities of yours, but even if that does not happen, keep up your conversation with God.

Spiritual Practice

Not Seen by Others

"Beware of practicing your piety before others in order to be seen by them; for then you have no reward from your Father in heaven.

"So whenever you give alms, do not sound a trumpet before you, as the hypocrites do in the synagogues and in the streets, so that they may be praised by others. Truly I tell you, they have received their reward. But when you give alms, do not let your left hand know what your right hand is doing, so that your alms may be done in secret; and your Father who sees in secret will reward you.

"And whenever you pray, do not be like the hypocrites; for they love to stand and pray in the synagogues and at the street corners, so that they may be seen by others. Truly I tell you, they have received their reward. But whenever you pray, go into your room and shut the door and pray to your Father who is in secret; and your Father who sees in secret will reward you.

"And whenever you fast, do not look dismal, like the hypocrites, for they disfigure their faces so as to show others that they are fasting. Truly I tell you, they have received their reward. But when you fast, put oil on your head and wash your face, so that your fasting may be seen not by others but by your Father who is in secret; and your Father who sees in secret will reward you."

Matthew 6:1–6, 16–18

IN THESE VERSES, we have Jesus' own interpretation of the traditional Jewish duties of almsgiving, prayer, and fasting. Performing such tasks for human approbation precludes any reward from the heavenly Father. Giving, praying, and fasting are even to be done in secret, removing the motivation to show off or display piety before others.

Today choose one of the three disciplines Jesus lists and practice it in secret. Pay close attention to how such a practice makes you feel, and how it may differ from the same action done more publicly.

Keeping Our Works Private

The Appearance of Righteousness

"[The scribes and Pharisees] do all their deeds to be seen by others; for they make their phylacteries broad and their fringes long. They love to have the place of honor at banquets and the best seats in the synagogues, and to be greeted with respect in the marketplaces, and to have people call them rabbi.

"Woe to you, scribes and Pharisees, hypocrites! For you are like whitewashed tombs, which on the outside look beautiful, but inside they are full of the bones of the dead and of all kinds of filth. So you also on the outside look righteous to others, but inside you are full of hypocrisy and lawlessness."

Matthew 23:5 7, 27–28

JESUS REPEATEDLY CONDEMNS playacting, which is what the word we translate "hypocrite" actually means. The dichotomy between appearance and reality, between word and deed, draws Jesus' most profound criticism. Here we see what the result of practicing the disciplines without secrecy can be. The Pharisees are so concerned with looking righteous to others that their study and service has ceased to be about God.

Reflect on these words and how they might apply to your life.

"Beginners in the spiritual life are apt to become very diligent in their exercises. The great danger for them will be to become satisfied with their religious works and with themselves. It is easy for them to develop a kind of secret pride. . . . But those who are at this time moving in God's way will counter this pride with humility. They will learn to think very little of themselves and their religious works. Instead, they will focus on how great and how deserving God is and how little it is that they can do for him. The Spirit of God dwells in such persons, urging them to keep their treasures secretly within themselves."

—John of the Cross, *The Dark Night of the Soul*[1]

In My Secret Heart

You desire truth in the inward being;
> therefore teach me wisdom in my secret heart.

Psalm 51:6

THE PSALMIST HERE makes a request to be taught in his secret heart. What do you think he means by "secret heart"? What connection does his request have to secrecy as we have defined it (refraining from having our good deeds and qualities generally known)?

Enter into your practice of secrecy today with this prayer:
> *O secret Christ,*
> *Lord of the rose of dawn,*
> *hide me within thy silent peace,*
> *that throughout the turmoil of day,*
> *I may abide within the quiet of the daybreak.*

—Anonymous

⟡ Keeping Our Works Private

He Could Not Escape Notice

From there [Jesus] set out and went away to the region of Tyre. He entered a house and did not want anyone to know he was there. Yet he could not escape notice.

Mark 7:24

TIME AND AGAIN we see Jesus trying to avoid the crowds, yet, as this passage states, no matter how he tried "he could not escape notice." All kinds and classes of people were "drawn to him" (see John 12:32)—and still are.

Dallas Willard writes, "One of the greatest fallacies of our faith, and actually one of the greatest acts of unbelief, is the thought that our spiritual acts and virtues need to be advertised to be known."[2] Jesus exemplified this concept. Think about his example as you say this prayer.

Father God, help me to follow the example of Jesus in his practice of secrecy. I want to revel in sharing secret time with you. I struggle sometimes, Lord, with wanting more recognition for my work, for my piety, for the things that I do for my family and friends. Help me to be grateful for those times when good things that I do escape notice, knowing that you see all that I do, all that is in me—the bad and also the good. In your name I pray. Amen.

The Light of the World

"You are the light of the world. A city built on a hill cannot be hid. No one after lighting a lamp puts it under the bushel basket, but on the lampstand, and it gives light to all in the house. In the same way, let your light shine before others, so that they may see your good works and give glory to your Father in heaven."

Matthew 5:14–16

THIS TEACHING, FROM the Sermon on the Mount, which might be better called the "Teaching, or Wisdom, from the Mount," is part of a large collection of some of Jesus' most memorable wisdom sayings. Even as Jesus attempted to keep his works private, his light shined so brightly that he could not escape from the crowds no matter how he tried. So too will his followers shine brightly if they allow God to be in charge of them. It is interesting that it is in the very next chapter of Matthew that Jesus warns so eloquently about not practicing piety in front of others in order to be seen by them. Letting our light shine is God's business, for his glory; a public show of piety is quite a different thing.

Reflect on this quote as you seek to find the balance between practicing secrecy and letting your light shine.

"People ought to learn to be free of their works as they perform them. For a man who has not practiced this, it is hard, learning to attain to a state in which the people around him and the works he performs are no hindrance—and much zeal is needed to achieve this—so that God is present to him and his light shines in him undiminished, whatever the occasion, whatever the environment."

—Meister Eckhart, *Selections from His Essential Writings*[3]

God Will Judge Our Secret Thoughts

All who have sinned apart from the law will also perish apart from the law, and all who have sinned under the law will be judged under the law. For it is not the hearers of the law who are righteous in God's sight, but the doers of the law who will be justified. When Gentiles, who do not posses the law, do instinctively what the law requires, these, though not having the law, are a law to themselves. They show that what the law requires is written on their hearts, to which their own conscience also bears witness; and their conflicting thoughts will accuse or perhaps excuse them on the day when, according to my gospel, God, through Jesus Christ, will judge the secret thoughts of all.

Romans 2:12–16

NO MATTER HOW far we advance while in this life on earth, we know only in part and we prophesy in part. We really do not have enough mind power, even under divine inspiration, to keep everything straight. But the complete is coming, and when it does, the partial will come to an end. "For now we see in a mirror, dimly," but we *will* see clearly (1 Cor 13:12). The book of Revelation 20:1–12 tells us that Christ himself will finally come on the scene as cosmic ruler to end the history-long battle of good and evil through his unquestioned victory and overwhelming presence. Human beings "great and small" will be judged. Accounts will be settled. Justice will be done.

Our definition of secrecy is abstaining "from having our good deeds and qualities generally known," but this verse is talking about all of our secrets—good and bad—being judged. What is the connection between keeping good deeds and qualities secret and having all of our secrets revealed and judged? Does thinking about this verse provide extra motivation to be quiet about the good works that we do?

Riches Hidden in Secret Places

I will give you the treasures of darkness
    and riches hidden in secret places,
so that you may know that it is I, the LORD
    the God of Israel, who call you by your name.

Isaiah 45:3

ISAIAH SHOWS US that God is powerfully and decisively—though hiddenly—engaged everywhere in the reality of the world. Once we acknowledge this claim, then the work of our faith is to relinquish in life, personal and public, all that contradicts the reality and purpose of God and to receive from God what we cannot generate ourselves.

Why are riches hidden in secret places? How might that make them more valuable?

Dear Lord, so often I fall into thinking that my worth is derived from the opinions of others. Teach me to seek riches hidden in secret places, so that I might understand better the joys of your company and your blessings for your sake alone. In your name I pray. Amen.

Hidden with God

O how abundant is your goodness
    that you have laid up for those who fear you,
and accomplished for those who take refuge in you,
    in the sight of everyone!
In the shelter of your presence you hide them
    from human plots;
you hold them safe under your shelter
    from contentious tongues.

Psalm 31:19–20

THE UTMOST CONFIDENCE here is stirring. The singer doesn't just put on a brave face, but lets this confidence break out in glad worship and singing. Keeping quiet about our own good qualities and good deeds can help us to shelter with God from "contentious tongues."

Reflect on what it means to be sheltered with God. How have you experienced secrecy as a form of shelter or protection?

Lord God,
grant us such faith that we can come to you
even in utter dearth of feelings and desires,
without a glow or an aspiration,
with the weight of low thoughts,
neglects, and wandering forgetfulness,
and still say to you:
"You are my refuge." Amen.

—George MacDonald

The Shelter of the Most High

You who live in the shelter of the Most High,
    who abide in the shadow of the Almighty,
will say to the LORD, "My refuge and my fortress;
    my God, in whom I trust."

Psalm 91:1–2

THE FIRST LINE of this verse is also translated, "He that dwelleth in the secret place of the most High" (KJV). Living in God, making the Most High our "dwelling place" (91:9), shows a deep trust, a stability that inspires the confidence in this psalm. For us to dwell in God as a refuge differs sharply from merely scampering into shelter when trouble strikes.

Living "in the shadow of the Almighty" reminds us of a child walking with a parent and making every effort to stay in the parent's shadow. It also hints of a condition where the child is so uninhibited and in love with the parent that he or she has no desire for public recognition. Abiding in someone's shadow means letting that person be the recipient of all glory and attention. After these last several days of trying to perform spiritual disciplines or good works in secrecy, how do you feel now about every good deed and quality of yours reflecting glory to God alone? If you are still having trouble abstaining from the compulsion to make your good deeds and qualities known, take it before your heavenly Father and ask for healing in this area of your life.

Praying for Others' Success

Now concerning love of the brothers and sisters, you do not need to have anyone write to you, for you yourselves have been taught by God to love one another; and indeed you do love all the brothers and sisters throughout Macedonia. But we urge you, beloved, to do so more and more, to aspire to live quietly, to mind your own affairs, and to work with your hands, as we directed you, so that you may behave properly toward outsiders and be dependent on no one.

1 Thessalonians 4:9–12

SOMETIMES IT IS hard to live quietly and mind our own affairs. We wish for recognition for the good things in our life and our family's lives; we also have trouble resisting pointing out what we see as flaws and failures in the lives of others. One of the best ways to practice the discipline of secrecy is to pray for success and honors for those around us, that they may be held up above ourselves. Dallas Willard writes, "If you want to experience the flow of love as never before, the next time you are in a competitive situation, pray that the others around you will be more outstanding, more praised, and more used of God than yourself. If Christians were universally to do this for each other, the earth would soon be filled with the knowledge of God's glory."[4] During the next ten days, whenever you find yourself in a competitive situation, whether it be at work, school, or among your peers, pray as Willard directs us.

Spiritual Practice

The One Who Is More Powerful Than I

John the baptizer appeared in the wilderness, proclaiming a baptism of repentance for the forgiveness of sins. And people from the whole Judean countryside and all the people of Jerusalem were going out to him, and were baptized by him in the river Jordan, confessing their sins. Now John was clothed in camel's hair, with a leather belt around his waist, and he ate locusts and wild honey. He proclaimed, "The one who is more powerful than I is coming after me; I am not worthy to stoop down and untie the thong of his sandals. I have baptized you with water; but he will baptize you with the Holy Spirit."

Mark 1:4–8

JOHN'S PREACHING STIRRED the people, who were accustomed to hearing a detailed set of laws they had to keep in order to achieve a faraway hope of a better day. Their teachers sat ensconced in the Temple. John preached in the desert, wearing the skin of a camel and eating insects and wild honey. He spoke of God's kingdom at hand and stressed repentance rather than laws. John differed from the scribes and Pharisees of his day in almost every respect. Most of all, John sought no prominent place for himself in the eyes of the people. Although he acquired a following over time and even had some "disciples," John quickly turned them toward the coming Messiah, claiming "He must increase, but I must decrease" (John 3:30). He did so with a sincere joy.

Say this prayer as you reflect on John the Baptist's humility and practice of heaping glory and attention on Jesus rather than himself:

Lord, I pray that of Your great goodness You would make known to me, and take from my heart, every kind and form and degree of pride, whether it be from evil spirits, or my own corrupt nature; and that You would awaken in me the deepest depth and truth of the humility that can make me capable of Your light and Holy Spirit.

—Andrew Murray, *Humility* [5]

Jesus Humbled Himself

Let the same mind be in you that was in Christ Jesus, / who, though
he was in the form of God, / did not regard equality with God / as
something to be exploited, / but emptied himself, / taking the form
of a slave, / being born in human likeness. / And being found in
human form, / he humbled himself / and became obedient to the
point of death— / even death on a cross.

Philippians 2:5–8

PAUL, USING THE words of an early Christian hymn, singles out Jesus'
own spirituality as the premier example of Christian life. Christian
spiritual formation is growing in con-*form*-ity to Christ. Jesus had it all.
Before becoming human, he was equal with God. Nonetheless, Jesus
did not "exploit" his status. He did not take advantage of his supreme
authority for selfish ends. Instead, he "emptied himself," giving himself
to others in life and in death. Jesus' spirituality was a spirituality of
humble obedience. And God recognized this life of obedience by exalting Jesus above all others. This Jesus is our model of spiritual formation, for status is gained not through "looking out for number one," but
rather by humbly sacrificing ourselves for others.

Hold this quotation before you as inspiration as you practice living quietly and putting others first:

"The humble man feels no jealousy or envy. He can praise God when
others are preferred and blessed before him. He can bear to hear others
praised and himself forgotten, because in God's presence he has learned
to say with Paul, "I be nothing" (2 Cor. 12:11). He has received the spirit
of Jesus, who did not please Himself and did not seek His own honor, as
the spirit of his life."

—Andrew Murray, *Humility*[6]

God's Splendor

Your fame spread among the nations on account of your beauty, for it was perfect because of my splendor that I had bestowed on you, says the LORD GOD. But you trusted in your beauty, and played the whore because of your fame, and lavished your whorings on any passer-by.

Ezekiel 16:14–15

THIS PASSAGE IS part of a lengthy allegory about the history of Jerusalem in which the prophet Ezekiel describes how God found Jerusalem, cared for her, and adopted her into the covenant by marriage. Now the history of Jerusalem takes a shocking turn. Jerusalem has convinced itself that it has long been God's faithful covenant partner. Ezekiel begs to differ. The prophet offers a radical new telling of Jerusalem's relationship with God. He offends his audience, calling the royal city a "whore." Jerusalem has been unfaithful with other gods and other nations. The children of the city have been sacrificed to other gods (16:20). In other words, they have been raised to place their trust and their future in the hands of gods that are frauds. At the same time the leaders of Jerusalem have been secretly having liaisons with the Egyptians, the Assyrians, and the Chaldeans (16:26, 28–29). Jerusalem has been unfaithful to God in its worship and in its politics. The threat to Jerusalem's covenant with God is both a spiritual and a political crisis.

In these words we find the basis for the discipline of secrecy. All that is good about us is from God. Just as Jerusalem's beauty was due to God's splendor, anything about us worthy enough to cause fame is also a gift from God. Therefore we have no reason to brag. Take a moment today to think of all the qualities and gifts that others have praised in you and thank God for them.

Let No One Boast

Do you not know that you are God's temple and that God's Spirit dwells in you? If anyone destroys God's temple, God will destroy that person. For God's temple is holy, and you are that temple.

Do not deceive yourselves. If you think that you are wise in this age, you should become fools so that you may become wise. For the wisdom of this world is foolishness with God. For it is written,

"He catches the wise in their craftiness,"

and again,

"The Lord knows the thought of the wise,
    that they are futile."

So let no one boast about human leaders.

1 Corinthians 3:16–21a

THE PROOFS OF spiritual attainment the Corinthians want so much to claim for themselves are not only illusions; they are altogether unnecessary. What is valuable and uplifting in life cannot be "attained" at all, only enjoyed freely through God's grace in the fellowship of Christ. One can almost hear Paul's relief and delight as he shares this liberating truth with his distant congregation. The first and most prominent theme of 1 Corinthians is that God alone is the source of the Spirit-filled life. From the Letter's first words of thanksgiving, Paul attributes all the benefits of the life of faith to God's saving initiative. It is God who calls, graces, strengthens, and sustains the with-God life, and Christ and the Spirit who are the agents of such gifts. Each time the Corinthians want to take credit for their own wisdom, insight, or spiritual abilities, Paul reminds them of the divine source of their blessings, "so that no one might boast in the presence of God" (1:29).

It is ironic that even those insights we receive while actively seeking God we are prone to crediting to ourselves. When have you claimed credit for something when it was due to God or another person?

Let Those Who Boast Boast in This

Thus says the LORD: Do not let the wise boast in their wisdom, do not let the mighty boast in their might, do not let the wealthy boast in their wealth; but let those who boast boast in this, that they understand and know me, that I am the LORD; I act with steadfast love, justice, and righteousness in the earth, for in these things I delight, says the LORD.

Jeremiah 9:23–24

THROUGH PROPHETS LIKE Jeremiah we learn that righteousness comes from the heart renewed in faith, not from outward ritual or legal obedience. We are called to a renewal of the covenant from the heart, not merely from the perspective of the formal observance of the law. God requires justice, mercy, and love, not merely outward sacrifice or formal obedience. We also learn that God is present with us during all of life's stages.

Dear God and Father, we thank you for your infinite goodness and love to us. You do continually keep us in your word, in faith, and in prayer. By this we know how to walk before you in humility and in fear. By this we are not proud of our own wisdom, righteousness, skill, and strength, but glory alone in your power. . . . To you be praise and thanks in eternity. Amen.

—Martin Luther, *Luther's Prayers*[7]

Boasting in Christ Jesus

For it is we who are the circumcision, who worship in the Spirit of God and boast in Christ Jesus and have no confidence in the flesh—even though I, too, have reason for confidence in the flesh.

If anyone else has reason to be confident in the flesh, I have more: circumcised on the eighth day, a member of the people of Israel, of the tribe of Benjamin, a Hebrew born of Hebrews; as to the law, a Pharisee; as to zeal, a persecutor of the church; as to righteousness under the law, blameless.

Yet whatever gains I had, these I have come to regard as loss because of Christ. More than that, I regard everything as loss because of the surpassing value of knowing Christ Jesus my Lord.

Philippians 3:3–8a

THE CHRISTIAN LIFE is not about "confidence in the flesh," Paul insists. Rather, it is about boasting in Christ Jesus. The source and the strength of the Christian life are found in the Spirit of God, not in our religious performance.

Paul's family heritage, training, and zeal would have secured him a place as one of the up-and-coming Jewish leaders. But when Paul stood face-to-face with the risen Christ, his résumé did nothing for him. And all that Paul had once considered assets he now counted as losses. What mattered now was relationship with God: knowing Christ and gaining Christ. Spiritual formation is learning to recognize and abandon those things that must be counted as losses in light of our encounter with Christ (possessions, credentials, attitudes, etc.) so that we might focus on the "gain" of relationship with Christ.

What is the difference between boasting in the flesh and boasting in Christ Jesus? How has trying to pray that those around you may be more outstanding and more successful than you helped you to let go of your own "confidence in the flesh"?

We Boast in Our Hope of Sharing the Glory of God

Therefore, since we are justified by faith, we have peace with God through our Lord Jesus Christ, through whom we have obtained access to this grace in which we stand; and we boast in our hope of sharing the glory of God. And not only that, but we also boast in our sufferings, knowing that suffering produces endurance, and endurance produces character, and character produces hope, and hope does not disappoint us, because God's love has been poured into our hearts through the Holy Spirit that has been given to us. But more than that, we even boast in God through our Lord Jesus Christ, through whom we have now received reconciliation.

Romans 5:1–3, 11

HERE PAUL BECOMES exuberant. Careful arguments give way to artesian praise. This justified-by-faith life, this life in which we live out of the abundance of God's grace instead of our own meager sin resources, is explosive with energetic thanksgiving. Paul uses the noisiest word he can find, "boast," to express the robust quality of his life; he uses it three times.

How have you been able to boast in God? Consider your practice of praying for the success of others. Is boasting about others a way of boasting in God?

"For a man ever to do well and to think little of himself is token of a meek soul. For a man not to wish to be comforted by any creature is a token of great purity and inward trust. He that seeketh no outward witness for himself, it appeareth only that he hath committed himself all wholly to God."

—Thomas à Kempis, *The Imitation of Christ*[8]

God Notices Us

Why, O Lord, do you stand far off?
    Why do you hide yourself in times of trouble?
In arrogance the wicked persecute the poor—
    let them be caught in the schemes they have devised.
For the wicked boast of the desires of their heart,
    those greedy for gain curse and renounce the Lord.
In the pride of their countenance the wicked say, "God will not seek
    it out";
    all their thoughts are, "There is no God."
But you do see! Indeed you note trouble and grief,
    that you may take it into your hands;
the helpless commit themselves to you;
    you have been the helper of the orphan.

Psalm 10:1–4, 14

HERE THE SINGER accuses God of being hidden, of letting the wicked prevail. The wicked themselves think God is no threat. Their statement "There is no God" is not real atheism, but a swaggering sense that God won't notice or do anything. But God not only sees, God notices and helps the people who are invisible to most folk—the helpless, the orphaned, the oppressed. People of faith learn to see through God's eyes and act in God's ways (cf. Matt 25:31–46).

It's easy to feel that all we do and hope for is for naught, that God does not even notice, much less work to change the situation. Has your practice of praying for others and trying to do good deeds without recognition caused you this kind of frustration? How does this passage help you in your understanding of God's reaction to those who claim he is not noticing or doing anything?

A God Who Hides

Thus says the LORD: / The wealth of Egypt and the merchandise of Ethiopia, / and the Sabeans, tall of stature, / shall come over to you and be yours, / they shall follow you; / they shall come over in chains and bow down to you. / They will make supplication to you, saying, / "God is with you alone, and there is no other; / there is no god besides him." / Truly, you are a God who hides himself, / O God of Israel, the Savior.

Isaiah 45:14–15

THE POET ACCEPTS that the God of Israel as the true God is one who remains hidden and is not readily available and transparent in the workings of creation. This statement is the foundation of an important theological trajectory that became crucial for the theological revolution of Martin Luther. The notion of *Deus absconditus,* the God who is hidden, was a correction to easier notions of God in which, when God revealed himself, everything was inexhaustibly known and available about God. Against that, the theology that grew out of the work of Martin Luther insists that apart from God's self-revelation in Jesus Christ, God retains unto his own self the ultimate mystery of his life and character. The hiddenness of God is a way of speaking about the theological awareness that God is not at the beck and call of human beings.

Lord God, as wonderful as it is to abide in your shadow, sometimes my limited understanding makes me feel that you are too hidden, and I long for you to reveal yourself. I long for recognition not just for myself but for you, Lord—for your glory to be revealed to all! Teach me patience, Lord, and continue to stretch my understanding of who you are and how you work in the world. Continue to cultivate within me the humility to know that your way is best. Amen.

For more verses on secrecy and ideas on how to practice the discipline of secrecy, see the Responding exercises and Spiritual Disciplines Index in *The Life with God Bible.*

Guidance

Experiencing an interactive friendship with God that gives direction and purpose to daily life

God wishes to be in relationship with us. One aspect of this interactive friendship with God is guidance. Throughout the Bible we see God providing continued guidance for the rough times and the good. Today, we often think this kind of interaction is no longer possible, but that is not the case. As Dallas Willard writes, "Today I continue to believe that people are meant to live in an ongoing conversation with God, speaking and being spoken to. . . . Given who we are by basic nature, we live—really live—only through God's regular speaking in our souls and thus 'by every word that comes from the mouth of God.'"[1]

These words from God can come to us in a variety of ways: through "the still small voice" (1 Kings 19:12, KJV), through others, through Scripture. As with so many of the disciplines, we often must cut through a lot of worldly static to hear God's voice. Like Moses and Jeremiah, we often resist God's will, in matters small and large.

But it's also important to realize that guidance is not just discerning God's will and direction for specific decisions, such as whether to marry a certain person, start a certain ministry, or pursue a particular career path. Having an interactive friendship with God means that divine will can pervade all areas of our life, so that even when we are not fully conscious of asking God whether to do a particular thing, we can still be within the scope of God's will. As Willard puts it, hearing God is about who God wants us to *be* as well as what God wants us to do.

When you turn to the right or when you turn to the left, your ears shall hear a word behind you, saying, "This is the way; walk in it."
—Isaiah 30:21

Guidance

Hearing God

Nevertheless I am continually with you; / you hold my right hand. /
You guide me with your counsel, / and afterward you will receive
me with honor.

Psalm 73:23–24

THE BIBLE ASSURES us, in this passage as well as many others, that
God's guidance and counsel are available to us. As this passage makes
clear, God does not guide us as a puppet master manipulates a puppet.
As missionary and theologian E. Stanley Jones writes:

> Obviously God must guide us in a way that will develop sponta-
> neity in us. The development of character, rather than direction
> in this, that, and the other matter, must be the primary purpose
> of the Father. He will guide us, but he won't override us. . . . The
> parent must guide in such a manner, and to the degree, that au-
> tonomous character, capable of making right decisions for itself,
> is produced. God does the same.[2]

Since guidance takes place within this type of relationship, how can
we practice it as a discipline? Although there is nothing we can do to
force a dream or a vision or God's still small voice, one way in which
we can open ourselves to God's guidance is by studying the way those in
the Bible have heard from God. Throughout the next ten days, we will
be studying various ways God has guided his people through the Bible
and also considering ways we have been and continue to be guided
by God. Be open to hearing God's counsel in many different ways: in
Scripture, in a still small voice, or in the words of another person. As
you read, try to imagine what it must have been like for these people
to hear God's voice. Look at how God approached them and how they
reacted. Then, as Dallas Willard writes, "We must pray for the faith and
for the experiences that would enable us to believe that *such things could
happen to us.* Only then will we be able to recognize, accept, and dwell
in them when they come."[3]

Spiritual Practice

You Shall Go

Now the word of the Lord came to [Jeremiah] saying,
"Before I formed you in the womb I knew you, / and before you were born I consecrated you; / I appointed you a prophet to the nations."
Then I said, "Ah, Lord God! Truly I do not know how to speak, for I am only a boy." But the Lord said to me,
"Do not say, 'I am only a boy'; / for you shall go to all to whom I send you, / and you shall speak whatever I command you. / Do not be afraid of them, / for I am with you to deliver you, / says the Lord."

Jeremiah 1:4–8

WHEN THE PROPHET speaks, in response to the call of God, his first word is a word of resistance. The one called for divine work immediately senses his limitations for that work. He tries to beg off, listing his inadequacies. Jeremiah was not being modest in saying, "I am only a boy"; he was simply being truthful. This is quite typical of the call for divine service, and quite beside the point. God tends, it would appear from stories of vocation in Scripture, almost always to call people who are too young, too timid, too old, or too immoral. The story is not about the singular virtues of the one being called. The story is about a risk-taking, bold sort of God who reaches in and calls people for divine service, giving them what they need for that service. Jeremiah need not work alone. God equips and stands beside those whom God calls. This is the sort of God who says, in effect, "I'm getting ready to change, revolutionize, renovate, and reorient the whole world—and guess who's going to help me?"

Too often we also think we are too young or too old, too busy or too underqualified to do God's work—or simply that someone else will. What limitations are you nursing as excuses for ignoring your divine vocation?

—• *Hearing God*

Here I Am

Now the boy Samuel was ministering to the LORD under Eli. The word of the LORD was rare in those days; visions were not widespread.

At that time Eli was lying down in his room; the lamp of God had not yet gone out, and Samuel was lying down in the temple of the LORD, where the ark of God was. Then the LORD called, "Samuel! Samuel!" and he said, "Here I am!" and ran to Eli, and said, "Here I am, for you called me." But he said, "I did not call; lie down again." So he went and lay down.

Now the LORD came and stood there, calling as before, "Samuel! Samuel!" And Samuel said, "Speak, for your servant is listening." Then the LORD said to Samuel, "See, I am about to do something in Israel."

As Samuel grew up, the LORD was with him and let none of his words fall to the ground. And all Israel from Dan to Beersheba knew that Samuel was a trustworthy prophet of the LORD.

1 Samuel 3:1–5, 10–11a, 19–20

THOUGH BUT A child, Samuel is nonetheless called by God. That God has not called Eli or his sons, the more obviously qualified adult candidates, but rather a child, is both ironic and startling, for it calls into question the deeply cherished assumption that the experienced, the educated, and the privileged are the vessels through which God works. In Israel's case, all of those types have wandered from the ways of Yahweh, and thus God chooses an almost laughable vessel, a child, through whom the word of the Lord will be delivered. It is a characteristic of this God, who chooses the second-born Jacob rather than the firstborn Esau and the politically and economically weak Israel rather than the rich and powerful Egypt, to align himself with such figures.

Father God, you who call the last people anyone would expect, here I am. As underqualified as I feel to do anything for your world, help me to do the work for which I was created. Give me the courage to hear and answer your call. Speak, for your servant is listening. Amen.

David Inquires of the Lord

When the Philistines heard that David had been anointed king over Israel, all the Philistines went up in search of David; but David heard about it and went down to the stronghold. David inquired of the LORD, "Shall I go up against the Philistines? Will you give them into my hand?" The LORD said to David, "Go up; for I will certainly give the Philistines into your hand." So David came to Baal-perazim, and David defeated them there. He said, "The LORD has burst forth against my enemies before me, like a bursting flood." The Philistines abandoned their idols there, and David and his men carried them away.

Once again the Philistines came up, and were spread out in the valley of Rephaim. When David inquired of the LORD, he said, "You shall not go up; go around to their rear, and come upon them opposite the balsam trees. When you hear the sound of marching in the tops of the balsam trees, then be on the alert; for then the LORD has gone out before you to strike down the army of the Philistines." David did just as the LORD had commanded him; and he struck down the Philistines from Geba all the way to Gezer.

2 Samuel 5:17, 19–20a, 21–25

DAVID'S MILITARY SUCCESS is rooted not in his great skill as a tactician or as a motivator of the troops, but rather in the fact that he submits his plans to Yahweh for approval first. This contrasts with the practice of the dead king, Saul, who instead consorted with a medium (1 Sam 28:3–20). So long as David continues in this faithful practice, he will live in a zone protected by the favor of Yahweh, the result of which will be prosperity for both himself and his people.

How do you feel about the Lord's giving direct guidance to us today? As you are considering this issue, read Isaiah 30:19–21, God's promise to Zion, and Acts 2:17–18, God's promise to Christians. What are the advantages in waiting for the Lord to speak before we act? The dangers?

~ Hearing God

Through the Mouth of a Donkey

That night God came to Balaam and said to him, "If the men have come to summon you, get up and go with them; but do only what I tell you to do." So Balaam got up in the morning, saddled his donkey, and went with the officials of Moab.

God's anger was kindled because he was going, and the angel of the LORD took his stand in the road as his adversary. Now he was riding on the donkey, and his two servants were with him. The donkey saw the angel of the LORD standing in the road, with a drawn sword in his hand; so the donkey turned off the road, and went into the field; and Balaam struck the donkey, to turn it back onto the road. Then the LORD opened the mouth of the donkey, and it said to Balaam, "What have I done to you, that you have struck me?" Balaam said to the donkey, "Because you have made a fool of me! I wish I had a sword in my hand! I would kill you right now!" But the donkey said to Balaam, "Am I not your donkey, which you have ridden all your life to this day? Have I been in the habit of treating you this way?" And he said, "No."

Then the LORD opened the eyes of Balaam, and he saw the angel of the LORD standing in the road, with his drawn sword in his hand; and he bowed down, falling on his face.

Numbers 22:20–23, 28–31

GOD CAN SPEAK even through the mouths of animals. God used the donkey to get Balaam's attention. And Peter repented after he heard the rooster's crow (Matt 26:34). Sometimes we fail to hear the voice of God because we are not listening. In the spiritual life, we learn to be attentive to the Lord's voice whenever and however he may speak. Here he not only speaks through a donkey, but to Balaam, a prophet of the Moabites. We cannot predict how or through whom God will speak. Developing listening ears is essential to spiritual growth.

What is the strangest way God has spoken to you?

Ananias Guides Saul

Now there was a disciple in Damascus named Ananias. The Lord said to him in a vision, "Ananias." He answered, "Here I am, Lord." The Lord said to him, "Get up and go to the street called Straight, and at the house of Judas look for a man of Tarsus named Saul. At this moment he is praying, and he has seen in a vision a man named Ananias come and lay his hands on him so that he might regain his sight." But Ananias answered, "Lord, I have heard from many about this man, how much evil he has done to your saints in Jerusalem; and here he has authority from the chief priests to bind all who invoke your name." But the Lord said to him, "Go, for he is an instrument whom I have chosen to bring my name before Gentiles and kings and before the people of Israel; I myself will show him how much he must suffer for the sake of my name." So Ananias went and entered the house. He laid his hands on Saul and said, "Brother Saul, the Lord Jesus, who appeared to you on your way here, has sent me so that you may regain your sight and be filled with the Holy Spirit." And immediately something like scales fell from his eyes, and his sight was restored. Then he got up and was baptized.

Acts 9:10–18

THIS PASSAGE IS preceded by Saul of Tarsus's famous blinding vision from Jesus on the road to Damascus. Saul's conversion depends on Ananias's obedience to his own vision: to help a great persecutor of Christians. Ananias's faithfulness is highlighted in his first word to Saul: "Brother." Here God guides his people not only through visions, but through the words and actions of others. It is instructive to see how God directs and blesses through his people.

How has God spoken to you through other people? How does it make you feel to think that God may be guiding others through you?

Peter's Vision

[Peter] saw the heaven opened and something like a large sheet coming down, being lowered to the ground by its four corners. In it were all kinds of four-footed creatures and reptiles and birds of the air. Then he heard a voice saying, "Get up, Peter; kill and eat." But Peter said, "By no means, Lord; for I have never eaten anything that is profane or unclean." The voice said to him again, a second time, "What God has made clean, you must not call profane."

Now while Peter was greatly puzzled about what to make of the vision that he had seen, suddenly the men sent by Cornelius appeared. The Spirit said to him, "Look, three men are searching for you. Now get up, go down, and go with them without hesitation, for I have sent them." So Peter went down to the men and said, "I am the one you are looking for; what is the reason for your coming?" They answered, "Cornelius, a centurion, an upright and God-fearing man, who is well spoken of by the whole Jewish nation, was directed by a holy angel to send for you to come to his house and to hear what you have to say."

The following day they came to Caesarea. Cornelius was expecting them and had called together his relatives and close friends. Then Peter began to speak to them: "I truly understand that God shows no partiality, but in every nation anyone who fears him and does what is right is acceptable to him."

Acts 10:11–15, 17a, 19b–22, 24, 34–35

PETER REALIZES THAT the good news of Jesus is not confined to the Jewish people. Here again God guides through visions and also with confirming words through other people. It takes Peter some time to realize his vision is not about food, but people. The full import of his original experience needed time to develop and be understood.

Have there been moments in your life when you did not understand God's guidance? What helped you to later see God's guiding hand?

You Are the Man!

But the thing that David had done displeased the LORD, and the LORD sent Nathan to David. He came to him, and said to him "There were two men in a certain city, the one rich and the other poor. The rich man had very many flocks and herds; but the poor man had nothing but one little ewe lamb, which he had bought. He brought it up, and it grew up with him and with his children; it used to eat of his meager fare, and drink from his cup, and lie in his bosom, and it was like a daughter to him. Now there came a traveler to the rich man, and he was loath to take one of his own flock or herd to prepare for the wayfarer who had come to him, but he took the poor man's lamb, and prepared that for the guest who had come to him." Then David's anger was greatly kindled against the man. He said to Nathan, "As the LORD lives, the man who has done this deserves to die; he shall restore the lamb fourfold, because he did this thing, and because he had no pity."

Nathan said to David, "You are the man! Why have you despised the word of the LORD, to do what is evil in his sight? You have struck down Uriah the Hittite with the sword, and have taken his wife to be your wife, and have killed him with the sword of the Ammonites." David said to Nathan, "I have sinned against the LORD."

2 Samuel 12:1–7a, 9, 13a

THE DIRECT CONFRONTATION of sin in the life of a person we know or work with, especially someone in a position of authority over us, is one of the most difficult and potentially hazardous social situations to negotiate. Yet, as the example of Nathan demonstrates, authentic spirituality will nevertheless issue forth in such situations when we say what needs to be said in spite of the discomfort or the consequences.

"If you cannot listen to your brother, you cannot listen to the Holy Spirit."

—Virgil Vogt, Reba Place Fellowship[4]

Guided by God's Strength

"In your steadfast love you led the people whom you redeemed;
you guided them by your strength to your holy abode."

Exodus 15:13

IN HIS BOOK *Hearing God,* Dallas Willard names several ways we receive guidance from God—dreams, visions, circumstances, conversations—but this verse recounts yet another way that God guided the Israelites, through his strength.

What do you think it means to be guided by God's strength? Does it have a sense of protection? Of looking after your needs? Of overcoming adversity? How can you be guided by God's strength? Reflect on this prayer:

Let your mighty hand, O Lord our Lord,
and outstretched arm, be our defense;
your mercy and loving-kindness
in Jesus Christ, your dear Son, be our salvation;
your all-true word be our instruction;
the grace of your life-giving Spirit
be our comfort and consolation;
to the end and in the end. Amen.

—John Knox

Guided by the Spirit

"I still have many things to say to you, but you cannot bear them now. When the Spirit of truth comes, he will guide you into all the truth; for he will not speak on his own, but will speak whatever he hears, and he will declare to you the things that are to come."

John 16:12–13

THE DEATH AND departure of Jesus and the coming of the Spirit upon the disciples was, in point of fact, a liberation of Christ from the self-imposed limitations of the divine presence in the individual life of a Jewish teacher and healer (Phil 2:5–8). With this liberation the person of Christ became free to move with the word of the gospel of the kingdom throughout the inner life of the disciples and about the world at large (e.g., Acts 6:7; 2 Tim 2:9; John 14:15–26; Col 3:16).

Here we have the why and the how of guidance. Christ through the Spirit guides us into understanding and truth.

Father God, I have seen these last days how faithful you are in guiding your people. Help me to rush to you with my arms open wide, seeking your Spirit at all times in your word, in other people, in Christ moving in the circumstances of my life. I ask for patience for those times when the way is murky. Clear away all the static in my life, so that I can hear you more clearly. In your name I pray. Amen.

Finding the Way

Truly, O people in Zion, inhabitants of Jerusalem, you shall weep no more. He will surely be gracious to you at the sound of your cry; when he hears it, he will answer you. Though the Lord may give you the bread of adversity and the water of affliction, yet your Teacher will not hide himself any more, but your eyes shall see your Teacher. And when you turn to the right or to the left, your ears shall hear a word behind you, saying, "This is the way; walk in it."

Isaiah 30:19–21

IT IS OFTEN difficult to hear that voice guiding us to the right path. Many of us *think* we know God's direction for a certain part of our lives, but we are not sure. Throughout the next ten days we will be seeking discernment about a major decision. Perhaps there is some leading you think you have felt or some issue about which you remain undecided—such as whether you should stay in or pursue a relationship with a certain person, or whether you should change vocation. Or perhaps you have not felt any real leadings from God about the direction your life should take and your task is not to confirm, but to ask God for a new direction. You can go about this task in a variety of ways. You might want to pray about the same thing every day, asking God for confirmation or direction, or, alternately, spend a block of time one day thinking and praying. Another option is to ask several trusted friends to meet with you to talk over and pray about your question. Quakers call such gatherings "meetings for clearness." Sometimes the Holy Spirit can speak to us more clearly in a group and can also reassure us that our inclination is of the Spirit and not of our own ego.

Throughout, as you seek confirmation that you are on the right path, consider that, in his *Rules for the Discernment of Spirits,* Ignatius of Loyola states that good influences provide courage and strength and produce peace and a greater feeling of love, while choices influenced by evil can be counted on to cause regret, sadness, and disquiet.[5] Reflect on these thoughts of Ignatius whenever you feel unsure.

Spiritual Practice

With Him I Speak Face to Face

While they were at Hazeroth, Miriam and Aaron spoke against Moses because of the Cushite woman whom he had married (for he had indeed married a Cushite woman); and they said, "Has the LORD spoken only through Moses? Has he not spoken through us also?" And the LORD heard it. Now the man Moses was very humble, more so than anyone else on the face of the earth. Suddenly the LORD said to Moses, Aaron, and Miriam, "Come out, you three, to the tent of meeting." So the three of them came out. Then the LORD came down in a pillar of cloud, and stood at the entrance of the tent, and called Aaron and Miriam; and they both came forward. And he said, "Hear my words:

When there are prophets among you,
   I the Lord make myself known to them in visions;
   I speak to them in dreams.
Not so with my servant Moses;
   he is entrusted with all my house.
With him I speak face to face—clearly, not in riddles;
   and he beholds the form of the LORD.

Why then were you not afraid to speak against my servant Moses?" And the anger of the LORD was kindled against them, and he departed.

Numbers 12:1–9

GOD'S STATEMENT THAT he speaks to Moses face-to-face is evoked by the jealousy of Miriam and Aaron over Moses's special relationship with God. Although God speaks to others in dreams and visions that are often shrouded in mystery, when he speaks with Moses his words are clear.

Do you struggle to determine God's purpose for your life, or do you feel sure that God has called you to a certain vocation, ministry, or task? Have you ever been jealous of a person who received clear, unmistakable guidance from God? If so, what might this be a symptom of? Read the passage again while asking the Lord for guidance in this area of your life.

Asking for a Sign

The angel of the LORD appeared to [Gideon] and said to him, "The LORD is with you, you mighty warrior. Go in this might of yours and deliver Israel from the hand of Midian; I hereby commission you." He responded, "But sir, how can I deliver Israel? My clan is the weakest in Manasseh, and I am the least in my family." The LORD said to him, "But I will be with you, and you shall strike down the Midianites, every one of them." Then he said to him, "If now I have found favor with you, then show me a sign that it is you who speak with me. Do not depart from here until I come to you, and bring out my present, and set it before you." And [the LORD] said, "I will stay until you return."

So Gideon went into his house and prepared a kid, and unleavened cakes. The angel of God said to him, "Take the meat and the unleavened cakes, and put them on this rock, and pour out the broth." And he did so. Then the angel of the LORD reached out the tip of the staff that was in his hand, and touched the meat and the unleavened cakes; and fire sprang up from the rock and consumed the meat and the unleavened cakes; and the angel of the LORD vanished from his sight. Then Gideon perceived that it was the angel of the LORD.

Judges 6:12, 14b–19a, 20–22a

GIDEON, A FARMER'S son, initially responds with skepticism and excuses when the Lord appears to him and commissions him to "deliver Israel from the hand of Midian." Even after the Lord tells him, "I will be with you," Gideon asks for a sign that it is the Lord speaking.

In seeking guidance from God, many of us struggle with being certain that a leaning or direction we feel is from God. What are some ways in which you have received confirmation that a certain guidance was from God? Have you ever asked for a sign from God concerning a major decision? What conditions prompted the request? What were the results?

Seeking False Guidance

So Saul died for his unfaithfulness; he was unfaithful to the LORD in that he did not keep the command of the LORD; moreover, he had consulted a medium, seeking guidance, and did not seek guidance from the LORD. Therefore the LORD put him to death and turned the kingdom over to David son of Jesse.

1 Chronicles 10:13–14

SAUL'S UNFAITHFULNESS ANTICIPATES the unfaithfulness of a number of kings, which resulted in the Babylonian exile (1 Chron 9:1; 2 Chron 36:14). Saul did not keep the word of Yahweh and he consulted a medium (1 Sam 28). Inquiring of a medium at a time of military danger seems to be comparable in the Chronicler's judgment to reliance on military alliances, which the Chronicler uniformly rejects. Above all it demonstrated distrust in Yahweh and disobedience to him.

When God doesn't give us clear answers, it's tempting to look elsewhere for reassurance that we're on the right path. Even Christians sometimes fall into such superstitious practices as "Bible roulette," in which one opens the Bible at random and looks for guidance in the first verse the finger falls on. How is this practice similar to Saul's consulting of a medium? What kinds of guidance or easy answers have you been tempted by? Say this prayer as you ask forgiveness for those times in which you let your anxiety and desire to know the future lead you down the wrong path:

Lord, your way is perfect: Help us always to trust in your goodness, so that, walking with you and following you in all simplicity, we may possess quiet and contented minds, and may cast all our care on you, for you care for us. Grant this, Lord, for your dear Son's sake, Jesus Christ. Amen.

—Christina Rossetti

The Fruit of the Spirit

By contrast, the fruit of the Spirit is love, joy, peace, patience, kindness, generosity, faithfulness, gentleness, and self-control. There is no law against such things. And those who belong to Christ Jesus have crucified the flesh with its passions and desires. If we live by the Spirit, let us also be guided by the Spirit.

Galatians 5:22–25

As Jesus pointed out, "The tree is known by its fruit" (Matt 12:33). Here Paul echoes the reality that fruit is a result of the nature of the tree, and for him that nature is the "new creation" (Gal 6:15). This metaphor of fruit is basic to spiritual formation. The fruit of the Spirit is the outward evidence of the inward reality of a heart "abiding" in Christ. In John 15 Jesus uses this metaphor to show that fruit is born as a result of relationship to the Vine. Therefore, we give our total energy and attention to grace-filled "training hard" by practicing the disciplines of being present to Jesus rather than in misguided "trying hard" to bear fruit. Through "abiding" (John 8:31–32, NKJV) we are set free to release the fruit of the Spirit.

Galatians tells us that we are on the right path if we show the fruit of the Spirit: love, joy, peace, patience, kindness, generosity, faithfulness, gentleness, and self-control. Write these qualities on an index card and put it in a place where you will come across it often. As you seek to be guided by God's will in your major life decisions at hand, prayerfully consider whether your choice will lead you closer to manifesting these qualities.

Asking for Help

When the king [Josiah] heard the words of the book of the law, he tore his clothes. Then the king commanded [them], saying, "Go, inquire of the LORD for me concerning the words of this book that has been found; for great is the wrath of the LORD that has been kindled against us, because our ancestors did not obey the words of this book."

So [they] went to the prophetess Huldah. She declared to them, "Thus says the LORD, the God of Israel: Tell the man who sent you to me, Thus says the LORD, I will indeed bring disaster on this place and on its inhabitants—all the words of the book that the king of Judah has read—because they have abandoned me and have made offerings to other gods. But as to the king of Judah, who sent you to inquire of the LORD, thus shall you say to him, Thus says the LORD, the God of Israel: Regarding the words that you have heard, because your heart was penitent, and you humbled yourself before the LORD, when you heard how I spoke against this place, and against its inhabitants, that they should become a desolation and a curse, and because you have torn your clothes and wept before me, I also have heard you, says the LORD. Therefore, I will gather you to your ancestors, and you shall be gathered to your grave in peace; your eyes shall not see all the disaster that I will bring on this place." They took the message back to the king.

2 Kings 22:11–12a, 13a, 14a, 15–17a, 18–20

EVEN THOUGH HE is the king, Josiah is humble enough to know that he needs to ask for help in understanding God's will about the book of the law that was found (probably an earlier form of Deuteronomy). Note that court officials must go outside the court to find the prophet who will speak these words.

Think about whose guidance you have found most helpful in your life. Today be open to hearing the Holy Spirit through anyone around you, especially those who display the fruit of the Spirit.

What Makes for Understanding

Elihu son of Barachel the Buzite answered: / "I am young in years, / and you are aged; / therefore I was timid and afraid / to declare my opinion to you. / I said, 'Let days speak, / and many years teach wisdom.' / But truly it is the spirit in a mortal, / the breath of the Almighty, that makes for understanding. / It is not the old that are wise, / not the aged that understand what is right. / Therefore I say, 'Listen to me; / let me also declare my opinion.'"

Job 32:6–10

IN THESE WORDS to Job, Elihu breaks the mold of the wisdom teacher by claiming it is the divine spirit, rather than the gray beard or hair, that makes for understanding. As Elihu speaks in the verses following this passage, we recognize in him a model spiritual director. He listens carefully, gives alternative explanations, suggests a reason for the current distress, and directs Job to God.

Under the discipline of guidance, by the spiritually mature in the local community of faith, we learn the secret of spiritual formation as we put off the old nature and "put on Jesus Christ" (Gal 3:27). When we "put on Christ," we do so in the spirit of love that forms the foundation of the universal community in which we encounter the reality of the risen Christ. As a result, we fall deeper and deeper in love with God and "love one another in truth and action" (1 John 3:11, 18).

Spiritual direction is an ancient practice gaining modern attention in which one Christian consults with another, spiritually experienced Christian. What qualities would you look for in a spiritual director? How might you know someone has the "breath of the Almighty"? Having considered these questions, is there someone you know who could serve as your spiritual director? Pray about whether this is an appropriate step for you to take in connection with your major life decision.

A Mentoring Influence

I am grateful to God—whom I worship with a clear conscience, as my ancestors did—when I remember you constantly in my prayers night and day. Recalling your tears, I long to see you so that I may be filled with joy. I am reminded of your sincere faith, a faith that lived first in your grandmother Lois and your mother Eunice and now, I am sure, lives in you. For this reason I remind you to rekindle the gift of God that is within you through the laying on of my hands; for God did not give us a spirit of cowardice, but rather a spirit of power and of love and of self-discipline.

Hold to that standard of sound teaching that you have heard from me, in the faith and love that are in Christ Jesus. Guard the good treasure entrusted to you, with the help of the Holy Spirit living in us.

2 Timothy 1:3–7, 13–14

PAUL AND TIMOTHY met during Paul's second missionary journey and worked together for some seventeen years. Although Timothy was young and probably fairly new to the Christian faith, he possessed a spiritual maturity beyond his years. After he became a Christian, Paul took him on as a companion, acting as a spiritual father to the young man.

In Paul Timothy found someone who could train him in his faith, someone who could love him and guide his growth while modeling a life lived in wholehearted service to Christ. We might call it mentoring or spiritual direction or holy friendship—whichever term we use, Timothy submitted to the discipline of guidance by opening his life to Paul and seeking growth through Paul's influence as they worked together.

"God's speaking in union with the human voice and human language is the primary *objective* way in which God addresses us. . . . This is best suited to the purposes of God precisely because it *most fully engages the faculties of free, intelligent beings who are socially interacting with agape love in the work of God as his colaborers and friends.*"

—Dallas Willard, *Hearing God*[6]

⌒ Finding the Way

Guiding the Nations

May God be gracious to us and bless us
    and make his face to shine upon us,
that your way may be known upon earth,
    your saving power among all nations.
Let the peoples praise you, O God;
    let all the peoples praise you.
Let the nations be glad and sing for joy,
    for you judge the people with equity
    and guide the nations upon earth.
Let the peoples praise you, O God;
    let all the peoples praise you.

Psalm 67:1–5

PSALM 67 IS a strong call to the nations and peoples to praise God. Clearly God's particular blessing has more than a narrow effect. God's action includes but reaches beyond a chosen people.

We are quick to acknowledge that God can guide individuals through things such as circumstances, signs, dreams, visions, and angels, but perhaps it is quite something else to consider that God may be able to lead a whole people or "guide the nations upon earth." Is it hard for you to think of God leading an entire group or nation? If so, why? How do you think God might be guiding your church? Your nation? If God can guide the nations, how does this impact your vision about how God can guide you in the greatest concerns of your life?

The Life God Wants for Us

Little children, let us love, not in word or speech, but in truth and
action. And by this we will know that we are from the truth and will
reassure our hearts before him whenever our hearts condemn us; for
God is greater than our hearts, and he knows everything. Beloved, if
our hearts do not condemn us, we have boldness before God; and we
receive from him whatever we ask, because we obey his commandments and do what pleases him.

1 John 3:18–22

WHAT A BEAUTIFUL description of the interactive friendship with God
that guidance is based on. We can have confidence that God hears and responds to our requests, which will reflect the Father's good pleasure even
as our lives are consistent with God's purposes. Our prayers and lives are
shaped by intimacy with God, who loved us while we were yet sinners.
They flow from, rather than qualify us for, a relationship with God.

Following God's will is less about specific actions than about living a
life that is consistent with God's purposes. How does this concept fit in
with your thoughts and experience of guidance these last twenty days?

"It may seem strange, but being in the will of God is very far removed from just doing what God wants us to do—so far removed, in
fact, that we can be solidly in the will of God, and be aware that we are,
without knowing God's preference with regard to various details of
our lives. . . . Generally speaking we are in God's will whenever we are
leading the kind of life he wants for us. And that leaves a lot of room for
initiative on our part, which is essential: our individual initiatives are
central to his will for us."

—Dallas Willard, *Hearing God*[7]

For more verses on guidance and ideas on how to practice the discipline of guidance, see
the Responding exercises and Spiritual Disciplines Index in *The Life with God Bible*.

Meditation

Prayerful rumination upon God, his Word, and his world

Many of us worry that "meditation" has a ring of the occult or of Eastern religions. Yet the Bible is filled with references to God's people meditating on his word, pondering Jesus or "higher things," reflecting on the beauty of creation. Unlike Eastern meditation, in which participants seek to empty themselves of attachment, in Christian meditation we seek to fill ourselves with God, to form a more complete attachment to Christ. "Christian meditation involves, not emptiness, but fullness," writes author Joyce Huggett. "It means being attentive to God."[1] Meditation is trying to focus on God with the aim of letting God direct our thoughts. Like so many of the disciplines, it is ultimately about seeking God's voice. And while meditation is closely linked with prayer and study, it focuses more on listening than on talking, is more devotional than analytical. In meditation, our emotions and our imaginations are as equally engaged as our minds.

Just as Enoch, Moses, the prophets, and countless others walked and talked with God, so too we seek to listen for God—whether in the slow savoring of God's word, in silent meditation, or in contemplation of creation or events in the world around us. Meditation is countercultural for many of us who tend to want to learn and pray and read as quickly as we can, so we can get to the next item on our to-do list. Reading slowly, pondering a flower, thinking about God with no set agenda—these are often difficult tasks for us, which shows just how essential they are for our formation.

On the glorious splendor of your majesty,
and on your wondrous works, I will meditate.

—*Psalm 145:5*

Meditation

Meditating on Scripture

Think over what I say, for the Lord will give you understanding in all things.

2 Timothy 2:7

FOR THE NEXT ten days, we will seek to meditate on a specific passage of Scripture—ponder it, think it over, and muse on it until it becomes a part of us. Unlike the longer passage you chose for the spiritual discipline of Study, here choose a very short passage, perhaps just a sentence in length. Any of these would work beautifully: one of Jesus' "I am" statements from the Gospel of John, a proverb, the first line or stanza of one of the psalms, or a teaching from a Letter.

Aim to enter the passage as an active participant, imagining yourself hearing Jesus say the words, experiencing the sights, sounds, and smells of that day. "Our task is not so much to study the passage as to be initiated into the reality of which the passage speaks," writes Richard Foster.[2] Remember that Christ assures us that he is still here with us, to teach and instruct us. Allow him to do this very thing with you. You may want to spend the entire ten days on the same passage. Or perhaps you would like to meditate on several different passages. You will find more about how to practice this type of "holy reading" in the devotions that follow.

Spiritual Practice

Holy Reading

Oh, how I love your law!
    It is my meditation all day long.
Your commandment makes me wiser than my enemies,
    for it is always with me.
I have more understanding than all my teachers,
    for your decrees are my meditation.

Psalm 119:97–99

LECTIO DIVINA, THE classic spiritual exercise of "holy reading," offers a way to let the Psalms shape us. We come to the text with an attitude of patient receptivity, in no hurry to get through the text. After all, it's not so much a question of how much we read as it is how well we read. Usually it helps to begin "holy reading" with silence, partly to quiet ourselves to listen and partly to consciously choose to read in a way much different from the way we normally read. Then we read, proceeding prayerfully, ready to stop, to soak in a word or a verse as God opens it to us, to brood gently over it, to take it in slowly like a mint melting in the mouth. This kind of listening to the text invites God to teach us in direct and transforming ways. We respond by pondering such teaching and acting on it.

Read this quotation for inspiration as you begin your meditation on Scripture:

"Prepare yourself for reading by purity of intention, singly aiming at the good of your soul, and by fervent prayer to God, that he would enable you to see his will and give you a firm resolution to perform it. . . . Labor to work yourself up into a temper correspondent with what you read, for that reading is useless which only enlightens the understanding without warming the affections. And therefore intersperse, here and there, earnest aspirations to God for his heat as well as his light."

—John Wesley, "Advice for Spiritual Reading"[3]

~ *Meditating on Scripture*

Meditate on It Day and Night

"Only be strong and very courageous, being careful to act in accordance with all the law that my servant Moses commanded you; do not turn from it to the right hand or to the left, so that you may be successful wherever you go. This book of the law shall not depart out of your mouth; you shall meditate on it day and night, so that you may be careful to act in accordance with all that is written in it. For then you shall make your way prosperous, and then you shall be successful."

Joshua 1:7–8

GOD'S WORDS TO Joshua at the beginning of Joshua's story suggest that effective leadership calls for concentrated meditation and musing on the law of God. This word was not to "depart" from his "mouth," for mortals do not live by bread alone, but by every word that proceeds from the mouth of God (Deut 8:3). Like Joshua, we are to talk about the word, think about the word, and obey the word (Ps 1:2–3). In a sense, every word from the Lord is also a call from the Lord. We read every verse of Scripture lovingly and attentively, because every verse is a potential summons from God. Perhaps when we read, we ought not to ask ourselves, "What do these words mean?" but "What is God summoning me to do through these words?"

Be guided by these words as you return to your meditation today:
"You must look up with the vision of the heart to the Person of Christ, and listen for the impress of His will on your will through His words, that is, through the Book of the Gospel that was written to be the means of communication with the souls of His people. As you become familiar with them He will by His Spirit bring them to your memory as you need them, to be your defence in the dangers of the way, even as David said in the Psalms: 'Thy word have I hid in my heart that I might not sin against Thee' (Ps 119:11, KJV)."

—Lilias Trotter, *The Way of the Sevenfold Secret* [4]

Mary Pondered the Words in Her Heart

In that region there were shepherds living in the fields, keeping watch over their flock by night. Then an angel of the Lord stood before them, and the glory of the Lord shone around them, and they were terrified. But the angel said to them, "Do not be afraid; for see—I am bringing you good news of great joy for all the people: to you is born this day in the city of David a Savior, who is the Messiah, the Lord. This will be a sign for you: you will find a child wrapped in bands of cloth and lying in a manger." And suddenly there was with the angel a multitude of the heavenly host, praising God and saying,

"Glory to God in the highest heaven,
     and on earth peace among those whom he favors!"

When the angels had left them and gone into heaven, the shepherds said to one another, "Let us go now to Bethlehem and see this thing that has taken place, which the Lord has made known to us." So they went with haste and found Mary and Joseph, and the child lying in the manger. When they saw this, they made known what had been told them about this child; and all who heard it were amazed at what the shepherds told them. But Mary treasured all these words and pondered them in her heart.

Luke 2:8–19

MARY SPENT HER whole life pondering the coming of Jesus into her life and treasuring the words she received about him and from him. Our last glimpse of Mary in the Bible finds her in constant prayer with Jesus' disciples, his brothers, and other women (Acts 1:14).

"Just as you do not analyze the words of someone you love, but accept them as they are said to you, accept the Word of Scripture and ponder it in your heart, as Mary did. That is all. That is meditation."

—Dietrich Bonhoeffer, *The Way to Freedom*[5]

~ Meditating on Scripture

The Beginning of Knowledge

The proverbs of Solomon son of David, king of Israel: / For
learning about wisdom and instruction, / for understanding words
of insight, / for gaining instruction in wise dealing, / righteousness,
justice, and equity; / to teach shrewdness to the simple, / knowledge
and prudence to the young— / let the wise also hear and gain in
learning, / and the discerning acquire skill, / to understand a
proverb and a figure, / the words of the wise and their riddles. /
The fear of the LORD is the beginning of knowledge; / fools despise
wisdom and instruction.

Proverbs 1:1–7

THE PROLOGUE EXPLAINS what the book of Proverbs is for; it is not just
a collection of clever sayings. No, these sayings—proverbs, parables, and
riddles—are to educate the young and inexperienced and to shape them
in right conduct. Proverbs, in short, is a book of spiritual and moral formation. No doubt in past times the wisdom sayings of Proverbs were committed to memory, to be summoned up in times of need. Elders might use
these sayings to instruct or reprove. Younger people might soak up these
counsels as a way of growing in spiritual strength. Contemporary people
can follow suit. If we read the book of Proverbs often, and devotionally,
certain texts will speak to us. Sometimes they hit so hard they even make
us laugh. With open, well-formed hearts, we will hear God's voice, if we
read slowly and prayerfully, letting the Lord speak to us through the text.
Intentional reading will help us to grow stronger in the virtuous life.

*Father God, I am so often in a hurry, skimming or reading as fast as I can,
so I can be on to the next thing. Help me to slow down, so I can be shaped
by the texts I turn my attention to this week. Help me to read prayerfully,
so that I can hear your voice through the words. In your name I pray.
Amen.*

Give Me Understanding

Teach me, O LORD, the way of your statutes, / and I will observe it
to the end. / Give me understanding, that I may keep your law / and
observe it with my whole heart. / Lead me in the path of your
commandments, / for I delight in it. / Turn my heart to your
decrees, / and not to selfish gain. / Turn my eyes from looking at
vanities; / give me life in your ways. / Confirm to your servant your
promise, / which is for those who fear you. / Turn away the disgrace
that I dread, / for your ordinances are good. / See, I have longed for
your precepts; / in your righteousness give me life.

Psalm 119:33–40

CHRISTIAN WRITERS THROUGHOUT history have insisted that the only
way we can come to understand the Psalms is by praying them and by
using them in ways that allow them to shape us. This involves a conscious
choice that contradicts common habits. It means that, instead of working on the text, we let the text work on us. It means reading formation-
ally rather than informationally, which is the habit we bring to reports,
newspapers, textbooks, and most of the other things we read. It means
embracing the text rather than holding it at arm's length. It means being
vulnerable to hear how God might address us through the text rather
than managing the text to serve our curiosity and need to control.

Think of the imagery in the following quote as you begin your meditation today. Is it helpful? Why or why not?

" 'Praying the Scripture' is not judged by *how much* you read but the
way you read. If you read quickly, it will benefit you little. You will be
like a bee that merely skims the surface of a flower. Instead, in this new
way of reading with prayer, you become as the bee who penetrates into
the *depths* of the flower. You plunge deeply within to remove its deepest
nectar."

—Madame Guyon, *Experiencing the Depths of Jesus Christ*[6]

— Meditating on Scripture

Knowing Jesus' Voice

"The one who enters by the gate is the shepherd of the sheep. The gate-keeper opens the gate for him, and the sheep hear his voice. He calls his own sheep by name and leads them out. When he has brought out all his own, he goes ahead of them, and the sheep follow him because they know his voice. They will not follow a stranger, but they will run from him because they do not know the voice of strangers.

"I am the good shepherd. I know my own and my own know me, just as the Father knows me and I know the Father. And I lay down my life for the sheep. I have other sheep that do not belong to this fold. I must bring them also, and they will listen to my voice. So there will be one flock, one shepherd."

John 10:2–5, 14–16

JOHN'S GOSPEL CITES the phrase "I am" together with seven sets of names to record metaphors for Christ. Jesus says, "I am the bread of life" (6:35, 48), "the light of the world" (8:12; 9:5), "the gate" (10:7, 9), "the good shepherd" (10:11, 14), "the resurrection and the life" (11:25), "the way, the truth, and the life" (14:6), and "the vine" (15:1, 5). All these pictures are expanded in ways that teach us more thoroughly about the triune grace that rescues, restores, establishes, nourishes, indwells, enlightens, guides, protects, saves, and raises us. Each of these statements provides ample ground for meditation. Jesus' description of himself as the shepherd also brings comfort and assurance to those of us struggling to discern his voice in our contemplative prayer. All those who are his sheep know his voice. He knows us and we know him. If we trust him to shepherd our lives, we will not follow a stranger.

Today meditate on one of Jesus' "I am" statements.

Lord, as I meditate on your word, I worry that I will not be able to recognize or discern your voice. Please help to make the way clear as I work to focus on you, my master, my shepherd. In your name I pray. Amen.

Knowledge of God's Mystery

For I want you to know how much I am struggling for you, and for those in Laodicea, and for all those who have not seen me face to face. I want their hearts to be encouraged and united in love, so that they may have all the riches of assured understanding and have the knowledge of God's mystery, that is, Christ himself, in whom are hidden all the treasures of wisdom and knowledge.

Colossians 2:1–3

THE KNOWLEDGE OF God, of course, is a mystery. It has been hidden throughout the ages, but is now revealed (1:26–27). This mystery is also understood to be the life of Christ within believers. Thus this is not a generalized mystery or a vague sense of the holy. It is Christ himself, who is the treasure of wisdom and knowledge. It is a truth not reducible to our categories of thought. And even though we see as in a mirror dimly (1 Cor 13:12), nonetheless we do actually see something of the truth, enough for knowing the love and salvation of God.

Meditate today on this passage about Christ as God's mystery, asking God to give you right understanding:

Lord God, dear Father, through your Holy Spirit you have taught and enlightened the hearts of your believers. Through the same Spirit give us a right understanding, to be glad at all times in his comfort and power, through your Son, Jesus Christ, our Lord. Amen.

—Martin Luther, *Luther's Prayers*[7]

I Search My Spirit

I cry aloud to God, / aloud to God, that he may hear me. / In the
day of my trouble I seek the Lord; / in the night my hand is
stretched out without wearying; / my soul refuses to be comforted. /
I think of God, and I moan; / I meditate, and my spirit faints. /
You keep my eyelids from closing; / I am so troubled that I cannot
speak. / I consider the days of old, / and remember the years of
long ago. / I commune with my heart in the night; / I meditate
and search my spirit: / "Will the Lord spurn forever, / and never
again be favorable? / Has his steadfast love ceased forever? / Are
his promises at an end for all time? / Has God forgotten to be
gracious? / Has he in anger shut up his compassion?" / And I say,
"It is my grief / that the right hand of the Most High has changed."

Psalm 77:1–10

THE STARK WORDS here portray the deep anguish of the singer. Moan-
ing at the thought of God and wondering if God's steadfast love has
ceased forever are apt examples of this darkness. In exploring lament
songs such as these, we can patiently reflect on why confessions of trust
are typically sandwiched between complaints and pleas for help.

Try to describe a time when your soul was bowed down from grief. If
you tried meditating on God and his deeds at that time, what effect
did it have on your soul? If you didn't meditate on them then, try to
remember to do so the next time your soul is weary.

Musing on God's Mighty Deeds

I will call to mind the deeds of the LORD; / I will remember your wonders of old. / I will meditate on all your work, / and muse on your mighty deeds. / Your way, O God, is holy. / What god is so great as our God? / You are the God who works wonders; / you have displayed your might among the peoples. / With your strong arm you redeemed your people, / the descendants of Jacob and Joseph.

Psalm 77:11–15

THIS PASSAGE IS the answer to the plaintive call of the previous verses. This hymn follows directly after the anguished words. Before, the singer was meditating and searching his spirit in an effort to find the reasons for his misfortune. Now he is meditating on all of God's work and musing on his mighty deeds. It seems the singer was suffering from grief about his situation and the recitation of God's deeds was the way to overcome it. The dramatic report of God's victory that follows would be stirring for us to ponder as we seek to recover hope in our dangerous world.

How has your practice of meditating on God's word in Scripture changed you? Do you feel better prepared to receive understanding about God and God's nature and work? Read this quote as inspiration for your continued practice of meditating on Scripture:

"Though God in this threefold revelation [of Scripture, nature, and Jesus Christ] has provided answers to our questions concerning Him, the answers by no means lie on the surface. They must be sought by prayer, by long meditation on the written Word, and by earnest and well-disciplined labor. However brightly the light may shine, it can be seen only by those who are spiritually prepared to receive it. 'Blessed are the pure in heart, for they shall see God.'"

—A.W. Tozer, *The Knowledge of the Holy*[8]

Setting Our Minds on God

So if you have been raised with Christ, seek the things that are above, where Christ is, seated at the right hand of God. Set your mind on the things that are above, not on things that are on earth.

Colossians 3:1–2

FOR THE NEXT ten days, we will try to set our minds on the things that are above, practicing clearing out from our minds the noise of daily life and focusing on hearing God's voice. Try to find a place that is as quiet and free of distractions as possible. Choose a comfortable position. Many prefer sitting on the floor or in a chair with feet flat on the ground. The idea is to be in a position comfortable enough that it requires no thought. You can close your eyes, or keep them open and focused on a religious item, perhaps a cross, or a tree or some other image from nature.

You might want to pick a word or phrase to keep your mind focused on God if you find yourself distracted by thoughts about work, household tasks, family, or a noise outside. "Jesus" or "Abba" is a good word to use. At first, you may find that your mind shoots out all kind of information at you, like a computer shutting down. Just try to relax as you work through this stage; keep repeating your word. Spiritual writer Madame Guyon writes: "Be assured that as your soul becomes more accustomed to withdrawing to inward things, this process will become easier. There are two reasons that you will find it easier each time to bring your mind under the subjection of the Lord. One is that the mind, after much practice, will form a new habit of turning deep within. The second is that you have a gracious Lord!"[9]

If you have not tried meditative prayer before, then start with five minutes or less. You can gradually work up to longer. You may find that God leads you to practical insights about your family or your life or events that have happened in your past or perhaps direct insights about God, his nature, and your relationship to him. The experience of meditative prayer is different for everyone. Many find it extremely helpful to keep a journal detailing their experiences and insights.

Spiritual Practice

The Meditation of My Heart

Let the words of my mouth and the meditation of my heart
  be acceptable to you,
  O LORD, my rock and my redeemer.

Psalm 19:14

THIS FAMILIAR VERSE invites God's scrutiny and correction (see 139:23–24). The word translated "meditation" here would be better rendered "whisperings" or "murmurings." Welcoming God's knowing and shaping of our inner talk deepens our vulnerability. It is a huge step in our formation.

Joyce Huggett writes, "We meditate to give God's words the opportunity to penetrate not just our minds, but our emotions—the places where we hurt—and our will—the place where we make choices and decisions. We meditate to encounter the Living Word, Jesus himself. We meditate so that every part of our being, our thoughts and our affections and our ambitions, are turned to face and honour and glorify him. Yet another reason for learning to meditate is so that we may become conversant with the will of God."[10] Use this quote as inspiration for your meditation today. Or you may wish to begin with this prayer.

Father God, today I come to you in meditative prayer. I ask that you open my heart to whatever you want to show me. Guide my meditations, my inner whispers, in the way that is acceptable and pleasing to you. I want so much for you to shape my inner being, yet I don't often seem to succeed at setting aside the time for you to do this work. Help me to be consistent in my meditations over the coming days, that I may come to you eagerly to learn, to be changed. In your name I pray. Amen.

~ *Setting Our Minds on God*

Think About These Things

Finally, beloved, whatever is true, whatever is honorable, whatever is just, whatever is pure, whatever is pleasing, whatever is commendable, if there is any excellence and if there is anything worthy of praise, think about these things. Keep on doing the things that you have learned and received and heard and seen in me, and the God of peace will be with you.

Philippians 4:8–9

THE SPIRITUAL LIFE is a cooperative transformation of thought and action. First, God is at work in us, enabling us "both to will and to work for his good pleasure" (2:13). Yet we also have a part to play. As Paul urges, we must choose to *think* of the things of God and choose to *do* the things of God. As we model our thoughts after the highest of standards and model our lives after the life and message of Paul himself, we will find that the "God of peace" himself accompanies us on our transforming journey.

Lord God, I return to you today to meditate on those things that are excellent and "worthy of praise." Throughout my day it seems that my thoughts are on everything but what is just, pure, pleasing, and commendable. Guide my thoughts, Lord; teach me about what is excellent and praiseworthy in your sight, that I may honor you in thought, word, and deed. Amen.

Resting and Reflecting

On the fifteenth day of the seven month you shall have a holy convocation; you shall not work at your occupations. It is a day for you to blow the trumpets.

Numbers 29:1

BUILT INTO THE religious calendar of the Israelites was a day to rest and blow the trumpets. Taking time to rest is important in the spiritual life. Rest is not merely the state of doing no work. Rest is a time for refreshment. It may be a time to reflect on the past or plan for the future. It is also a time for worshiping God. The Sabbath is an intentional time set apart for worship. Our souls receive true peace and strength when we worship God. Rest is a Spiritual Discipline that requires and also restores our trust in God. Our trust grows as we see how God fulfills our needs even when we are working. We realize we don't need to earn God's provision. Rest helps us reside in the unconditional, unfailing, and forgiving love of God.

Meditation is a wonderful way to rest in God. Today think of your meditative prayer time as resting in God, seeking the refreshment only God can give. Relax, close your eyes, even allow yourself to fall asleep if that is what your body wants. When you awake, thank God for the gift of rest.

Meditating in the Watches of the Night

My soul is satisfied as with a rich feast,
    and my mouth praises you with joyful lips
when I think of you on my bed,
    and meditate on you in the watches of the night;
for you have been my help,
    and in the shadow of your wings I sing for joy.
My soul clings to you;
    your right hand upholds me.

Psalm 63:5–8

PSALM 63 CALLS especially for focused attention on God. Far from being boring or a chore, the singer finds the experience to be one of joy. When the disciple looks upon God, thinks of him, and meditates on him, his "soul is satisfied as with a rich feast."

Have you found your meditative prayer practice to be joyful?

Only to sit and think of God,
    Oh what a joy it is!
To think the thought, to breathe the Name
    Earth has no higher bliss.

—Frederick W. Faber[11]

When Life Hinders Meditation

Then Eliphaz the Temanite answered:
"Should the wise answer with windy knowledge,
    and fill themselves with the east wind?
Should they argue in unprofitable talk,
    or in words with which they can do no good?
But you are doing away with the fear of God,
    and hindering meditation before God.
For your iniquity teaches your mouth,
    and you choose the tongue of the crafty.
Your own mouth condemns you, and not I;
    your own lips testify against you."

Job 15:1–4

IN THIS PASSAGE Job's friend Eliphaz accuses Job of "hindering meditation before God." He argues that Job has no right to question God, that such talk is "unprofitable." Listening, quiet rumination before God, would be the better way to deal with Job's situation, he seems to be saying. But the central problem for Job is that God will not talk to him, will not explain to him why this disproportionate suffering has been visited upon him. The silence of God is a theological problem in the book of Job. We honor the mysteries of God by allowing our confusion, anger, hopelessness, and grief to mount along with Job's as the book develops.

Has there ever been a time in your life when what one person said or did seemed to hamper your ability to meditate on the things of God or talk with God?

God, there are times when I feel that you will not talk to me, to explain to me why I feel a certain way or why a certain thing has happened. Lord, help me to keep asking, to keep opening my heart to you and asking you to shape it. In your name I pray. Amen.

~ *Setting Our Minds on God*

A Walking Meditation

Now Isaac had come from Beer-lahai-roi, and was settled in the Negeb. Isaac went out in the evening to walk in the field; and looking up, he saw camels coming. And Rebekah looked up, and when she saw Isaac, she slipped quickly from the camel, and said to the servant, "Who is the man over there, walking in the field to meet us?" The servant said, "It is my master." So she took her veil and covered herself. And the servant told Isaac all the things that he had done. Then Isaac brought her into his mother Sarah's tent. He took Rebekah, and she became his wife; and he loved her. So Isaac was comforted after his mother's death.

Genesis 24:62–67

AFTER THE DEATH of his mother, Sarah, Isaac goes out into the field in the evening, perhaps to mourn for her or talk to God about what the future now holds for him. The meaning of the Hebrew word translated "walk" above is unclear, so it is often translated "meditate." It is during one of these evening meditations or walks that he meets Rebekah, the very woman Isaac's father's servant has brought for Isaac to marry.

Sometimes open fields or spaces stimulate our desire to meditate. Today, if at all possible spend your time of meditation outside.

Lord God, what a pleasant habit it is to walk and enjoy your creation while thinking of you. Thank you for the grass and the trees, the sun and the clouds, the moon and the stars. Such beauty is hard for the mind to grasp. How well you must think of us to create such a beautiful place for us to live. It makes me ponder what wonders heaven has in store. Thank you, Father God, for this world. In your name I pray. Amen.

Meditating on God's Works

You make springs gush forth in the valleys; / they flow between
the hills, / giving drink to every wild animal; / the wild asses
quench their thirst. / By the streams the birds of the air have their
habitation; / they sing among the branches. / From your lofty abode
you water the mountains; / the earth is satisfied with the fruit of
your work. / You cause the grass to grow for the cattle, / and plants
for people to use, / to bring forth food from the earth, / and wine
to gladden the human heart, / oil to make the face shine, / and
bread to strengthen the human heart. / O Lord, how manifold are
your works! / In wisdom you have made them all; / the earth is full
of your creatures. / May my meditation be pleasing to him, / for
I rejoice in the Lord.

Psalm 104:10–15, 24, 34

God's lavish and orderly care for all the creatures brings them joy,
and they rely on the steady care day to day. We do well to marvel at the
creation and bless God for the power, wisdom, and generosity we see in
it. It can help ward off complacency, self-sufficiency, and even a false
sense of entitlement. We do well to remember that each moment, each
breath, is a gift.

During your meditative prayer today, reflect on these words:

"All created beauty, all beauty of nature, the beauty of the sunset, of
the sea lying like a mirror beneath the blue sky, of the dark forest, of the
garden of flowers, of the mountains and the great spaces of the desert,
of the snow and the ice, the beauty of a rare soul reflected in a beautiful
face, all these beauties are but the palest reflection of Yours, my God.
All that has ever charmed my eyes in this world is but the poorest, the
humblest reflection of Your infinite beauty."

—Charles de Foucauld[12]

Reflecting on Jesus

Therefore, brothers and sisters, holy partners in a heavenly calling, consider that Jesus, the apostle and high priest of our confession, was faithful to the one who appointed him, just as Moses also "was faithful in all God's house." Yet Jesus is worthy of more glory than Moses, just as the builder of a house has more honor than the house itself. (For every house is built by someone, but the builder of all things is God.) Now Moses was faithful in all God's house as a servant, to testify to the things that would be spoken later. Christ, however, was faithful over God's house as a son, and we are his house if we hold firm the confidence and the pride that belong to hope.

Hebrews 3:1–6

SPIRITUAL EXISTENCE IS not isolated existence. The work of Jesus reconciles believers to God, but it also forms them into a new community, a "house" far greater than was possible through the law of Moses. Believers are urged to "consider . . . Jesus." The Greek word for "consider" means to think about in a careful and reflective manner. The relation of Jesus to his "house" is different from the relation of Moses to his "house." Jesus is the Son and thus the true heir, whereas Moses was a servant. Moses "had" a house, that is, the law possessed believers; Christ and believers "are" a house, a new community of Sanctifier and sanctified (2:11), one with the Lord and with each other.

Spend some time today meditating on this passage about Jesus. Begin with this prayer for understanding:

O heavenly Father, / the author and fountain of all truth, / the bottomless sea of all understanding: / Send your Holy Spirit into our hearts, / and lighten our understandings / with the beam of your heavenly grace. / We ask this, O merciful Father, / for the sake of your dear Son, / our Savior Jesus Christ. Amen.

—Nicholas Ridley

Setting Our Sights on Jesus

Therefore, since we are surrounded by so great a cloud of witnesses, let us also lay aside every weight and the sin that clings so closely, and let us run with perseverance the race that is set before us, looking to Jesus the pioneer and perfecter of our faith, who for the sake of the joy that was set before him endured the cross, disregarding its shame, and has taken his seat at the right hand of the throne of God.

Consider him who endured such hostility against himself from sinners, so that you may not grow weary or lose heart. In your struggle against sin you have not yet resisted to the point of shedding your blood.

Hebrews 12:1–4

THE FAITH OF other believers throughout space and time supports and encourages our own faith. We draw strength from the "great cloud of witnesses" that has gone faithfully before us. We do not concentrate on the faith per se, but we set our sights deliberately on "Jesus the pioneer and perfecter of our faith." Jesus pioneers a way for believers through the uncharted territory of this world, perfecting our faith as we follow him. We must, like pilgrims, travel light by laying "aside every weight and the sin that clings so closely," willingly enduring hardships until we joyfully reach "the heavenly Jerusalem, and . . . the assembly of the firstborn who are enrolled in heaven" (12:22–23).

Today try doing meditative prayer by sitting in silence and repeating Jesus' name.

Lord, what better focus for my meditation than Jesus. I place my gaze firmly on him as I ponder the meaning of his life, death, and resurrection. Thank you for his perfecting work in me. In your name I pray. Amen.

For more verses on meditation and ideas on how to practice the discipline of meditation, see the Responding exercises and Spiritual Disciplines Index in *The Life with God Bible*.

Solitude

The creation of an open, empty space in our lives by purposefully abstaining from interaction with other human beings, so that, freed from competing loyalties, we can be found by God

The Gospels tell us that Jesus' very public ministry was interspersed with periods of solitude during which he, either completely by himself or with the disciples, left the crowds behind to pray. These times of solitude appeared to nourish Jesus for those times when he was in the public eye. He began his ministry with forty days in the desert, just after he was baptized. And he continued the practice of going off alone to pray, often just at the times when his ministry seemed to demand the most from him.

Solitude is not about becoming a hermit or misanthrope. Indeed, times of solitude can enhance our times of fellowship with others. Neither is solitude loneliness. It is time spent with God. Put this way, it sounds so natural, yet for most of us this time does not just *happen*. One of the keys to the definition above is the phrase "the creation of an open, empty space." We must work to create this space, to "purposefully" withdraw even when—especially when—it seems that we have no time to do so. We can all learn from Jesus' example and take time to focus on our relationship with God, replenishing and nourishing ourselves for busy lives.

Come away to a deserted place all by yourselves and rest a while.
—Mark 6:31

Solitude

Withdrawing to a Deserted Place

But now more than ever the word about Jesus spread abroad; many crowds would gather to hear him and to be cured of their diseases. But he would withdraw to deserted places and pray.

Luke 5:15–16

EACH DAY FOR the next ten days, seek to do exactly what Jesus did. Withdraw to a place where you can be alone with God and use that time to pray. When possible, try to have these times of solitude immediately before or after times where you are around many others. If it is an extremely busy time for you—*especially* if that is the case—work to create time to be alone with God, even if all you can manage is a solitary cup of coffee in the morning or a few moments of prayer in your car before your drive to work. Remind yourself that these times of solitude will nourish and refresh you. Perhaps you already set aside time each day to be with God in a place that is quiet and deserted. If so, perhaps you will want to challenge yourself to withdraw even more. For example, if you usually pray in a room in your house, perhaps you could try driving or walking to a park or a place where you can be almost certain that you won't be interrupted. You might want to begin your time of solitude with this prayer from the Northumbria Community:

> *Here am I, Lord,*
> > *I've come to do Your Will.*
> *Here am I, Lord,*
> > *in your presence I'm still.*

—Celtic Daily Prayer[1]

Spiritual Practice

The Tent of Meeting

Now Moses used to take the tent and pitch it outside the camp, far off from the camp; he called it the tent of meeting. And everyone who sought the Lord would go out to the tent of meeting, which was outside the camp. Whenever Moses went out to the tent, all the people would rise and stand, each of them, at the entrance of their tents and watch Moses until he had gone into the tent. When Moses entered the tent, the pillar of cloud would descend and stand at the entrance of the tent, and the Lord would speak with Moses. When all the people saw the pillar of cloud standing at the entrance of the tent, all the people would rise and bow down, all of them at the entrance of their tent. Thus the Lord used to speak to Moses face to face, as one speaks to a friend.

Exodus 33:7–11a

WITH MOSES GOD chose to be present and not distant, to show his glory, to get up close and personal as when one speaks with a friend. Moses was able to meet "face to face" with God in the tent of meeting. The Israelites too could come daily to God—approach God, learn God's name, and call upon that name. The major formational advantage of this individual communion with God is the good effect of God's direct presence. Our lives find their direction when God *is* present with us, and we are directionless without him. Intimate, individual communication with God is something that cannot be overlooked in spiritual formation. We must constantly seek it out. We need the full assurance of God's greatness and goodness that comes only from his direct presence. This, frankly, cannot be derived from any other source.

Do you have a favorite location that serves as your "tent of meeting," where you go to seek communion with God? If so, how do you find that prayer in this place differs from prayer elsewhere? If not, try to practice your time of solitude today in a spot that would serve as such a place to regularly seek God in solitude.

Wrestling with God

The same night [Jacob] got up and took his two wives, his two maids, and his eleven children, and crossed the ford of the Jabbok. He took them and sent them across the stream, and likewise everything that he had. Jacob was left alone; and a man wrestled with him until daybreak. When the man saw that he did not prevail against Jacob, he struck him on the hip socket; and Jacob's hip was put out of joint as he wrestled with him. Then he said, "Let me go, for the day is breaking." But Jacob said, "I will not let you go, unless you bless me." So he said to him, "What is your name?" And he said, "Jacob." Then the man said, "You shall no longer be called Jacob, but Israel, for you have striven with God and with humans, and have prevailed." Then Jacob asked him, "Please tell me your name." But he said, "Why is it that you ask my name?" And there he blessed him. So Jacob called the place Peniel, saying, "For I have seen God face to face, and yet my life is preserved."

Genesis 32:22–30

WHEN JACOB DELIBERATELY created space to be alone, God joined him. The nighttime wrestling match with Someone divine is obscured in the shadows of mystery. What is clear is that, although Jacob prevails, he also acquires a new name and a limp. Insisting that he be blessed by the midnight stranger, Jacob receives the new name Israel, indicating that "God rules," "God preserves," "God protects," or "God strives." Filled with mystery, this encounter with God is also characterized by remarkable intimacy. Notice that the wrestling stranger refuses to be named. God comes so close we cannot even see exactly who or what has gotten hold of us. However, after such an encounter we go forward blessed—wounded perhaps, but always changed.

Why does the word "alone" often strike fear into the hearts of the bravest of us? Pick the one reason that best describes why you fear being alone. Talk to God about that fear as you practice your time of solitude.

Spending the Night in Prayer

Now during those days [Jesus] went out to the mountain to pray; and he spent the night in prayer to God. And when day came, he called his disciples and chose twelve of them, whom he also named apostles: Simon, whom he named Peter, and his brother Andrew, and James, and John, and Philip, and Bartholomew, and Matthew, and Thomas, and James son of Alphaeus, and Simon, who was called the Zealot, and Judas son of James, and Judas Iscariot, who became a traitor.

Luke 6:12–16

TWO SIGNIFICANT EMPHASES in Luke are prayer and solitude. All the Gospel writers mention prayer, of course, but Luke takes care to show how Jesus' prayer practice was often linked to solitude: "[Jesus] would withdraw to deserted places and pray" (5:16); "At daybreak he departed and went into a deserted place" (4:42). Other Gospel writers mention his calling of the twelve apostles, but they don't tell us Jesus prayed all night about it, as we see here. And they relate his challenge to the disciples, "Who do the crowds say that I am?" but not that he was praying by himself before he put the question: "Jesus was praying alone, with only the disciples near him" (9:18).

When have you spent time in solitude and prayer before making a big decision? What was the result?

— *Withdrawing to a Deserted Place*

Hide Yourself

Now Elijah the Tishbite, of Tishbe in Gilead, said to Ahab, "As the LORD the God of Israel lives, before whom I stand, there shall be neither dew nor rain these years, except by my word." The word of the LORD came to him, saying, "Go from here and turn eastward, and hide yourself by the Wadi Cherith, which is east of the Jordan. You shall drink from the wadi, and I have commanded the ravens to feed you there." So he went and did according to the word of the LORD; he went and lived by the Wadi Cherith, which is east of the Jordan. The ravens brought him bread and meat in the morning, and bread and meat in the evening; and he drank from the wadi.

1 Kings 17:1–6

TWO EXTRAORDINARY PERIODS in the Old Testament were marked by multiple miracles—the time of Moses and the exodus, and the years of the prophets Elijah and Elisha. Just as Moses spent forty years tending sheep before leading the Israelites from Egypt and then spent time alone with God throughout the trek in the desert, Elijah also spent important time in solitude before and during his role as a messenger of God. His story opens with the above prophecy to Israel's King Ahab, and Elijah then gets a personal instruction from God to go and hide himself. Elijah is sent away from places of royal power and provision to places that seem to promise little: here, a brook with ravens, and in the verses that follow, a Phoenician town with a widow.

Can you imagine a place so remote that the only food available is delivered by ravens? Yet that was God's hiding place for Elijah. Think of the most remote place in your town or building, somewhere you can't imagine running into any other people. Go there for your time of solitude.

Lord, teach me to seek out those places where I can be alone with you. Help me to appreciate the lack of people, noise, and busyness, and the opportunity this solitude gives me to hear you. In your name I pray. Amen.

I Alone Am Left

Ahab told Jezebel all that Elijah had done, and how he had killed all the prophets [of Baal] with the sword. Then Jezebel sent a messenger to Elijah, saying, "So may the gods do to me, and more also, if I do not make your life like the life of one of them by this time tomorrow." Then he was afraid; he got up and fled for his life.

But he himself went a day's journey into the wilderness, and came and sat down under a solitary broom tree. He asked that he might die. Then he lay down under the broom tree and fell asleep. Suddenly an angel touched him and said to him, "Get up and eat." He looked, and there at his head was a cake baked on hot stones, and a jar of water. He got up, and ate and drank; then he went in the strength of that food forty days and forty nights to Horeb the mount of God. At that place he came to a cave, and spent the night there.

Then the word of the LORD came to him, saying "What are you doing here, Elijah?" He answered, "I have been very zealous for the LORD, the God of hosts; for the Israelites have forsaken your covenant, thrown down your altars, and killed your prophets with the sword. I alone am left, and they are seeking my life, to take it away."

1 Kings 19:1–3a, 4a, 5–6a, 8–10

ONCE AGAIN ELIJAH goes into the wilderness for refuge. Elijah wasn't necessarily trying to find God; he fled because he was afraid. But even in Elijah's running away, God met him in his solitude. Elijah lived a fantastic life, seeing God's might firsthand as few others have. Yet even Elijah needed times of solitude, where God could meet him alone, giving refreshment and guidance.

Have you ever sought solitude for a reason other than trying to meet God and had an experience of God anyway? What is it about being alone that allows God to come to us more easily?

I Sat Alone

O Lord, you know; / remember me and visit me, / and bring down retribution for me on my persecutors. / In your forbearance do not take me away; / know that on your account I suffer insult. / Your words were found, and I ate them, / and your words became to me a joy / and the delight of my heart; / for I am called by your name, / O Lord, God of hosts. / I did not sit in the company of merrymakers, / nor did I rejoice; / under the weight of your hand I sat alone, / for you had filled me with indignation. / Why is my pain unceasing, / my wound incurable, / refusing to be healed?

Jeremiah 15:15–18a

JEREMIAH HAS BEEN made a prophet, a spokesperson for the truth, because God's word came to him. At first that word was sweet delight. He devoured those good words. Yet because the prophet has dared to utter those words—all of them, including the ones not so sweet—he bears a heavy burden: he is alone. He has had to deliver the hard news that Israel is about to go into exile (chaps. 13–14). Here we hear about the cost of fidelity to God. The blessing of divine vocation can also be a great burden. Those who work for God, who dare to say yes to the divine summons, who dare to speak up for God, are often persecuted, victimized, and made lonely. It is good for us to be reminded, by Jeremiah's lament, of the cost of faithful discipleship and good to ask ourselves: Are we prepared to bear such a burden?

As the lives of the prophets so richly illustrate, divine vocation does not always lead to earthly happiness. But it does often lead to solitude. Why are those so close to God so intimate with solitude?

He Is with Me

So Jesus said, "When you have lifted up the Son of Man, then you will realize that I am he, and that I do nothing on my own, but I speak these things as the Father instructed me. And the one who sent me is with me; he has not left me alone, for I always do what is pleasing to him."

John 8:28–29

THE FATHER WAS with the Son in every situation, and Jesus promises that the Advocate, the Holy Spirit, will be with us forever (14:16). Why does solitude make us more aware of the indwelling Holy Spirit's sustaining presence?

Reflect on this quote as you seek to meet God in solitude today:

"Solitude is not merely a negative relationship. It is not merely the absence of people or of presence with people. True solitude is a participation in the solitariness of God—Who is in all things. Solitude is not a matter of being something *more* than other men, except by accident: for those who cannot be alone cannot find their true being and they are less than themselves. Solitude means withdrawal from an artificial and fictional level of being which men, divided by original sin, have fabricated in order to keep peace with concupiscence and death. But by that very fact the solitary finds himself on the level of a more perfect spiritual society—the city of those who have become real enough to confess and glorify God (that is, life) in the teeth of death."

—Thomas Merton, from his journals[2]

~ Withdrawing to a Deserted Place

Yet I Am Not Alone

Jesus answered them, "Do you now believe? The hour is coming, indeed it has come, when you will be scattered, each one to his home, and you will leave me alone. Yet I am not alone because the Father is with me. I have said this to you, so that in me you may have peace. In the world you face persecution. But take courage; I have conquered the world!"

John 16:31–33

AGAIN, JESUS TELLS the disciples that although the people around him will desert him, he will not be alone because God is with him. History is replete with stories of Christians who have been alone for extended periods of time—voluntarily in deserts or involuntarily in prison—but who came through the experience knowing that God was with them.

What do Jesus' words teach you about the difference between loneliness and solitude? In days and weeks ahead, if you have not already done so, read a book about the desert fathers and mothers to inform your understanding of solitude. You might want to start with John Chryssavgis's *In the Heart of the Desert: The Spirituality of the Desert Fathers and Mothers,* a compilation of their sayings accompanied by original commentary by Chryssavgis.

Opening Ourselves

I, John, your brother who share with you in Jesus the persecution and the kingdom and the patient endurance, was on the island called Patmos because of the word of God and the testimony of Jesus. I was in the spirit on the Lord's day, and I heard behind me a loud voice like a trumpet saying, "Write in a book what you see and send it to the seven churches, to Ephesus, to Smyrna, to Pergamum, to Thyatira, to Sardis, to Philadelphia, and to Laodicea."

Revelation 1:9–11

THE REVELATION TO John is a scary book. Not only is it full of malicious monsters, but some of the settings—glassy seas, bottomless pits, rivers of blood—are like nothing we've seen before, nor are we sure we ever want to. Jesus himself, whom we are used to envisioning as a man in a simple peasant caftan, transmogrifies into strange shapes throughout this vision. Often we see him as a bloody, slaughtered lamb (5:6); later, as a warrior with fiery eyes, arrayed in an equally bloody robe, with a sword protruding from his mouth (19:11–16). But when you open yourself to a vision, as John did on that barren, volcanic, prison island of Patmos, you don't get to choose its contents.

Unlike John, who was exiled to the island of Patmos, most of us will never experience an intense, extended period of solitude in our lives. And even for shorter periods, we often tell ourselves that we are too busy to consistently create an open, empty space in which we can meet God, but perhaps there are other reasons why many of us fill every minute of our day with people, work, TV, noise. Is it possible that the thought of truly being alone with God is a little frightening? After all, we know that most of the people in the Bible who saw God or heard his voice initially reacted with fear. Consider your experiences practicing solitude the last few days. Did you approach them reluctantly? How did you feel about the time of solitude when you were able to practice it?

Retreat with God

Immediately [Jesus] made the disciples get into the boat and go on ahead to the other side, while he dismissed the crowds. And after he had dismissed the crowds, he went up the mountain by himself to pray. When evening came, he was there alone.

Matthew 14:22–23

MOST OF US probably live too far from mountains to climb one regularly to pray, but we have other ways to be alone with God. Sometime within the next ten days, build on your practice of daily solitude by taking an entire day or at least an afternoon to spend alone with God. If you absolutely cannot get away now, plan the time when you will do it, mark it on your calendar, and make a promise to yourself, to God, and to another person that you will honor it. It is so easy to let the rhythm of our daily lives carry us away. Remind yourself that this time alone with God will be to refresh and nourish you for the rest of your life, that it will not be time wasted when you could be doing other necessary things, but rather time that you need in order to get rest and direction. Author and former executive Emilie Griffin writes, "When there is no time to do it, that's when you most need to unclutter the calendar and go apart to pray. When the gridlock of your schedule relentlessly forbids it is the time you most need retreat. That is when your heart beats against the prison walls of your enslavement and says, 'Yes, Lord, I want to spend time with you.'"[3]

You can take a solitary hike (up a mountain, just as Jesus did, if that is possible for you and appeals to you), drive out to a forest, or visit another quiet place. Another option is to look into staying at a retreat center for a night or an entire weekend. Take your Bible if you wish, but you may prefer just spending the time praying or talking to God. A good resource for preparation is Emilie Griffin's *Wilderness Time*. But do not feel the need to plan too much; just remember that you are deliberately creating an open, empty space in which you can be found by God.

Spiritual Practice

In the Wilderness

Jesus, full of the Holy Spirit, returned from the Jordan and was led by the Spirit in the wilderness, where for forty days he was tempted by the devil.

Luke 4:1–2a

THE SOLITUDE OF the wilderness gives Jesus strength. It is not simply a place of negation or temptation. It is also a place of preparation and perception, absent of human power structures and controls, a wild place where supernatural forces move unfettered—a place that can empower, depending upon how the experience is handled. The spiritual formation process requires time spent in the wilderness. The wilderness is a strange and difficult place. It is in the wilderness that we are most aware of our need for God's provision and protection. When we are open to God, then we can best hear his voice. The wilderness is also quiet, desolate, and lonely. We can hear God more easily there. Thus, the wilderness is God's special meeting and training place for his people. Our wildernesses and deserts are not our endings. It is the Spirit of God who leads us about in them. They are our opportunities.

Reflect on these words as you think about the ways you might benefit from your time "in the wilderness":

"It is a difficult lesson to learn today—to leave one's friends and family and deliberately practice the art of solitude for an hour or a day or a week. For me, the break is the most difficult. Parting is inevitably painful, even for a short time. It is like an amputation, I feel. A limb is being torn off, without which I shall be unable to function. And yet, once it is done, I find there is a quality to being alone that is incredibly precious. Life rushes back into the void, richer, more vivid, fuller than before."

—Anne Morrow Lindbergh, *Gift from the Sea*[4]

I Will Bring Her into the Wilderness

Therefore, I will now allure her,
  and bring her into the wilderness,
  and speak tenderly to her.
From there I will give her her vineyards,
  and make the Valley of Achor a door of hope.
There she shall respond as in the days of her youth,
  as at the time when she came out of the land of Egypt.

Hosea 2:14–15

GOD TELLS US here that he will woo Israel by bringing her "into the wilderness." Up to this point God has been condemning Israel for her worship of other gods. This startling turn in God's intention from condemnation to mercy is made all the more surprising by its being introduced with the word "therefore." Far from following as a logical consequence, this move of divine grace is diametrically opposed to what has preceded it. As both thwarted lover and deserted parent, God has poured out his heart's emotion toward Israel, reminiscing, chastising, lamenting, warning of Israel's grim future, and, finally, in these verses, promising to take her back, heal her, and cause her to flourish.

Why do you think God chooses the wilderness as the scene for this reconciliation? Have you ever gone on a retreat to be reconciled with God? Is it helpful to think of your upcoming time of solitude this way?

Shaping the Soul

Moses was keeping the flock of his father-in-law Jethro, the priest of Midian; he led his flock beyond the wilderness, and came to Horeb, the mountain of God. There the angel of the LORD appeared to him in a flame of fire out of a bush; he looked, and the bush was blazing, yet it was not consumed. When the LORD saw that he had turned aside to see, God called to him out of the bush, "Moses, Moses!" And he said, "Here I am." Then he said, "Come no closer! Remove the sandals from your feet, for the place on which you are standing is holy ground." He said further, "I am the God of your father, the God of Abraham, the God of Isaac, the God of Jacob." And Moses hid his face, for he was afraid to look at God.

Then the LORD said, "The cry of the Israelites has now come to me; I have also seen how the Egyptians oppress them. So come, I will send you to Pharaoh to bring my people, the Israelites, out of Egypt."

Exodus 3:1–2, 4–7a, 9–10

MOSES IS ENGAGED in the lonely job of tending the flock. When he takes the flock "beyond the wilderness," the angel of God appears to him. More often than we know, God works in the uneventful routines of our lives. For decades Moses took care of his father-in-law's livestock. An extreme challenge would one day occur at a burning bush, at an Egyptian throne, on a night of blood and death, on a mountain that thundered with God. Something had formed in Moses during the long years that enabled him, despite an initial reluctance, to stand before Pharaoh's throne and declare, "Thus says the LORD: 'Let my people go!'" (5:1). The soul of Moses was being shaped by the Spirit of God long before Mt. Horeb and the burning bush. It is no different for us.

Many times God or his angel appears to those who tend flocks. Is there something about the solitude or the remote places necessitated by this job that "shapes the soul" for experiences of God? Where does your job fit in the spectrum between solitude and constant interaction?

The Crowds Were Looking for Jesus

At daybreak [Jesus] departed and went into a deserted place. And the crowds were looking for him; and when they reached him, they wanted to prevent him from leaving them. But he said to them, "I must proclaim the good news of the kingdom of God to the other cities also; for I was sent for this purpose." So he continued proclaiming the message in the synagogues of Judea.

Luke 4:42–44

LUKE TAKES GREAT pains to make Christ's life of prayer an example to us. He also highlights the interludes of quiet and solitude that Christ secures in the middle of a strenuous preaching and healing ministry.

Sometimes we think that practicing solitude is selfish or denies the value of community, but Jesus shows us how to successfully integrate time alone with God with time spent in active ministry to others. Reflect for a few minutes on this quote about how solitude can show us the worth of our fellow human beings. How does this correlate with your own experience?

"In solitude we can come to the realization that we are not driven together but brought together. In solitude we come to know our fellow human beings not as partners who can satisfy our deepest needs, but as brothers and sisters with whom we are called to give visibility to God's all-embracing love. In solitude we discover that community is not a common ideology, but a response to a common call. In solitude we indeed realize that community is not made but given."

—Henri J. M. Nouwen, *Clowning in Rome*[5]

Rising Early to Pray

That evening, at sunset, they brought to [Jesus] all who were sick or possessed with demons. And the whole city was gathered around the door. And he cured many who were sick with various diseases, and cast out many demons; and he would not permit the demons to speak, because they knew him.

In the morning, while it was still dark, he got up and went out to a deserted place, and there he prayed. And Simon and his companions hunted for him. When they found him, they said to him, "Everyone is searching for you." He answered, "Let us go on to the neighboring towns, so that I may proclaim the message there also; for that is what I came out to do." And he went throughout Galilee, proclaiming the message in their synagogues and casting out demons.

Mark 1:32–39

JESUS' FAME HAD spread to the point that "the whole city" was gathered to watch him heal. Yet in the midst of this hectic time Jesus rises early to go pray in a deserted place; so intent is he on solitude that even the disciples do not know where he has gone. When they find him, Jesus is ready, refreshed enough from his time alone with God to continue his work in the neighboring towns. This instance is one of several in which Mark mentions that Jesus and the disciples go to a deserted place to rest and pray. Our own spiritual formation will be strengthened if, in our busy, crowded, and noisy lives, we find regular times and places for quiet, for prayer, for listening to God. Time alone with God gives us renewed energy to live fully engaged with the world again.

Do you neglect your need to be alone to recharge?

"Every so often I need OUT; something will throw me into total disproportion, and I have to get away from everybody—away from all those people I love most in the world—in order to regain a sense of proportion."

—Madeleine L'Engle, *A Circle of Quiet*[6]

Come Away and Rest a While

[Jesus] said to [the disciples], "Come away to a deserted place all by yourselves and rest a while." For many were coming and going, and they had no leisure even to eat. And they went away in the boat to a deserted place by themselves. Now many saw them going and recognized them, and they hurried there on foot from all the towns and arrived ahead of them. As he went ashore, he saw a great crowd; and he had compassion for them, because they were like sheep without a shepherd; and he began to teach them many things. When it grew late, the disciples came to him and said, "Send them away so that they may go into the surrounding country and villages and buy something for themselves to eat." But he answered them, "You give them something to eat." Then he ordered them to get all the people to sit down in groups on the green grass. Taking the five loaves and the two fish, he looked up to heaven, and blessed and broke the loaves. And all ate and were filled; and they took up twelve baskets full of broken pieces and of the fish. Those who had eaten the loaves numbered five thousand men.

Immediately he made his disciples get into the boat and go on ahead to the other side, to Bethsaida, while he dismissed the crowd. After saying farewell to them, he went up on the mountain to pray. When evening came, the boat was out on the sea, and he was alone on the land.

Mark 6:31–35a, 36–37a, 41a, 42–47

THE STORY OF the loaves and fishes, one of Jesus' best-remembered crowd experiences, is both preceded and followed by a time of solitude. Jesus craves solitude and rest not for selfish reasons, but because this is where the spiritual resources for ministry are found.

"It is in deep solitude that I find the gentleness with which I can truly love my brothers. The more solitary I am, the more affection I have for them."

—Thomas Merton, from his journals[7]

I Went Away at Once

But when God, who had set me apart before I was born and called me through his grace, was pleased to reveal his Son to me, so that I might proclaim him among the Gentiles, I did not confer with any human being, nor did I go up to Jerusalem to those who were already apostles before me, but I went away at once into Arabia, and afterwards I returned to Damascus.

Then after three years I did go up to Jerusalem to visit Cephas and stayed with him fifteen days; but I did not see any other apostle except James the Lord's brother. In what I am writing to you, before God, I do not lie! Then I went into the regions of Syria and Cilicia, and I was still unknown by sight to the churches of Judea that are in Christ; they only heard it said, "The one who formerly was persecuting us is now proclaiming the faith he once tried to destroy." And they glorified God because of me.

Galatians 1:15–24

THE ELEMENTS IN Paul's story are common to every spiritual journey toward freedom in Christ: life without Christ; encounter with Christ; formation through solitude; sharing the story; mission in the world; and transformed relationships with friends and enemies. After his conversion Paul "at once" retreated to Arabia to begin the process of learning from Jesus how to live this new life of grace and freedom. Through intentional withdrawal into silence and solitude we process and assimilate what God is doing in our lives. Solitude is both a "vacation with God" and a "furnace of transformation."

"The further the soul is from the noise of the world, the closer it may be to its Creator, for God, with his holy angels, will draw close to a person who seeks solitude and silence. It is better to remain alone and to care for your soul than to neglect yourself and work miracles."

—Thomas à Kempis, *The Imitation of Christ* [8]

Preparation Time

When [Paul] had come to Jerusalem, he attempted to join the disciples; and they were all afraid of him, for they did not believe that he was a disciple. But Barnabas took him, brought him to the apostles, and described for them how on the road he had seen the Lord, who had spoken to him, and how in Damascus he had spoken boldly in the name of Jesus. So he went in and out among them in Jerusalem, speaking boldly in the name of the Lord. He spoke and argued with the Hellenists; but they were attempting to kill him. When the believers learned of it, they brought him down to Caesarea and sent him off to Tarsus.

Acts 9:26–30

SOON AFTER PAUL had his vision and conversion experience, his bold preaching about Jesus put his life in danger. In the previous reading, we learned that Paul spent three years in Arabia, and here we learn that he fled to his old hometown of Tarsus for a number of years. It was approximately thirteen years from the time of Paul's conversion until he reappeared at Antioch (13:1). This is the hidden preparation through which God puts his ministers.

When Paul withdrew from public ministry God used this time to prepare him for the challenges and glories ahead. The record of Paul's work we have in his Letters amply demonstrates the fruits of that preparation. When you undertake your time of solitude, consider using some of the time to reevaluate your life goals and directions. What new projects or goals would you like to undertake? These can range from reading all the works of an author you enjoy, to taking up a new hobby, to something as life-changing as trying a new vocation or ministry. You might want to try to undertake a retreat of this nature several times a year. But if this type of retreat does not appeal to you now, do not hesitate to make your time of solitude just about solitude, with no particular agenda.

Down from the Mountaintop

Six days later, Jesus took with him Peter and James and John, and led them up a high mountain apart, by themselves. And he was transfigured before them, and his clothes became dazzling white, such as no one on earth could bleach them. And there appeared to them Elijah with Moses, who were talking with Jesus. Then Peter said to Jesus, "Rabbi, it is good for us to be here; let us make three dwellings, one for you, one for Moses, and one for Elijah." He did not know what to say, for they were terrified. Then a cloud overshadowed them, and from the cloud there came a voice, "This is my Son, the Beloved; listen to him!" Suddenly when they looked around, they saw no one with them any more, but only Jesus.

As they were coming down the mountain, he ordered them to tell no one about what they had seen, until after the Son of Man had risen from the dead.

Mark 9:2–9

JESUS AND HIS inner circle, Peter, James, and John, have a "mountaintop experience" in which everything seems so clear and perfect and close to God. They cannot stay up there forever, however. Jesus leads them down to the challenges and opportunities of the daily life of faith. We can be grateful when we have such soaring experiences of closeness to God too. Yet our lives are lived in the daily pains and pleasures of this world.

Father God, help me to parlay my experiences with you into strength and encouragement for doing your kingdom work in my daily life. Remind me to continue to find moments of solitude in the middle of life and to have the courage to take time out when my soul needs refreshing. In your name I pray. Amen.

For more verses on solitude and ideas on how to practice the discipline of solitude, see the Responding exercises and Spiritual Disciplines Index in *The Life with God Bible*.

Fellowship

Engaging with other disciples in the common activities of worship, study, prayer, celebration, and service, which sustain our life together and enlarge our capacity to experience more of God

From the first pages of Genesis, when God created a mate for Adam, through the pages of Paul's Letters, with his timeless advice on living together in joy and love, to the final pages of Revelation, where we see a glimpse of the company we will keep in heaven, it's clear that the Christian life is to be a life lived together. Although Jesus often prayed in solitude, he did not travel Judea alone during his ministry, but called the disciples to travel and minister with him. Paul's description of the Church as the Body of Christ (Rom 12:5; 1 Cor 12:12–26; Eph 4) makes it clear that each of us has different gifts and abilities and only together can the Church run smoothly for God's glory.

Fellowship can bring us great joy, encouragement, and comfort. It can also bring frustration and disappointment, as we bump up against each other's sins, shortcomings, and failures to hear and follow God's voice in our lives. The amount of text that Paul devotes to solving the problems of community living is testimony to just how hard it can be. One way we can sustain our fellowship and focus it upon God is by sharing Communion together. Jesus commanded us to gather together and remember him when we ate the bread and drank of the cup. Following Jesus' example at the Last Supper and the example of the early Church, this sharing is one way we focus our fellowship on Jesus.

The whole body, joined and knit together by every ligament with which it is equipped, as each part is working properly, promotes the body's growth in building itself up in love.

—Ephesians 4:16

Fellowship

Recognizing Christ in Others

Only, live your life in a manner worthy of the gospel of Christ, so that, whether I come and see you or am absent and hear about you, I will know that you are standing firm in one spirit, striving side by side with one mind for the faith of the gospel. If then there is any encouragement in Christ, any consolation from love, any sharing in the Spirit, any compassion and sympathy, make my joy complete: be of the same mind, having the same love, being in full accord and of one mind. Do nothing from selfish ambition or conceit, but in humility regard others as better than yourselves.

Philippians 1:27; 2:1–3

WHEN COMMUNITY WORKS, it is Paul's support and his joy. When it doesn't work, it is the bane of Paul's life—and ours as well. Spiritual formation involves not only individuals, but also groups. Paul's Letters are letters of formation written to *communities.* He advertises a new citizenship (3:20). It is one thing to aim toward personal spiritual growth. It is another to strive as a community toward spiritual maturity. We are to be of "one mind" and "one spirit." He gives us a key as to how to achieve this community-mindedness in this last verse: "In humility regard others as better than yourselves." Truly regarding others as better can help us to move away from self-interest and toward unity of spirit.

One way to put community-mindedness into action is to recognize and appreciate the efforts of those around us. For the next ten days, when you engage in your regular prayer time or at the end of the day, ask yourself who you saw Christ in that day. You may find yourself thinking of your spouse or child or even the checker at the grocery store. Next, review with God how you treated your neighbors that day. Were you loving, patient, kind, and generous, or did you act with impatience or a lack of respect or love? Ask forgiveness if you need to. Finally, ask God to continue to teach you how to love your neighbors and to regard others as better than yourself.

Spiritual Practice

The Good Work of Unity

How very good and pleasant it is
    when kindred live together in unity!
It is like the precious oil on the head,
    running down upon the beard,
on the beard of Aaron,
    running over the collar of his robes.
It is like the dew of Hermon,
    which falls on the mountains of Zion.
For there the LORD ordained his blessing,
    life forevermore.

Psalm 133:1–3

"KINDRED" IN THE psalmist's time meant those who could trace their ancestry to Abraham, Isaac, and Jacob, but in our day it can refer to our brothers and sisters in Christ. Perhaps sung by pilgrims gathered from across Israel in festivals of worship, this psalm celebrates the unity of God's people. It's better than the anointing of a guest's head with oil, better than the abundant dew of beautiful Mt. Hermon, the highest mountain in the whole region. It reminds us to celebrate and work for such refreshing unity.

Unity is also the goal Paul sets out for Christian community in the passage from Philippians in the previous reading. What do you think it means to live in unity? What would it look like in your home? In your church? As you begin your practice of recognizing Christ in others and considering others as better than yourself, think about whether it makes you feel more united with your fellow Christians.

⌐ *Recognizing Christ in Others*

Growing Together

In that day, says the LORD,
  I will assemble the lame
and gather those who have been driven away,
  and those whom I have afflicted.
The lame I will make the remnant,
  and those who were cast off, a strong nation;
and the LORD will reign over them in Mount Zion
  now and forevermore.

Micah 4:6–7

THE "REMNANT" IS an important theme in Micah's prophecy (see also 2:12; 5:7–8; 7:18). The covenant-keeping King will gather out of the world a remnant of believing people for his praise. The truth is that individuals within this redeemed solidarity need each other in order to grow spiritually and minister effectively. We are born anew as individuals, but we grow together. The royal road to knowing God runs through human community.

"Without community our hearts close up and die," says Jean Vanier, founder of the worldwide L'Arche community. Today, prayerfully explore how you can exchange the Western world's rugged individualism and self-reliance for the powerful sense of community that existed in the early Church (Acts 2:42–47; 4:32–35). Remember that Scripture describes the People of God as a family, a household, a body, a flock, a holy nation.

Building Up Christ's Body

I therefore, the prisoner in the Lord, beg you to lead a life worthy of the calling to which you have been called, with all humility and gentleness, with patience, bearing with one another in love, making every effort to maintain the unity of the Spirit in the bond of peace. There is one body and one Spirit, just as you were called to the one hope of your calling, one Lord, one faith, one baptism, one God and Father of all, who is above all and through all and in all.

But speaking the truth in love, we must grow up in every way into him who is the head, into Christ, from whom the whole body, joined and knit together by every ligament with which it is equipped, as each part is working properly, promotes the body's growth in building itself up in love.

Ephesians 4:1–6, 15–16

THE COMMUNITY OF faith has been established to bring us into living communion with God and abiding fellowship with one another. We seek God and find him most often through the ministry of a local church. Here we experience, in real and concrete ways, the love of Christ and learn how we are to love one another despite disagreements and imperfections. This love, witnessed by those outside the community and proclaimed by word and sacrament, draws the world to God. This *is* the community of loving persons intended from the beginning of time.

Why does Paul use the metaphor of a body when trying to describe the relationship of Christians to one another? Today as you think about those you have seen Christ in, think about what each person's role might be in the Body of Christ. What do you see as your role in the Body of Christ? What have you done to help the Body as a whole work properly and to promote love? What else could you do?

Many Members, One Body

For just as the body is one and has many members, and all the members of the body, though many, are one body, so it is with Christ.

Indeed, the body does not consist of one member but of many. If the foot would say, "Because I am not a hand, I do not belong to the body," that would not make it any less a part of the body. And if the ear would say, "Because I am not an eye, I do not belong to the body," that would not make it any less a part of the body. If the whole body were an eye, where would the hearing be? If the whole body were hearing, where would the sense of smell be? But as it is, God arranged the members in the body, each one of them, as he chose. If all were a single member, where would the body be? As it is, there are many members, yet one body. The eye cannot say to the hand, "I have no need of you," nor again the head to the feet, "I have no need of you." On the contrary, the members of the body that seem to be weaker are indispensable, and those members of the body that we think less honorable we clothe with greater honor, and our less respectable members of the body are treated with greater respect; whereas our more respectable members do not need this. But God has so arranged the body, giving the greater honor to the inferior member, that there may be no dissension within the body, but the members may have the same care for one another.

1 Corinthians 12:12, 14–25

IN COMMUNITY WE learn of our individual responsibilities to God and our corporate responsibilities to one another. There are exceptions, to be sure, but sustaining a life with God without an active, living connection to a visible expression of the Body of Christ is virtually impossible and is not a goal to be sought after.

Have you ever been tempted to try to travel the path of faith alone? If so, what caused those feelings? Consider making a list of all the ways church fellowship has helped or could help you to grow closer to God.

How to Live in Community

For as in one body we have many members, and not all the members have the same function, so we, who are many, are one body in Christ, and individually we are members one of another. We have gifts that differ according to the grace given to us: prophecy, in proportion to faith; ministry, in ministering; the teacher, in teaching; the exhorter, in exhortation; the giver, in generosity; the leader, in diligence; the compassionate, in cheerfulness.

Live in harmony with one another; do not be haughty, but associate with the lowly; do not claim to be any wiser than you are. Do not repay anyone evil for evil, but take thought for what is noble in the sight of all. If it is possible, so far as it depends on you, live peaceably with all.

Romans 12:4–8, 16–18

SPIRITUAL FORMATION CAN never take place in isolation or develop in impersonal or functional ways. Spiritual formation is never just between me and God. Persons, persons-in-relationship, are necessarily involved. Paul spends much of the Letter to the Romans dealing with the fact that in the Roman congregation Jews are feeling superior to Gentiles and Gentiles are feeling superior to Jews. Neither group has anything to be proud of. All are first-class sinners; all are miraculously "grafted" into God's olive-tree Church. There is neither motive nor excuse now for Jews to push Gentiles into the background or for Gentiles to elbow Jews to the sidelines. Yes, we are all the same, sharing a common Christ identity, yet we are all different; each of us is uniquely gifted to live out this endlessly creative identity in fresh and particular ways.

As you continue to look for Christ in others, focus on those who are different from you, reminding yourself that we are all one in Christ Jesus.

Dear Lord, teach me to live in harmony even with those with whom I can see no common ground. Teach me to love all of your people equally, that we may be one, working in harmony as your Body. Amen.

~ Recognizing Christ in Others

Joy in Fellowship

We declare to you what was from the beginning, what we have heard, what we have seen with our eyes, what we have looked at and touched with our hands, concerning the word of life—this life was revealed, and we have seen it and testify to it, and declare to you the eternal life that was with the Father and was revealed to us—we declare to you what we have seen and heard so that you also may have fellowship with us; and truly our fellowship is with the Father and with his Son Jesus Christ. We are writing these things so that our joy may be complete.

1 John 1:1–3

THE LIFE THAT is in Jesus Christ is the solid foundation from which the confidence, concerns, and challenges of 1 John flow. This "word of life" is both eternal and has been made so tangible that the author refers four times to what he has seen and twice to what he has heard. The goal of drawing attention to Jesus Christ is not to emphasize readers' religious experiences of him, but to draw them into fellowship with one another and God. This is what joy is all about, for eternal life can be experienced here and now.

What is the most joyous experience of fellowship you have ever had? Did you see it as fellowship with the Father and the Son as well? How might it change your ideas about fellowship to always see it that way? Reflect on this quote about why we engage in fellowship:

"There is probably no Christian to whom God has not given the up-lifting *experience* of genuine Christian community at least once in his life. But in this world such experiences can be no more than a gracious extra beyond the daily bread of Christian community life. . . . It is not the experience of Christian brotherhood, but solid and certain faith in brotherhood that holds us together."

—Dietrich Bonhoeffer, *Life Together* [1]

Passing Judgment on One Another

We do not live to ourselves, and we do not die to ourselves. If we live, we live to the Lord, and if we die, we die to the Lord; so then, whether we live or whether we die, we are the Lord's. For to this end Christ died and lived again, so that he might be Lord of both the dead and the living.

Why do you pass judgment on your brother or sister? Or you, why do you despise your brother or sister? For we will all stand before the judgment seat of God. For it is written,

"As I live, says the Lord, every knee shall bow to me,

and every tongue shall give praise to God."

So then, each of us will be accountable to God.

Let us therefore no longer pass judgment on one another, but resolve instead never to put a stumbling block or hindrance in the way of another.

Romans 14:7–13

FOR A COMMUNITY that lives, every last one of us, solely by forgiveness and grace, keeping up a running commentary on what we disapprove of or dislike in one another is outrageous. Critical barbs and gossipy asides are corrosive and corrupting. Every judgmental word out of our mouths violates an eternal soul for whom Christ died.

Where have you seen fellowship destroyed by judgmental criticisms and gossip? As you talk with God today about your interactions with others, be especially aware of any criticism or gossip you may have passed on.

Father God, too often I say things out of jealousy or unkindness or perhaps out of a desire to focus on someone else's shortcomings rather than my own. Instead, help me to speak words of encouragement and hope that build community rather than tear it down. In your name I pray. Amen.

Recognizing Christ in Others

Loving Our Brothers and Sisters

God is light and in him there is no darkness at all. If we say that we have fellowship with him while we are walking in darkness, we lie and do not do what is true; but if we walk in the light as he himself is in the light, we have fellowship with one another, and the blood of Jesus his Son cleanses us from all sin.

Whoever says, "I am in the light," while hating a brother or sister, is still in the darkness. Whoever loves a brother or sister lives in the light, and in such a person there is no cause for stumbling. But whoever hates another believer is in the darkness, walks in the darkness, and does not know the way to go, because the darkness has brought on blindness.

1 John 1:5b–7; 2:9–11

THIS PASSAGE STATES that to have genuine fellowship with one another and with God, we must walk in the light of God "as he himself is in the light." Hatred of one's brother or sister means one is in the darkness rather than in the light. Those who abandon the fellowship also walk without the light and thus stumble in blindness and cause others to stumble. We must choose whether we will live in God's guiding light, and so love others, or dwell in the realm of darkness and reject our brothers and sisters. We cannot do both.

Why does John use the metaphor of light in describing God and Christian fellowship? Pray that God will fill you with that light and help you walk in it.

Pleasing Our Neighbors

We who are strong ought to put up with the failings of the weak, and not to please ourselves. Each of us must please our neighbor for the good purpose of building up the neighbor. For Christ did not please himself; but, as it is written, "The insults of those who insult you have fallen on me." May the God of steadfastness and encouragement grant you to live in harmony with one another, in accordance with Christ Jesus, so that together you may with one voice glorify the God and Father of our Lord Jesus Christ.

Romans 15:1–3, 5–6

DO WE THINK that the people with whom we worship should be "our kind"—affable and congenial fellow Christians who think well of us and make us feel at home? And if they do not please us, do we go off looking for others who will? This is a weak view of the Church, and certainly not what Christ experienced. Paul puts the shoe on the other foot: *we* are to be the ones out to please others. We come to church not to get our needs met, but to meet the needs of our neighbor.

Is this the way you normally approach church—as a place to meet others' needs? If so, how does it affect your experiences there? If not, how might this attitude change the way you feel about church? For this last day of our spiritual practice of recognizing Christ in others, consider whether this practice is one you would like to continue incorporating in your life on a daily basis. To remember this practice, write one of the verses from this section on a bookmark or index card and put it someplace where you will come across it often. Finally, as you engage in your practice today, pay particular attention to how you reflect Christ to others throughout the day and can model Christ for others tomorrow and going forward.

Where Two or Three Are Gathered

"Again, truly I tell you, if two of you agree on earth about anything you ask, it will be done for you by my Father in heaven. For where two or three are gathered in my name, I am there among them."

Matthew 18:19–20

WE DON'T NORMALLY think that a gathering of two or three people constitutes a fellowship and that Jesus could be in our midst there as much as he is at our large gatherings. Yet Jesus assures us that his presence will be there whenever we gather together in his name.

Sometime in the next ten days invite a couple of your friends to gather with you for fellowship and prayer. Enjoy part of your time together however you like—playing a game or going for a hike—but remember that the central purpose of your visit is to pray. Before praying, write out all the prayer requests that you agree on. Challenge yourself and your friends to honestly ask for the things that you need, even if they are personal. Part of fellowship is opening ourselves to one another. Pay special attention to any issues that may be affecting your fellowship—whether it is a small disagreement between two of you or a larger issue that is driving your church apart. Then pray together until you have covered everything on the list. You may find that the Holy Spirit directs you to pray for other things too.

If you have not prayed like this with Christian friends before, you might find it a little awkward, but remember that prayer is something we need to work on doing in all kinds of ways in order for it to become as natural as breathing. Think how much more powerful your prayer can become when prayed with the whole hearts of several people.

Ask your friends to make a special effort to be aware of the Spirit of Jesus moving among and within you during this fellowship in prayer. Then reflect on whether you sensed that Jesus' presence was stronger when there were several of you together. You might want to end your time together with a meal, breaking bread together as the early Christians did in their Communion practice.

Spiritual Practice

Devoted Fellowship

Peter said to them, "Repent, and be baptized every one of you in the name of Jesus Christ so that your sins may be forgiven; and you will receive the gift of the Holy Spirit. For the promise is for you, for your children, and for all who are far away, everyone whom the Lord our God calls to him." And he testified with many other arguments and exhorted them, saying, "Save yourselves from this corrupt generation." So those who welcomed his message were baptized, and that day about three thousand persons were added. They devoted themselves to the apostles' teaching and fellowship, to the breaking of bread and to prayers.

Acts 2:38–42

THE LAST VERSE summarizes the Church's inner life. Each activity reappears in Acts 3–6. The apostles' teaching was of Jesus. Fellowship was the "common life" or partnership, which included not only meeting together, but attending to each other's needs. The "breaking of bread" was likely the Lord's Supper. Prayer characterizes the community's life. Unlike our individualistic culture, the ethos of the first century was communal. In Acts, Luke depicts the Christian community as the locus of divine activity. His understanding of the Church is charismatic; that is, through the Holy Spirit, God directs the Church. The events in Acts are, finally, the work of God and not the product of the individual human ingenuity of Peter or Tabitha or Paul or Lydia or Priscilla and Aquila.

It is hard for us even to conceive of the communal nature of the early Church. Reflect for a few moments on how this quote speaks to your life:

"The deep disease of man, the self-contradiction in which he is involved as individual and member of human societies, is his denial of the law of his being. He seeks to possess within or by himself, whether in the form of physical or spiritual goods, what he can have only in the community of receiving and giving."

—H. Richard Niebuhr, *Christ and Culture*²

━ *Where Two or Three Are Gathered*

Life Among the Believers

Day by day, as they spent much time together in the temple, they broke bread at home and ate their food with glad and generous hearts, praising God and having the goodwill of all the people. And day by day the Lord added to their number those who were being saved.

Acts 2:46–47

THE EARLY CHURCH continued to be closely connected with Judaism (of which it was thought to be a "sect," 28:22), but members also met in private homes for Christian celebration of the Lord's Supper. Gratitude ("glad and generous hearts") is the hallmark of true Christian spirituality. Luke wants us to understand and act as members who are in unity with one another, charitable to all, and held in high esteem. He describes a community in which fellowship includes economic responsibility for one another. He shows us how early Christians gathered to hear the word, break bread, and pray, and how they went out from their meetings to bring others into the Christian community. And he expects us to "go and do likewise."

As you prepare to gather in your home like the believers of the early Church, meditate on this quote about why believers need one another:

"The Christian needs another Christian who speaks God's Word to him. He needs him again and again when he becomes uncertain and discouraged, for by himself he cannot help himself without belying the truth. He needs his brother man as a bearer and proclaimer of the divine word of salvation. He needs his brother solely because of Jesus Christ. The Christ in his own heart is weaker than the Christ in the word of his brother; his own heart is uncertain, his brother's is sure. And that also clarifies the goal of all Christian community: they meet one another as bringers of the message of salvation."

—Dietrich Bonhoeffer, *Life Together* [3]

The Worldwide Community

Do not lie to one another, seeing that you have stripped off the old self with its practices and have clothed yourselves with the new self, which is being renewed in knowledge according to the image of its creator. In that renewal there is no longer Greek and Jew, circumcised and uncircumcised, barbarian, Scythian, slave and free; but Christ is all and in all!

As God's chosen ones, holy and beloved, clothe yourselves with compassion, kindness, humility, meekness, and patience. Bear with one another and, if anyone has a complaint against another, forgive each other; just as the Lord has forgiven you, so you also must forgive. Above all, clothe yourself with love, which binds everything together in perfect harmony. And let the peace of Christ rule in your hearts, to which indeed you were called in the one body. And be thankful. Let the word of Christ dwell in you richly; teach and admonish one another in all wisdom; and with gratitude in your hearts sing psalms, hymns, and spiritual songs to God. And whatever you do, in word or deed, do everything in the name of the Lord Jesus, giving thanks to God the Father through him.

Colossians 3:9–17

BECAUSE BELIEVERS ARE in relationship with Jesus Christ, their fullness or perfection is the goal of Paul's teaching and preaching. Believers today worship and pray and serve in company with a vast array of people. No one worships, prays, or serves alone. Christians are a worldwide community of believers who transcend historical boundaries as the communion of saints. When we sit in a quiet place to pray and reflect upon the Scriptures (Matt 6:6), we do so participating in a wonderful spiritual dialectic: at once alone, yet joined to the great throng of the faithful across the world and throughout history.

The words of this passage are excellent directions for your time together. Pray and rejoice together that we as Christians are never alone.

⌐ Where Two or Three Are Gathered

Meeting Together

Therefore, my friends, since we have confidence to enter the sanctuary by the blood of Jesus, by the new and living way that he opened for us through the curtain (that is, through the flesh), and since we have a great priest over the house of God, let us approach with a true heart in full assurance of faith, with our hearts sprinkled clean from an evil conscience and our bodies washed with pure water. Let us hold fast to the confession of our hope without wavering, for he who has promised is faithful. And let us consider how to provoke one another to love and good deeds, not neglecting to meet together, as is the habit of some, but encouraging one another, and all the more as you see the Day approaching.

Hebrews 10:19–25

As believers we are exhorted to five spiritual practices. First, we may freely and confidently approach God in faith. Second, we are urged to be steadfast and not waver from the faithful promises of God. Third, we should constantly encourage one another in love and good works. Fourth, we should commit to gather regularly in fellowship. Finally, we are warned not to reject the work of Christ, but recall how God has faithfully preserved us in the past (10:26–35). Rejecting these exhortations leads to spiritual timidity and perdition, whereas following them results in spiritual endurance and the safekeeping of our souls (10:39).

Meditate on this quote as you continue to prepare for or reflect on your time together:

"Remember that God's intention is that we each come to a fuller knowledge of him as we deepen our personal fellowship with one another."

—Richard J. Foster and others, eds., *The Life with God Bible*[4]

Bearing One Another's Burdens

My friends, if anyone is detected in a transgression, you who have received the Spirit should restore such a one in a spirit of gentleness. Take care that you yourselves are not tempted. Bear one another's burdens, and in this way you will fulfill the law of Christ. So then, whenever we have an opportunity, let us work for the good of all, and especially for those of the family of faith.

Galatians 6:1–2, 10

THE LIFE OF freedom is developed and demonstrated in community—in relationships of truth, trust, and grace. It is in the all-inclusive, God-created loving community that the gospel is experienced, stories are shared, faith is developed, and the Spirit works. Spiritual formation is always in the context of community. God's forming work in an individual is extremely personal, but not private. Our freedom and formation stories are to be shared for the enriching of our brothers and sisters. In so doing we both challenge and encourage one another. Paul, in the Letter to the Galatians, speaks powerfully, yet lovingly, into the lives of his fellow Christians in order to build a community without distinctions and hierarchies in which all are one in Christ Jesus.

What does it mean to you to bear another's burdens? In praying for someone, how do you bear his or her burden? Have you ever felt that by praying for someone you have physically taken on that person's burden?

Lord God, give me the wisdom, gentleness, and strength to help bear the burdens of my brothers and sisters in community. Teach me what it means to restore a brother in a way that is best for the entire family of faith. Above all, I ask that you give me the love necessary to pray for and care for my sister in the same way you care for me. In your name I pray. Amen.

⌒ Where Two or Three Are Gathered

Pray for One Another

Are any among you suffering? They should pray. Are any cheerful? They should sing songs of praise. Are any among you sick? They should call for the elders of the church and have them pray over them, anointing them with oil in the name of the Lord. The prayer of faith will save the sick, and the Lord will raise them up; and anyone who has committed sins will be forgiven. Therefore confess your sins to one another, and pray for one another, so that you may be healed. The prayer of the righteous is powerful and effective. Elijah was a human being like us, and he prayed fervently that it might not rain, and for three years and six months it did not rain on the earth. Then he prayed again, and the heaven gave rain and the earth yielded its harvest.

My brothers and sisters, if anyone among you wanders from the truth and is brought back by another, you should know that whoever brings back a sinner from wandering will save the sinner's soul from death and will cover a multitude of sins.

James 5:13–20

JAMES FOCUSES ON community life here, underscoring the importance of congregational care for each member. Those who are suffering distress or experiencing sickness are worthy of visitation, prayer, and the benefits of listening or conversing. If sin has occasioned the sickness—confession and prayer aid healing. Recovery, renewal, and reinstatement are the works of divine compassion and should be prime concerns within the fellowship. Corporate faith, steadfast living, fervent prayer, and corporate care are contagious evidences of spiritual health, and James writes to encourage Christians to cultivate these in the Church.

"A simple question such as 'What would you like prayer for?' can at times be tremendously revealing. Remember, prayer is a way of loving others, and so courtesy, grace, and respect are always in order."

—Richard J. Foster, *Prayer: Finding the Heart's True Home*[5]

Sharing in the Lord's Supper

For I received from the Lord what I also handed on to you, that the Lord Jesus on the night when he was betrayed took a loaf of bread, and when he had given thanks, he broke it and said, "This is my body that is for you. Do this in remembrance of me." In the same way he took the cup also, after supper, saying, "This cup is the new covenant in my blood. Do this, as often as you drink it, in remembrance of me." For as often as you eat this bread and drink this cup, you proclaim the Lord's death until he comes.

1 Corinthians 11:23–26

JUST AS JESUS allowed himself to be handed over to those who would try to execute him, Paul now hands over the tradition of Jesus, who repeatedly established community for people who were denied community or cast in the position of outsiders. Paul refers to the tradition of Jesus in order to insist that the Corinthian churches eat the Lord's Supper in a manner that eliminates all false social divisions.

The actions of the Lord's Supper—taking, giving thanks, breaking, and giving—are actions that those who eat the meal receive from the Lord as gifts of grace. The Church receives the gift of the meal, has its brokenness restored, and is then enabled to pass the thanksgiving, breaking, and giving on in mission. All creative power for restoration and mission lies with God in Jesus. This process is a crucial element in our formation into Christlikeness.

Sharing in the Lord's Supper is a communal activity, a visible way of demonstrating that we are all on equal footing before the Lord. The next time you join in the Lord's Supper at your church, examine the way it makes you think about your community. Does it give you a sense of being more connected to your fellow Christians? As you eat the bread and drink from the cup, offer a prayer for unity, that all those in your church and the Church around the world may be one.

⁀ Where Two or Three Are Gathered

Be at Peace Among Yourselves

But we appeal to you, brothers and sisters, to respect those who labor among you, and have charge of you in the Lord and admonish you; esteem them very highly in love because of their work. Be at peace among yourselves. And we urge you, beloved, to admonish the idlers, encourage the faint-hearted, help the weak, be patient with all of them. See that none of you repays evil for evil, but always seek to do good to one another and to all. Rejoice always, pray without ceasing, give thanks in all circumstances; for this is the will of God in Christ Jesus for you. Do not quench the Spirit. Do not despise the words of prophets, but test everything; hold fast to what is good; abstain from every form of evil.

1 Thessalonians 5:12–22

THIS LAUNDRY LIST of counsels is pregnant with spiritual formation implications. It describes the effective functioning of community life. Note how counsels for ordinary tasks mingle with counsels on matters of deep spiritual import. In the community of disciplined grace, respecting co-workers and helping the weak are just as essential as praying without ceasing and not quenching the Spirit.

Reflect on the idea that respecting your colleagues and helping the weak are just as important as praying without ceasing and not quenching the Spirit. Does this statement resonate with you? Does it bother you? Does your church value both sides of community life equally?

That They May Be One

"I have made your name known to those whom you gave me from the world. They were yours, and you gave them to me, and they have kept your word. Now they know that everything you have given me is from you; for the words that you gave to me I have given to them, and they have received them and know in truth that I came from you; and they have believed that you sent me. I am asking on their behalf; I am not asking on behalf of the world, but on behalf of those whom you gave me, because they are yours. All mine are yours, and yours are mine; and I have been glorified in them. And now I am no longer in the world, but they are in the world, and I am coming to you. Holy Father, protect them in your name that you have given me, so that they may be one, as we are one."

John 17:6–11

PONDER ALL THAT we learn of the Trinity's work and our own as Jesus prays for his disciples. Too often we fail to realize how much God wants the Christian community to be one as part of the triune character. The community follows Jesus in abiding in the Father's word; how much more of an impact the Church would have on the world if we didn't belong to it so much! Are we willing to die for the world? To live for its sake? To give our all at great cost?

Father God, you sent your Son to this earth that we may be one, and yet we fail so miserably. We look out for our own interests first and put your work last. We allow ourselves to be separated by jealousy and bitterness and misunderstanding. Forgive us for our failures. Teach us to hold Jesus before us always, with the knowledge and understanding that only through him can our fellowship work and magnify your name. Amen.

For more verses on fellowship and ideas on how to practice the discipline of fellowship, see the Responding exercises and Spiritual Disciplines Index in *The Life with God Bible*.

Fasting

The voluntary abstention from an otherwise normal function—
most often eating—for the sake of intense spiritual activity

Fasting was an integral part of the lives of the people we read about in
the Bible. They fasted during times of mourning, in repentance, or to
seek blessing, answers, or guidance. Everyone fasted together on the
Day of Atonement. A normal fast during biblical times involved abstention from all food and liquid except for water, but during extreme
circumstances even water was declined (see Esther 4:16).

Jesus undertook an extreme fast of forty days and forty nights when
he experienced the temptation in the desert. He also speaks of fasting as
a normal part of life for his followers (Matt 6:16–18). Later, in response
to a question about why his followers do not fast, he answers that wedding guests do not fast while the bridegroom is with them, but that "the
days will come when the bridegroom is taken away from them, and
then they will fast" (Matt 9:15). From these words it seems clear that
Jesus expected his followers to practice the discipline of fasting.

So why is fasting less common today? Probably the main reason is
that we rarely deny ourselves anything, whether food or drink or material goods or entertainment. Fasting forces us to take attention from our
desires in order to focus on God. Jesus tells his disciples that his food
is to "do the will of him who sent me and to complete his work" (John
4:34). Fasting can be a humbling experience, as we see just how con-
trolled we are by our appetites. But it also teaches us that what sustains
us is not the food we eat or the pleasures we feel, but God alone.

> Yet even now, says the LORD, / return to me with all your heart, /
> with fasting, with weeping, and with mourning.
>
> —Joel 2:12

Fasting

Humbling Our Souls Through Fasting

It is zeal for your house that has consumed me;
 the insults of those who insult you have fallen on me.
When I humbled my soul with fasting,
 they insulted me for doing so.

Psalm 69:9–10

THIS PASSAGE FROM Psalms explains both the purpose of fasting and one of the reasons why many of us would prefer not to do it. Fasting humbles our soul; it helps to see our weaknesses and frailties with more honesty and clarity than we are accustomed to. And, as in the passage, sometimes the way people react to fasting can be off-putting. If people were to learn that you were fasting today, they might say how unhealthy or foolish fasting is or simply respond with incredulity. Or in circles familiar with fasting, perhaps the temptation would be to advertise that you are fasting so that others can be impressed by your piety, as did the Pharisees Jesus spoke of in Matthew 6:16–17. So for the next ten days we will attempt to combine two Spiritual Disciplines: fasting and secrecy.

Choose something from which to fast for the next ten days. Do not undertake a full fast from food. A fast of this extent and duration should only be undertaken with very clear direction from God and a good deal of preparation. Instead, perhaps fast from one specific type of food or drink or from using the Internet, watching TV, reading novels, or something similar. And, as Jesus advised, try as much as possible to keep your fast secret except from those with whom you live. You do not need to lie about it; just try to keep yourself from talking about your practice so others will think well of you. And the time you would usually spend doing what you have given up—use that time for prayer, reading the Bible, or otherwise being with God.

Spiritual Practice

Not by Bread Alone

Remember the long way that the LORD your God has led you these forty years in the wilderness, in order to humble you, testing you to know what was in your heart, whether or not you would keep his commandments. He humbled you by letting you hunger, then by feeding you with manna, with which neither you or your ancestors were acquainted, in order to make you understand that one does not live by bread alone, but by every word that comes from the mouth of the LORD.

Deuteronomy 8:2–3

IN THIS PASSAGE we learn that God imposed fasting on the Israelites. He then provided them with manna, a food they did not recognize, in order to teach them that life consisted of more than satisfying physical appetites, that they also had a spiritual hunger that only God could satisfy.

As you participate in your time of fasting today, consider spending the time you normally would have used doing the activity you have given up in studying a Bible passage such as 1 Corinthians 13. Reflect on what it means to live by "every word that comes from the mouth of the LORD." Which needs usually take precedence in your life—the physical or the spiritual?

Humbling Our Souls Through Fasting

David Fasts and Pleads with God

The LORD struck the child that Uriah's wife bore to David, and it became very ill. David therefore pleaded with God for the child; David fasted, and went in and lay all night on the ground. On the seventh day the child died. And the servants of David were afraid to tell him that the child was dead; for they said, "While the child was still alive, we spoke to him, and he did not listen to us; how then can we tell him the child is dead? He may do himself some harm." But when David saw that his servants were whispering together, he perceived that the child was dead; and David said to his servants, "Is the child dead?" They said, "He is dead."

Then David rose from the ground, washed, anointed himself, and changed his clothes. He went into the house of the LORD, and worshiped; he then went to his own house; and when he asked, they set food before him and he ate. Then his servants said to him, "What is this thing that you have done? You fasted and wept for the child while it was alive; but when the child died, you rose and ate food." He said, "While the child was still alive, I fasted and wept; for I said, 'Who knows? The LORD may be gracious to me, and the child may live.' But now he is dead; why should I fast? Can I bring him back again? I shall go to him, but he will not return to me."

2 Samuel 12:15b–16, 18–23

DAVID'S ACTIONS WERE exactly the opposite of what people expected of him: he fasted from food while the child was sick and ate after he died. David's fasting was not ritualized mourning, but a way of focusing on his plea to God. It does not even need to be spelled out in the text that his fasting was accompanied by prayer, since it was understood that fasting was always accompanied by prayer. The theological significance of fasting is that the denial of bodily needs for specified periods of time focuses the soul for greater attentiveness to God.

Why do fasting and prayer make such a powerful combination?

A Communal Fast

When Mordecai learned [of the king's edict to kill all the Jews], Mordecai tore his clothes and put on sackcloth and ashes, and went through the city, wailing with a loud and bitter cry; he went up to the entrance of the king's gate, for no one might enter the king's gate clothed with sackcloth. In every province, wherever the king's command and his decree came, there was great mourning among the Jews, with fasting and weeping and lamenting, and most of them lay in sackcloth and ashes.

Esther 4:1–3

AS DID DAVID when his child was sick, all the Jewish people in the kingdom fasted when they heard the terrible news of the king's edict for their extinction. Unlike David's, however, theirs was a public and communal fast. Like Esther's people, we also often abstain from food during times of crisis or mourning, perhaps because we lose our appetites or because we view eating, particularly sharing a meal, as a way of celebrating.

At your next meal, take time to consider your attitude toward food. Does it represent fuel to make your body healthy? Is it a symbol of shared time with family and friends? Does eating bring feelings of guilt about your appearance? Is it too important in your life, or is it not appreciated enough?

⌐ *Humbling Our Souls Through Fasting*

Ahab Fasts and Humbles Himself

Ahab said to Elijah, "Have you found me, O my enemy?" He answered, "I have found you. Because you have sold yourself to do what is evil in the sight of the LORD, I will bring disaster on you; I will consume you, and will cut off from Ahab every male, bond or free, in Israel; and I will make your house like the house of Jeroboam son of Nebat, and like the house of Baasha son of Ahijah, because you have provoked me to anger and have caused Israel to sin."

When Ahab heard those words, he tore his clothes and put sackcloth over his bare flesh; he fasted, lay in the sackcloth, and went about dejectedly. Then the word of the LORD came to Elijah the Tishbite: "Have you seen how Ahab has humbled himself before me? Because he has humbled himself before me, I will not bring the disaster in his days; but in his son's days I will bring the disaster on his house."

1 Kings 21:20–22, 27–29

THE TEXT GOES out of the way to tell us how sinful Ahab was, yet Ahab's humbling himself before the Lord through fasting was enough to make God postpone his judgment. Surely this is a lesson to us about how God views such discipline.

One reason fasting humbles and also frees us is that it helps show God's provision for us. How have you found your fast humbling? How have you experienced God's provision during times of fasting?

Dear God, why should I be anxious and worry about my body and its food? How do you raise up the grain on the field and all the fruits? The world with all its wisdom and power is not able to make a stalk, a tiny leaf, or a flower. In you I have a Lord who can multiply one loaf as much as you please, without the aid of a farmer, a miller, or a baker. As you do this day by day, why should I worry whether you can or will supply my bodily needs! Amen.

—Martin Luther, *Luther's Prayers*[1]

Sanctify a Fast

Put on sackcloth and lament, you priests;
>   wail, you ministers of the altar.
Come, pass the night in sackcloth,
>   you ministers of my God!
Grain offering and drink offering
>   are withheld from the house of your God.
Sanctify a fast,
>   call a solemn assembly.
Gather the elders
>   and all the inhabitants of the land
to the house of the LORD your God,
>   and cry out to the LORD.

Joel 1:13–14

JOEL'S PROPHECY COMES at a time of complete environmental disaster for Judah: locusts, drought, fires, and famine. The nation of Judah looks and feels like a war zone. Worship services are suspended, because there is not enough grain or wine to make the daily offerings. Joel summons the people to make their mourning and desperation holy by turning to God for help. The discipline of fasting, entered into with a whole heart, imparts a spiritual vulnerability to God. God transforms the hearts of those willing to take this radical step toward him. Joel instructs the people to gather in God's house and purposefully direct their laments to God. Those who suffer have no difficulty immersing themselves in agony, but the People of God are to carry their pain into God's presence. Authentic turning to God is the only fruitful activity in times of horrible calamity.

How does it help your understanding to think of fasting as "carrying your pain into God's presence"? Is it a good description of your current fast?

~ *Humbling Our Souls Through Fasting*

Fasting for Victory

After this the Moabites and the Ammonites, and with them some of the Meunites, came against Jehoshaphat for battle. Messengers came and told Jehoshaphat, "A great multitude is coming against you from Edom, from beyond the sea; already they are at Hazazon-tamar" (that is, Engedi). Jehoshaphat was afraid; he set himself to seek the LORD, and proclaimed a fast throughout all Judah. Judah assembled to seek help from the LORD; from all the towns of Judah they came to seek the LORD.

2 Chronicles 20:1–4

ATTACKED BY A coalition of eastern neighbors, Jehoshaphat seeks Yahweh. Jehoshaphat understands that his victory will come from God, not from his military. Instead of preparing for a potential invasion with battle plans and arms, he proclaims a fast throughout his entire kingdom. God responds to this fasting and prayer with instructions for Jehoshaphat's army to stand still during the battle and watch "the victory of the LORD" (20:17). Jehoshaphat's piety delivers a victory that has nothing to do with his military might.

Have you ever fasted to prepare for something? If so, what was the result? Think of something coming up that frightens you—a doctor's appointment, a plane trip, an exam or presentation. Pray about it during your time of fasting today.

"Is fasting ever a bribe to get God to pay more attention to the petitions? No, a thousand times no. It is simply a way to make clear that we sufficiently reverence the amazing opportunity to ask help from the everlasting God, the Creator of the universe, to choose to put everything else aside and concentrate on worshiping, asking forgiveness, and making our requests known—considering His help more important than anything we could do ourselves in our own strength and with our own ideas."

—Edith Schaeffer, L'Abri[2]

I Afflicted Myself with Fasting

Malicious witnesses rise up;
>   they ask me about things I do not know.
They repay me evil for good;
>   my soul is forlorn.
But as for me, when they were sick,
>   I wore sackcloth;
>   I afflicted myself with fasting.
I prayed with head bowed on my bosom,
>   as though I grieved for a friend or a brother;
I went about as one who laments for a mother,
>   bowed down and in mourning.

Psalm 35:11–14

OBVIOUSLY IN THIS instance the psalmist refers to fasting from food. What is interesting is that he does so in response to the sickness of his enemies. How difficult would it be to deny ourselves one of life's pleasures so that we could spend extra time praying for the health of those we don't like and may even consider enemies?

Today direct your time of fasting outward by using it to pray for an "enemy"—whether that is someone you dislike or someone you feel is repaying you evil for good.

Father God, I find it so hard to pray for those I dislike. As I try to turn my attention from my desires, soften my heart toward those whom I have judged and found wanting. In your name I pray. Amen.

⌒ Humbling Our Souls Through Fasting

Joyful Fasting

The word of the LORD of hosts came to [Zechariah], saying: Thus says the LORD of hosts: The fast of the fourth month, and the fast of the fifth, and the fast of the seventh, and the fast of the tenth, shall be seasons of joy and gladness, and cheerful festivals for the house of Judah: therefore love truth and peace.

Zechariah 8:18–19

BY THE TIME of Zechariah Jews practiced the four regular fasts mentioned in this passage. In contrast to the fasts tied to mourning that we see in many other passages, these fasts are to be "seasons of joy and gladness." Here we find an interesting conjoining of two Spiritual Disciplines not usually thought of as going together: fasting and celebration.

Many of those who have fasted describe the experience in joyful terms. Dallas Willard writes, "In fasting, we learn how to suffer happily as we feast on God."[3] Augustine of Hippo writes, "In his fasting, therefore, let a man rejoice inwardly in the very fact that by his fasting he is turning away from the pleasures of the world to make himself subject to Christ."[4] Today as you near the end of your ten-day fast, think of your abstention as a joyful thank-you to God for a blessing in your life.

Rejecting the Royal Rations

Then the king commanded his palace master Ashpenaz to bring some of the Israelites of the royal family and of the nobility to serve in the king's palace. The king assigned them a daily portion of the royal rations of food and wine. Among them were Daniel, Hananiah, Mishael, and Azariah, from the tribe of Judah.

But Daniel resolved that he would not defile himself with the royal rations of food and wine. Then Daniel asked the guard whom the palace master had appointed: "Please test your servants for ten days. Let us be given vegetables to eat and water to drink. You can then compare our appearance with the appearance of the young men who eat the royal rations, and deal with your servants according to what you observe." At the end of ten days it was observed that they appeared better and fatter than all the young men who had been eating the royal rations. So the guard continued to withdraw their royal rations and the wine they were to drink, and gave them vegetables. To these four young men God gave knowledge and skill in every aspect of literature and wisdom; Daniel also had insight into all visions and dreams.

Daniel 1:3, 4b, 5a, 6, 8a, 11a, 12–13, 15–17

DANIEL'S CHOICE TO receive food from God's earth instead of the king's table shows who he trusts to provide for his needs. He knows that faithfulness is accompanied by a constant craving that the world cannot meet. Perhaps better than any other Old Testament character, Daniel modeled a person committed to a life of unceasing discipline, and he experienced great freedom as a result. His disciplined, God-directed eating and drinking habits produced the freedom of a healthy, robust body and his appointment to rule over others.

Daniel modeled an alternative kind of fast: fasting from all food and drink except vegetables and water. After your "fast" of the last ten days, what are some other alternative fasts you think might help you?

Fasting from Food

Then Jesus was led up by the Spirit into the wilderness to be tempted by the devil. He fasted forty days and forty nights, and afterwards he was famished. The tempter came and said to him, "If you are the Son of God, command these stones to become loaves of bread." But he answered, "It is written,

'One does not live by bread alone,
> but by every word that comes from the mouth of God.'"

Matthew 4:1–4

IF FOR NO other reason, simply the fact that Jesus did it should convince us that trying a fast from food is worthwhile, although of course few if any of us will be called to attempt a forty-day fast. Sometime within the next ten days attempt a fast from food. Since the Scripture tells us that Jesus was famished, we assume that he was drinking water, as was customary during fasts. You might want to drink just water or only fruit juices during your fast. If you have never fasted before, a good way to begin is to try abstaining from food from after dinner one evening until dinner the next day, skipping two meals. If you are more experienced with fasting, perhaps you would prefer to undertake a twenty-four-hour fast or even a fast of two or three days.

Of course if you are an expectant mother, are nursing an infant, or have a physical condition that prevents you from fasting, you will not be able to undertake this type of fast. Instead, consider spending the whole day with your cell phone, computer, TV, or radio (or all of these things!) turned off.

Keep a journal of your experiences, recording how you feel and whether you find yourself more attuned to God. As you did with your previous fast, try to spend the time you would have used eating in prayer, meditation, or study.

Spiritual Practice

Ezra Proclaims a Fast

Those who went up with me from Babylonia, in the reign of King Artaxerxes, I gathered by the river that runs to Ahava, and there we camped three days.

Then I proclaimed a fast there, at the river Ahava, that we might deny ourselves before our God, to seek from him a safe journey for ourselves, our children, and all our possessions. For I was ashamed to ask the king for a band of soldiers and cavalry to protect us against the enemy on our way, since we had told the king that the hand of our God is gracious to all who seek him, but his power and his wrath are against all who forsake him. So we fasted and petitioned our God in this, and he listened to our entreaty.

Ezra 8:1b, 15a, 21–23

WHEN IT CAME to living out faithful obedience, Ezra "walked the talk." Preparing for his journey to Jerusalem, Ezra uncovered several critical issues. One was that Ezra and his entourage were defenseless in their trek across hostile territory. Some scholars have theorized that the Jews were carrying enough silver and gold to equal the yearly income of between a hundred and five hundred thousand people. In response to this problem, Ezra trusted the "hand of God" (8:18) and called his people to a time of fasting and prayer. The Church can learn much from the life of Ezra. Spending time being attentive to the Spirit of God through fasting and prayer is a far more effective way to solve church problems than endless hours in debate and confrontation.

Passages like this one make it clear that "denying ourselves before our God," deliberately turning away from the needs of our bodies, is an effective and powerful way to focus our prayers. What demands of your body are you most attuned to? What would your prayer life be like if you could focus on God with the same intensity?

Right Reverence

Yet day after day they seek me
　　and delight to know my ways,
as if they were a nation that practiced righteousness
　　and did not forsake the ordinance of their God;
they ask of me righteous judgments,
　　they delight to draw near to God.
"Why do we fast, but you do not see?
　　Why humble ourselves, but you do not notice?"
Is this not the fast that I choose:
　　to loose the bonds of injustice,
　　to undo the thongs of the yoke,
to let the oppressed go free,
　　and to break every yoke?
Is it not to share your bread with the hungry,
　　and bring the homeless poor into your house;
when you see the naked, to cover them,
　　and not to hide yourself from your own kin?

Isaiah 58:2–3a, 6–7

A FAST IS a religious discipline, but the kind of "fast" God would like to see has to do with the breaking of oppression and with concern for the suffering of those who lack food, clothing, and shelter. Indeed, the last phrase of this passage, in Hebrew, goes beyond calling the poor and homeless "your own kin," as in English; it calls them "your own flesh." That is, the ones addressed by the poetry must stand in profound solidarity with the needy.

Fasting does no good when we engage in it with the wrong attitude. As you prepare for your time of fasting, pray for right intentions and right reverence. Even as you turn inward, ask God to show you any parts of your life that are not in accord with God's will.

Was It for Me That You Fasted?

In the fourth year of King Darius, the word of the LORD came to Zechariah on the fourth day of the ninth month, which is Chislev. Now the people of Bethel had sent Sharezer and Regem-melech and their men, to entreat the favor of the LORD, and to ask the priests of the house of the LORD of hosts and the prophets, "Should I mourn and practice abstinence in the fifth month, as I have done for so many years?" Then the word of the LORD of hosts came to me: Say to all the people of the land and the priests: When you fasted and lamented in the fifth month and in the seventh, for these seventy years, was it for me that you fasted? And when you eat and when you drink, do you not eat and drink only for yourselves?

Thus says the LORD of hosts: Render true judgments, show kindness and mercy to one another; do not oppress the widow, the orphan, the alien, or the poor; and do not devise evil in your hearts against one another.

Zechariah 7:1–6, 9–10

THIS ORACLE DESCRIBES the community's religious practices—mourning, fasting, and lament. Yet these have apparently become empty, performed not for the Lord, but for the people themselves. We are reminded of the hollowness of piety if it is not for the Lord's worship. Along with the people, we are told that devout faith is demonstrated not in rote ritual, but in rendering "true judgments" and showing "kindness and mercy." We are to act on behalf of the powerless in our world, taking particular care not to do harm to widows, orphans, aliens, and the poor.

A question we should constantly ask ourselves about our fasting, our worship, our study, our service—any of our disciplines—is, "Is it for God?"

"If our fasting is not unto God, we have failed. Physical benefits, success in prayer, the enduing with power, spiritual insights—these must never replace God as the center of our fasting."

—Richard J. Foster, *Celebration of Discipline* [5]

~ Fasting from Food

Fasting in Solidarity

Mordecai told [Hathach, Esther's servant] all that had happened to him, and the exact sum of money that Haman had promised to pay into the king's treasuries for the destruction of the Jews. Mordecai also gave him a copy of the written decree issued in Susa for their destruction, that he might show it to Esther, explain it to her, and charge her to go to the king to make supplication to him and entreat him for her people.

Then Esther spoke to Hathach and gave him a message for Mordecai, saying, "All the king's servants and the people of the king's provinces know that if any man or woman goes to the king inside the inner court without being called, there is but one law—all alike are to be put to death." When they told Mordecai what Esther had said, Mordecai told them to reply to Esther, "Do not think that in the king's palace you will escape any more than all the other Jews. For if you keep silence at such a time as this, relief and deliverance will rise for the Jews from another quarter, but you and your father's family will perish. Who knows? Perhaps you have come to royal dignity for just such a time as this." Then Esther said in reply to Mordecai, "Go, gather all the Jews to be found in Susa, and hold a fast on my behalf, and neither eat nor drink for three days, night or day. I and my maids will also fast as you do. After that I will go to the king."

Esther 4:7–8, 10–11a, 12–16a

ESTHER COMMANDS A fast by all the Jews of Susa and says that she and her maids will do likewise. The discipline of fasting can be a means of creating solidarity among people who are separated from one another. Fasting also reminds us that spirituality cannot be divorced from physical, embodied experience. As she prepares to confront the king, she knows her community is with her in spirit *and* in body.

We too can be in solidarity with others when we fast. If you are fasting today, spend one time when you would have been eating praying for those who must fast because they do not have enough food.

Fasting After Saul's Death

The next day, when the Philistines came to strip the dead, they found Saul and his three sons fallen on Mount Gilboa. They cut off his head, stripped off his armor, and sent messengers throughout the land of the Philistines to carry the good news to the houses of their idols and to the people. They put his armor in the temple of Astarte; and they fastened his body to the wall of Beth-shan. But when the inhabitants of Jabesh-gilead heard what the Philistines had done to Saul, all the valiant men set out, traveled all night long, and took the body of Saul and the bodies of his sons from the wall of Beth-shan. They came to Jabesh and burned them there. Then they took their bones and buried them under the tamarisk tree in Jabesh, and fasted seven days.

1 Samuel 31:8–13

A CONTEMPORARY PARALLEL to the fast that the inhabitants of Jabesh-gilead undertook after the burial of Saul and his sons are the times of mourning that nations experience following the death or assassination of their leaders. However, the customs vary widely—military funerals, wakes, public demonstrations, religious services.

Have you ever fasted after a national leader or someone you loved died? If so, did the process help with your grief? If you have not tried this, do you think fasting from food might be helpful in dealing with grief?

~ *Fasting from Food*

The People Assemble with Fasting

Now on the twenty-fourth day of this month the people of Israel were assembled with fasting and in sackcloth, and with earth on their heads.

Nehemiah 9:1

THE PEOPLE OF Israel are celebrating the eighth day of the Festival of Booths, a "solemn assembly" (8:18) in which they listen to the Word, confess, and worship. The actions described here—refraining from eating, wearing sackcloth (from which funeral shrouds were made), and covering the head with dirt—all symbolize death.

As we saw in yesterday's devotion, God's people often fasted after someone died. Here we see that the practice of fasting is itself symbolically tied to death. What insight has your fasting practice given you about dying or dying to self? What does reflecting on death teach you about life?

Return to Me

Yet even now, says the LORD,
    return to me, with all your heart,
with fasting, with weeping, and with mourning;
    rend your hearts and not your clothing.
Return to the LORD, your God,
    for he is gracious and merciful,
slow to anger, and abounding in steadfast love,
    and relents from punishing.

Joel 2:12–13

EVEN THOUGH JUDGMENT is at hand, there is hope. It is not too late to change God's mind. Ancient Near Eastern people expressed mourning by tearing their clothes and putting on sackcloth. God exhorts the people to convert external actions into a radical reorientation of the heart and mind and will. The antidote for spiritual destitution is still the same. God invites his people into passionate communion with him through fasting, weeping, mourning, and the rending of our hearts.

God calls his people to return to him through the external discipline of fasting. In your practice, have you found fasting to be a powerful means of reconciliation? Reflect on this quote and how it speaks to your practice:

"Do you have a hunger for God? If we don't feel strong desires for the manifestation of the glory of God, it is not because we have drunk deeply and are satisfied. It is because we have nibbled so long at the table of the world. Our soul is stuffed with small things, and there is no room for the great. If we are full of what the world offers, then perhaps a fast might express, or even increase, our soul's appetite for God. Between the dangers of self-denial and self-indulgence is the path of pleasant pain called fasting."

—John Piper[6]

Fasting for the Church

After [Barnabas and Paul] had proclaimed the good news to [Derbe] and had made many disciples, they returned to Lystra, then on to Iconium and Antioch. There they strengthened the souls of the disciples and encouraged them to continue in the faith, saying, "It is through many persecutions that we must enter the kingdom of God." And after they had appointed elders for them in each church, with prayer and fasting they entrusted them to the Lord in whom they had come to believe.

Acts 14:21–23

PAUL SUPPOSED THAT the purpose of ministry was to "equip the saints" (Eph 4:12–13). We are commanded not only to make disciples, but also to teach them to obey everything that Jesus had commanded (Matt 28:20). Here we see that Barnabas and Paul did what they could to strengthen the new disciples, teaching and encouraging them and appointing elders to help lead them. Then they entrusted them to God with prayer and fasting. Interestingly, in a previous chapter we see that members of the church at Antioch had been fasting when they received the message from the Holy Spirit that Paul and Barnabas were to undertake this very missionary journey. Then the two were sent off with another period of prayer and fasting (Acts 13:2–3).

In this passage we see prayer and fasting as integral to the creation of a new church as well as to the selection and installation of Barnabas and Paul as missionaries. Today worship and prayer are common in the ordination of pastors and the installation of missionaries, but fasting is not. Why do you think fasting has been dropped from the preparation for these times of consecration? Why do you think the members of the early Church participated in fasting as part of these events? Have you ever experienced communal fasting as a church? How might it affect your church as a whole and as individuals if you included fasting as part of the next ordination or installation service in your fellowship?

They Fasted That Day

Then Samuel said to all the house of Israel, "If you are returning to the Lord with all your heart, then put away the foreign gods and the Astartes from among you. Direct your heart to the Lord, and serve him only, and he will deliver you out of the hand of the Philistines." So Israel put away the Baals and the Astartes, and they served the Lord only.

Then Samuel said, "Gather all Israel at Mizpah, and I will pray to the Lord for you." So they gathered at Mizpah, and drew water and poured it out before the Lord. They fasted that day, and said, "We have sinned against the Lord." And Samuel judged the people of Israel at Mizpah.

1 Samuel 7:3–6

THE SPIRITUAL DISCIPLINE of fasting as preparation for an encounter with the holy is an ancient one, as this text illustrates. By turning from the needs of the body toward the needs of the soul, the community is able to see in much sharper relief its need for repentance and restoration. In our own society, overfed yet spiritually malnourished as we have become, the recovery of such a practice may well be necessary for the community once again to come to this point.

Do you agree that denying our body food and focusing on the needs of our soul help us "see in much sharper relief" our need for repentance and restoration? What other lessons have surfaced while you fasted from food?

Father God, I am so used to satisfying my desires that it's hard for me to see that I am increasingly ruled by them. Help me to continue to deliberately turn away from my wants and toward you. In your name I pray. Amen.

For more verses on fasting and ideas on how to practice the discipline of fasting, see the Responding exercises and Spiritual Disciplines Index in *The Life with God Bible*.

Chastity

Purposefully turning away for a time from dwelling upon or engaging in the sexual dimension of our relationship to others—even our husband or wife—and thus learning how not to be governed by this powerful aspect of our life

God created us with bodies, and our sexuality is a wonderful gift, a blessing, that comes with our embodiedness. From the very first chapter of Genesis, where God created Adam and Eve in their glorious nakedness, to the Song of Solomon and its celebration of faithful and very physical love, we see that sexuality is part of God's good plan.

Yet a gift so powerful can also be misused and improperly directed. To try to keep our sexual impulses in check, the law grew to contain many rules about sex, which various teachers added on to, so that by the time of Jesus some groups were teaching that married couples could only engage in intercourse one or two nights a week. Even among the early Christians were some who argued that all believers should be celibate (1 Tim 4:3), a misconception even the celibate Paul was quick to clear up.

Practicing chastity is not about denying our sexuality. Rather, as Dallas Willard writes, chastity should be viewed as "the proper disposal of sexual acts, feelings, thoughts, and attitudes within our life as a whole, inside of marriage and out."[1] What is also clear from the biblical witness is that our sexuality is best expressed within a faithful and committed relationship with our spouse. Always we see underlying these directives to faithfulness and exclusivity in our human relationship with our spouse the parallel to our relationship with God. God is to be our one and only God.

I am my beloved's, / and his desire is for me.

—*Song of Solomon 7:10*

Chastity

Viewing Everyone as Sisters and Brothers

Do not speak harshly to an older man, but speak to him as to a father, to younger men as brothers, to older women as mothers, to younger women as sisters—with absolute purity.

1 Timothy 5:1–2

THIS ADVICE PAUL gives to Timothy seems to be at least in part to help him avoid sexual temptation. It is excellent counsel for all of us about how to properly direct our sexuality. If we view all those around us as our parents or siblings, we are working to treat each person with the affection, respect, and love he or she deserves without bringing sexual feelings into the picture. For the next ten days, with the exception of your spouse if you are married, try to view all those around you, especially those of the opposite sex, as members of your family. How does this change the way you react to people or treat them? Does it make any difference for you with regard to feelings of sexual attraction or temptation? Take notice also of those times when you are responding to someone with inappropriate sexual feelings. When does this happen? Under what circumstances? Do you learn anything about how you can avoid being tempted in the future?

Spiritual Practice

One Flesh

Then the LORD God said, "It is not good that the man should be alone; I will make him a helper as his partner." The man gave names to all the cattle, and to the birds of the air, and to every animal of the field; but as for the man there was not found a helper as his partner. So the LORD God caused a deep sleep to fall upon the man, and he slept; then he took one of his ribs and closed up its place with flesh. And the rib that the LORD God had taken from the man he made into a woman and brought her to the man. Then the man said,

"This at last is bone of my bones / and flesh of my flesh; / This one shall be called Woman, / for out of Man this one was taken."

Therefore a man leaves his father and his mother and clings to his wife, and they become one flesh. And the man and his wife were both naked, and were not ashamed.

Genesis 2:18, 20–25

HUMAN BEINGS ARE meant to live in community. The garden with all of its living abundance is not enough. Even though human beings were created to be in relationship with God and given a vocation like that of God to use speech to name the animals, still they are not meant to be alone. The creation of woman begins in God's recognition of the human need for companionship. Only after man and woman are created are human words recorded and the goodness of creation spoken about in human speech. It is important to note that the Hebrew term translated "helper as his partner" (*ezer*) literally means "one corresponding to." It is a word bristling with implications for community. There is not the slightest hint of subordination in the term, and it is wrong and a tragedy that it has often been used in that way.

Father God, thank you for your gift of helpers and partners. Help me to see my spouse, and anyone I may be guilty of viewing as inferior to me, as my partner in your kingdom work. In your name I pray. Amen.

I Am My Beloved's

I am my beloved's,
  and his desire is for me.

Song of Solomon 7:10

THIS PHRASE IS a statement of the mutual affection shared by the man and the woman. She gives herself wholly to him in this exclusive relationship. Married love is exclusive. Spouses belong to one another in a way they do not belong to any other person on earth.

The exclusive fidelity of a marriage is a form of chastity, a sacred commitment that can sometimes be eroded as time passes. If you are single, reflect on the role of chastity in your life. How do you express your sexuality? How do you keep from being governed by it? If you are married, to give your commitment the attention it deserves, consider copying out your marriage vows or this line of Scripture on an index card or piece of paper. Place it somewhere where you will see it often—in your Bible as a bookmark, in your wallet, in your medicine cabinet. Each time you see it, as you are able, reflect on how well you are honoring your vows.

Faithfulness to Each Other and to God

When the LORD first spoke through Hosea, the LORD said to Hosea, "Go, take for yourself a wife of whoredom and have children of whoredom, for the land commits great whoredom by forsaking the LORD." So he went and took Gomer daughter of Diblaim, and she conceived and bore him a son.

Hosea 1:2–3

IN THE BOOK of Hosea we find perhaps the most dramatic example of how our relationships parallel our relationship to God. The pain we feel when someone we love is not faithful to us gives us some insight into how we affect God when we turn our attentions elsewhere. God resorts here to drastic, even scandalous measures to reach a covenant people who have themselves scandalized the sacred covenant. God's word, God's prophet, even God's own reputation are all put at risk in God's desperate desire for relationship with his people.

Today, as you try to view everyone you meet as your brother and sister, take it one step further. Try to see everyone the way God sees them—their good qualities, why they are worthy of love. See them as people God sent his only son to die for in order that he might have relationship with them.

Father God, it is sobering to think that our relationships here on earth parallel our relationships with you. Help me to treat those around me with the respect and honor that I would accord to you. Above all, forgive me for those times when I have not been faithful to you in word, thought, or deed. I love you, Lord, and I want only you. In your name I pray. Amen.

Viewing Everyone as Sisters and Brothers

I Promised You in Marriage

I feel a divine jealousy for you, for I promised you in marriage to one husband, to present you as a chaste virgin to Christ. But I am afraid that as the serpent deceived Eve by its cunning, your thoughts will be led astray from a sincere and pure devotion to Christ.

2 Corinthians 11:2–3

PAUL HERE PUTS himself in the place of the dramatically flamboyant prophet Hosea, who promises to take a woman mired in prostitution as his wife forever, in righteousness and faithfulness (Hos 2:19–20). Paul is thus making a powerful commitment to the Corinthians with this statement. Just as Hosea did with Gomer, Paul transforms the identity of those he betroths to Christ. Being married to Christ became a powerful expression of the desire for union with God in the Middle Ages.

Here again we see a clear parallel between the earthly marriage relationship and our relationship with God. How does devoting ourselves to a life with God help us keep our sexuality in proper perspective?

"Sex is like a great river that is rich and deep and good as long as it stays within its proper channels. The moment a river overflows its banks, it becomes destructive, and the moment sex overflows its God-given banks, it too becomes destructive. Our task is to define as clearly as possible the boundaries placed upon our sexuality and to do all within our power to direct our sexual responses into that deep, rich current."

—Richard J. Foster, *The Challenge of the Disciplined Life*[2]

Joseph and Potiphar's Wife

Now Joseph was handsome and good-looking. And after a time his master's wife cast her eyes on Joseph and said, "Lie with me." But he refused and said to his master's wife, "Look, with me here, my master has no concern about anything in the house, and he has put everything that he has in my hand. He is not greater in this house than I am, nor has he kept anything back from me except yourself, because you are his wife. How then could I do this great wickedness and sin against God?" And although she spoke to Joseph day after day, he would not consent to lie beside her or to be with her. One day, however, when he went into the house to do his work, and while no one else was in the house, she caught hold of his garment, saying, "Lie with me!" But he left his garment in her hand, and fled and ran outside. When she saw that he had left his garment in her hand and had fled outside, she called out to the members of her household and said to them, "See, my husband has brought among us a Hebrew to insult us! He came in to me to lie with me, and I cried out with a loud voice; and when he heard me raise my voice and cry out, he left his garment beside me, and fled outside."

Genesis 39:6b–15

WHEN HIS MASTER'S wife propositioned him, Joseph refused to "sin against God." Insulted, Potiphar's wife made Joseph look guilty of seducing her, causing him to be sent to prison. Still, "the LORD was with Joseph and showed him steadfast love" (39:21).

As we are trying to do in our spiritual practice, Joseph seems to view Potiphar as a friend or a brother, which gives him the conviction to resist the advances of Potiphar's wife. What other ways can you think of to keep your sexual responses within their proper channels?

Adultery in the Heart

"You have heard that it was said, 'You shall not commit adultery.' But I say to you that everyone who looks at a woman with lust has already committed adultery with her in his heart. If your right eye causes you to sin, tear it out and throw it away; it is better for you to lose one of your members than for your whole body to be thrown into hell. And if your right hand causes you to sin, cut it off and throw it away; it is better for you to lose one of your members than for your whole body to go into hell."

Matthew 5:27–30

NOTE THAT JESUS says, "*If* the eye or hand offends." He never says *that* those external members offend. In fact, he taught just the opposite. He said that it is not what goes into the body that offends, but what is in the heart (15:11). It was the scribes and Pharisees who said external matters are what count. In fact, there was one exceedingly strict group, called "the bruised and battered Pharisees," who would shut their eyes upon merely seeing a woman, therefore earning their nickname by bumping into walls and posts. Jesus, as the master Teacher, simply uses a *reductio ad absurdum;* he takes their own teachings on externals and pushes it to the point of absurdity. "If the eyes offend, don't just close them, dig them out; cut off your arms and legs and roll into heaven a mutilated stump!" That is the logic of the external righteousness of the scribes and Pharisees.

Jesus cares not just about how we act, but how we think about those around us because it reflects what is in our heart. Meditate on this quote as you continue your practice of viewing others as brothers and sisters:

"Lust produces bad sex, because it denies relationship. Lust turns the other person into an object, a thing, a nonperson. Jesus condemned lust because it cheapened sex, it made sex less than it was created to be. For Jesus, sex was too good, too high, too holy, to be thrown away by cheap thoughts."

—Richard J. Foster, *The Challenge of the Disciplined Life*[3]

Loving and Respecting Each Other

Wives, be subject to your husbands as you are to the Lord. For the husband is the head of the wife just as Christ is the head of the church, the body of which he is the Savior. Just as the church is subject to Christ, so also wives ought to be, in everything, to their husbands.

Husbands, love your wives, just as Christ loved the church and gave himself up for her, in order to make her holy by cleansing her with the washing of water by the word, so as to present the church to himself in splendor, without a spot or wrinkle or anything of the kind—yes, so that she may be holy and without blemish. In the same way, husbands should love their wives as they do their own bodies. He who loves his wife loves himself. For no one ever hates his own body, but he nourishes and tenderly cares for it, just as Christ does for the church, because we are members of his body. "For this reason a man will leave his father and mother and be joined to his wife, and the two will become one flesh." This is a great mystery, and I am applying it to Christ and the church. Each of you, however, should love his wife as himself, and a wife should respect her husband.

Ephesians 5:22–33

SERIOUS SEEKERS OF the Christ life will take these countercultural instructions seriously. Paul's comparison of the spousal relationship with that between Christ and the Church and his abiding concern for the relationship between the gospel and culture require it. Spiritual formation requires that every part of our lives be under a Christ scrutiny.

Instead of telling couples they should not commit adultery, Paul gives positive guidance that, if followed, will overcome the temptation to be unfaithful. Why is positive instruction more effective than a negative command? If you are married, examine your relationship with your spouse. Why is mutual submission integral to chastity (fidelity)?

If My Heart Has Been Enticed by a Woman

"I have made a covenant with my eyes;
   how then could I look upon a virgin?
What would be my portion from God above,
   and my heritage from the Almighty on high?
Does not calamity befall the unrighteous,
   and disaster the workers of iniquity?
Does he not see my ways,
   and number all my steps?
If my heart has been enticed by a woman
   and I have lain in wait at my neighbor's door;
then let my wife grind for another,
   and let other men kneel over her.
For that would be a heinous crime;
   that would be a criminal offense;
for that would be a fire consuming down to Abaddon,
   and it would burn to the root all my harvest."

Job 31:1–4, 9–12

CHAPTER 31 IS Job's long oath of innocence or defense of his earlier conduct. Convinced that God is still in the wrong, Job hopes that God will recognize his integrity and moral uprightness. In his challenge to God Job names adultery as an action he should be punished for if he were guilty of committing it. Job names two actions in his culture—heart following eyes and being enticed by a woman—that lead to adultery.

How does adultery damage the relationship between husband and wife? Consider making a list of the ways you can avoid the temptation of being unfaithful to your spouse or future spouse.

Keep Your Way Far from Her

My child, be attentive to my wisdom;
  incline your ear to my understanding,
so that you may hold on to prudence,
  and your lips may guard knowledge.
For the lips of a loose woman drip honey,
  and her speech is smoother than oil;
but in the end she is bitter as wormwood,
  sharp as a two-edged sword.
Her feet go down to death;
  her steps follow the path to Sheol.
She does not keep straight to the path of life;
  her ways wander, and she does not know it.
And now, my child, listen to me,
  and do not depart from the words of my mouth.
Keep your way far from her,
  and do not go near the door of her house;
or you will give your honor to others,
  and your years to the merciless.

Proverbs 5:1–9

THIS IS A strong warning against the dangers of adultery. The stratagems of the "loose woman" lead to bitter conflict, bloodshed, and death.

The Teacher here offers advice about how to avoid temptation. Literally, keep far away from someone to whom you are attracted. Is this good advice? How might it have worked for you in a situation in which you were tempted to sin? How does this advice differ from the spiritual practice of trying to view everyone as brothers and sisters?

Shunning Youthful Passions

Shun youthful passions and pursue righteousness, faith, love and peace,
along with those who call on the Lord from a pure heart.

2 Timothy 2:22

WE OFTEN THINK of chastity as something for the young to worry
about before they are married and their "youthful passions" are safely
channeled into a marriage partnership. But if we think of chastity as
not being governed by our sexual impulses, then it is clear that it is a
lifelong task for all of us. Sometime within the next ten days, sit down
with a journal or a large piece of paper and chart how you have or have
not been governed by your sexuality over time. You could draw a visual
representation, such as a time line, or write your thoughts out in words.
Focus especially on times when you realize that you were particularly
tempted or not tempted by sexual sin. What made those times different? Was it a particular person or influence in your life? Was it a time
when you had a church home and close friends? Were you rested or
overworked and exhausted? Perhaps this exercise will help you recognize how to better govern your sexuality. If you find yourself haunted
by a particular sexual sin in your past or present, take time now to confess and talk to God about it.

Spiritual Practice

Widows Young and Old

Let a widow be put on the list if she is not less than sixty years old and has been married only once; she must be well attested for her good works, as one who has brought up children, shown hospitality, washed the saints' feet, helped the afflicted, and devoted herself to doing good in every way. But refuse to put younger women on the list; for when their sensual desires alienate them from Christ, they want to marry, and so they incur condemnation for having violated their first pledge. Besides that, they learn to be idle, gadding about from house to house; and they are not merely idle, but also gossips and busybodies, saying what they should not say. So I would have younger widows marry, bear children, and manage their households, so as to give the adversary no occasion to revile us.

1 Timothy 5:9–14

A CHURCH IS judged by its care of its more vulnerable. At the time 1 Timothy was written, widows were the epitome of need and dependency; therefore, the Letter expends much text dealing in detail with the community's responsibility for them. The list Paul mentions is of those who receive aid from the church. He wants only older widows to be placed on the list; younger widows are to remarry because of their "sensual desires." The importance Paul places on sexuality is evident by his concern that sexuality have proper channels. When it is not directed properly, he sees all kinds of repercussions—alienation from Christ, idleness, a tendency to gossip.

Paul makes a distinction between young and old widows. As you start your journaling or time line, think about the different ways you might have struggled with your sexuality during different stages in your life. How did your temptations change?

⁓ Shunning Youthful Passions

Be Chaste and Self-Controlled

But as for you, teach what is consistent with sound doctrine. Tell the older men to be temperate, serious, prudent, and sound in faith, in love, and in endurance.

Likewise, tell the older women to be reverent in behavior, not to be slanderers or slaves to drink; they are to teach what is good, so that they may encourage the young women to love their husbands, to love their children, to be self-controlled, chaste, good managers of the household, kind, being submissive to their husbands, so that the word of God may not be discredited.

Likewise, urge the younger men to be self-controlled. Show yourself in all respects a model of good works, and in your teaching show integrity, gravity, and sound speech that cannot be censured; then any opponents will be put to shame, having nothing evil to say of us.

Titus 2:1–8

PAUL DIRECTS YOUNG women to love their husbands *and* to be "chaste." Clearly chastity here has a more nuanced meaning than simply refraining from sexual activity. Scripture such as this Letter reminds us that the Christian faith is not only something we believe, but also something we practice. In too many contemporary communities, there is a reluctance to make moral judgments upon anyone's behavior. Who am I to judge you? Your brother or sister in Christ, that's who. The Letter to Titus suffers no reservations in making specific moral demands upon new Christians. The world is quite right in assuming that if the way of Christ is true and life-giving, it ought to be able to look at our lives and see that way personified in what we do and say. Titus helps guide us toward the personification of the way of Christ.

How can we embody chastity in our lives? When in your life have you best exemplified chaste self-control? As you reflect, ask God to show you the way to love God, your neighbor, and yourself more completely.

Control Your Own Body

Finally, brothers and sisters, we ask and urge you in the Lord Jesus that, as you learned from us how you ought to live and to please God (as, in fact, you are doing), you should do so more and more. For you know what instructions we gave you through the Lord Jesus. For this is the will of God, your sanctification: that you abstain from fornication; that each one of you know how to control your own body in holiness and honor, not with lustful passion, like the Gentiles who do not know God; that no one wrong or exploit a brother or sister in this matter, because the Lord is an avenger in all these things, just as we have already told you beforehand and solemnly warned you. For God did not call us to impurity but in holiness. Therefore whoever rejects this rejects not human authority but God, who also gives his Holy Spirit to you.

1 Thessalonians 4:1–8

PAUL URGES THE Thessalonians to live here and now as men and women and as married folk in a way that honors God, because Jesus Christ has given them his grace. Paul urges the Christians to live in marriage with tenderness and honor. The health of marriages is a major pastoral concern for Paul. For us too.

Sanctification, that is, our growth in grace, is here directly applied to sexual purity, and specifically to the problem of fornication—sexual intercourse between people who are not married to each other. And we thought times had changed!

Paul speaks of fornication as something that one can use to wrong or exploit a brother or sister. In what ways can sexual sin do so? Have you ever sexually wronged or exploited another or been wronged?

Father God, sexuality is a wonderful gift that gives us so much pleasure, yet we can also use it to wrong or exploit others. Please forgive me for those people I have seen as sexual objects. I humbly ask today for purity of thought and the ability to control my body in holiness and honor. Amen.

A Temple of the Holy Spirit

The body is meant not for fornication but for the Lord, and the Lord for the body. And God raised the Lord and will also raise us by his power. Do you not know that your bodies are members of Christ? Should I therefore take the members of Christ and make them members of a prostitute? Never! Do you not know that whoever is united to a prostitute becomes one body with her? For it is said, "The two shall be one flesh." But anyone united to the Lord becomes one spirit with him. Shun fornication! Every sin that a person commits is outside the body; but the fornicator sins against the body itself. Or do you not know that your body is a temple of the Holy Spirit within you, which you have from God, and that you are not your own? For you were bought with a price; therefore glorify God in your body.

1 Corinthians 6:13b–20

WHAT WE DO with our bodies matters. The physical world, including the human body, is beautiful, powerful, and holy under God. The physical world is the dwelling place of spiritual life—and of God himself when he became enfleshed in Jesus Christ. The physical world mediates the presence of God-with-us in many ways, but above all it is the place where we learn to live in union with the kingdom of God. We seek and find the kingdom of God, first, in Jesus himself, but then in every detail of ordinary life (Matt 6:33). The character of Jesus descends on our body as we progress in spiritual formation and it—that is, our body—becomes the bearer and showplace of the fruit of the Spirit.

This is perhaps the most often quoted text about chastity in the Bible. What does it mean to you that your body is a "temple of the Holy Spirit"? Has your perspective on this verse changed in different periods of your life? What disciplines other than chastity might this understanding have bearing on?

Do Not Deprive One Another

Now concerning the matters about which you wrote: "It is well for a man not to touch a woman." But because of cases of sexual immorality, each man should have his own wife and each woman her own husband. The husband should give to his wife her conjugal rights, and likewise the wife to her husband. For the wife does not have authority over her own body, but the husband does; likewise the husband does not have authority over his own body, but the wife does. Do not deprive one another except perhaps by agreement for a set time, to devote yourself to prayer, and then come together again, so that Satan may not tempt you because of your lack of self-control. This I say by way of concession, not of command. I wish that all were as I myself am. But each has a particular gift from God, one having one kind and another a different kind.

To the unmarried and the widows I say that it is well for them to remain unmarried as I am. But if they are not practicing self-control, they should marry. For it is better to marry than to be aflame with passion.

1 Corinthians 7:1–9

SOMEONE AMONG THE Corinthians is asserting that sexual abstinence should be the norm for all church members, married and unmarried. Paul disagrees. Not only does sexual intercourse prevent immorality; marriage partners have an equal right to sexual fulfillment.

Paul does say that an agreed-upon period of abstinence is okay within a marriage. What effect might a time of abstinence have?

"Any marriage has times of separation, ill-health, or just plain crankiness, in which sexual intercourse is ill-advised. And it is precisely the skills of celibate friendship—fostering intimacy through letters, conversations, performing mundane tasks together (thus rendering them pleasurable), savoring the holy simplicity of a shared meal, or a walk together at dusk—that can help a marriage survive the rough spots."

—Kathleen Norris, *The Cloister Walk*[4]

Rejoice in the Wife of Your Youth

Drink water from your own cistern, / flowing water from your own
well. / Should your springs be scattered abroad, / streams of water
in the streets? / Let them be for yourself alone, / and not for sharing
with strangers. / Let your fountain be blessed, / and rejoice in the
wife of your youth, / a lovely deer, a graceful doe. / May her breasts
satisfy you at all times; / may you be intoxicated always by your
love. / Why should you be intoxicated, my son, by another woman /
and embrace the bosom of an adulteress? / For human ways are
under the eyes of the LORD, / and he examines all their paths. / The
iniquities of the wicked ensnare them / and they are caught in the
toils of their sin.

Proverbs 5:15–22

THIS PROVERB ELOQUENTLY describes the beauty of faithful married
love. Married love and fidelity will bring secure happiness. Even those of
us who are married are meant to remain chaste, in the sense of remain-
ing faithful to one's husband or wife—in thought, word, and deed.

With the advent of the Internet, sexual temptation is sometimes literally at our fingertips. Is there a sexual temptation in your life? If so,
meditate on this prayer:

*God, I find myself in a constant struggle with sexual temptation. I am
ashamed of my sin and I long to be free. Please forgive me and teach me
how to remain chaste in thought, word, and deed. Show me what steps
I need to take to overcome this temptation—whether there is someone I
need to talk to about it or some way I can minimize its influence in my life.
In your name I pray. Amen.*

Set Me as a Seal Upon Your Heart

Set me as a seal upon your heart, / as a seal upon your arm; / for love is strong as death, / passion fierce as the grave. / Its flashes are flashes of fire, / a raging flame. / Many waters cannot quench love, / neither can floods drown it. / If one offered for love / all the wealth of one's house, / it would be utterly scorned.

Song of Solomon 8:6–7

BEING CHASTE DOES not mean being celibate. Within a marriage relationship it means giving ourselves fully, and permanently, to our spouse in the same way we give ourselves fully to God. In this passage the woman desires that the man take full possession of her. She surrenders herself to him, yearning for "one flesh" union. The seal in ancient Israelite society was typically a stamp that was pressed on soft clay to leave an impression that served as a person's identification. She wants to be marked as belonging to her beloved, with all her inward ("your heart") and outward ("your arm") being. Our own sense of individuality often rebels against this idea, and the danger is great in a fallen world, but the woman expresses a desire that we all have to be intimate and safe in the presence of another. Such an intense feeling explains why the ideal relationship between a man and a woman serves so well as a metaphor for our relationship with God.

Reflect on this quote. How do you feel about this kind of permanence? Is it frightening? Comforting?

"The loyalty pictured in the Song should remind [us] that there's no way out of this. There's no rip cord that can be pulled, no ejection seat that can be triggered. They are in it together, bound to each other forever with covenantal loyalty."

—David Hubbard, "Love and Marriage"[5]

Let Marriage Be Held in Honor

Let mutual love continue. Let marriage be held in honor by all, and let the marriage bed be kept undefiled; for God will judge fornicators and adulterers.

Hebrews 13:1, 4

HEBREWS 13 CONTAINS a checklist of spiritual exercises. The cardinal virtue of all is love of those inside the fellowship of faith (the sense of the Greek word *philadelphia,* "mutual love"). Marriage must be honored, remembering that God will judge the sexually immoral, whether fornicators or adulterers.

It can be difficult to reconcile honoring marriage and expressing "mutual love" with others we care about. Indeed, how to express appropriately our sexuality outside the marriage relationship is a struggle for almost everyone. Richard Foster writes, "This does not mean that we repress our sexuality outside marriage. Oh, no, hardly anything will damage the marriage more. We must be human; we need intimacy, touch, meaningful conversation, and much more outside the marriage bonds. Otherwise we will be asking the marriage to carry more than is reasonable for even the healthiest relationship."[6] How can you express your sexuality in a healthy way with those other than your spouse? What are the lines you cannot cross?

The Greatest of These Is Love

If I speak in the tongues of mortals and of angels, but do not have love, I am a noisy gong or a clanging cymbal. And if I have prophetic powers, and understand all mysteries and all knowledge, and if I have faith, so as to remove mountains, but do not have love, I am nothing. If I give away all my possessions, and if I hand over my body so that I may boast, but do not have love, I gain nothing.

Love is patient; love is kind; love is not envious or boastful or arrogant or rude. It does not insist on its own way; it is not irritable or resentful; it does not rejoice in wrongdoing, but rejoices in the truth. It bears all things, believes all things, hopes all things, endures all things. And now faith, hope, and love abide, these three; and the greatest of these is love.

1 Corinthians 13:1–7, 13

As a pastor speaking to a specific situation in his former congregation, Paul here offers a statement on love unequaled in spiritual writing. Though he presents an ideal seldom attained by any community, his very words uplift and inspire. The love outlined here is what Paul wants the Corinthians to show toward one another in all their behavior, that they might experience such love themselves. We too experience and are sustained by the love we are able to show others.

Dallas Willard writes, "To practice chastity, then, we must first practice love, practice seeking the good of those of the opposite sex we come in contact with."[7]

Lord God, just as you love us, you call us to love one another. Thank you for this wonderful gift. Teach me to love others chastely, with patience and endurance, but also with rejoicing, recognizing in all I meet my brothers and sisters. In your name I pray. Amen.

For more verses on chastity and ideas on how to practice the discipline of chastity, see the Responding exercises and Spiritual Disciplines Index in *The Life with God Bible*.

Submission

Subordination to the guidance of God; within the Christian fellowship, a constant mutual subordination out of reverence for Christ, which opens the way for particular subordination to those who are qualified to direct our efforts toward Christlikeness and who then add the weight of their wise authority on the side of our willing spirit to help us do the things we would like to do and refrain from doing the things we don't want to do

Submission does not mean blindly following anyone who tells us to do something. Rather, the best biblical description of submission comes from Jesus himself when he says, "If any want to become my followers, let them deny themselves and take up their cross and follow me" (Luke 9:23). Self-denial is an unfamiliar concept for many of us today, and we worry that it requires losing our individuality. But all self-denial means is realizing that we do not always have to have our own way, that our happiness does not depend on getting what we want.[1] Subordinating our own will to another's can be gloriously freeing. When we give up the need to always get our own way, we can hold the things of this world lightly. We always submit first to God, but submitting to others frees us to value our brothers and sisters in a way that is difficult if not impossible when we are thinking only of our own self-interest. As in all the disciplines we have no better example to follow than Jesus.

We must, however, be watchful for those times when submission becomes destructive. Here we trust the Holy Spirit to help us discern when we must refuse to submit to humans or human authority.

Here am I, the servant of the Lord; let it be with me according to your word.

—*Luke 1:38*

Submission

Your Will Be Done

"Pray then in this way:
Our Father in heaven,
    hallowed be your name.
Your kingdom come,
Your will be done,
    on earth as it is in heaven."

Matthew 6:9–10

Spiritual Practice

MANY OF US pray for God's will to be done, even while silently or unconsciously adding a coda to our request: *As long as your will is the same as my own.* Yet one of the fundamental lessons of the Christian life is that God knows better than we ourselves what will truly make us happy. For the next ten days we will try to experience the freedom that comes from setting aside our own will and self-interest. Do not focus so much on asking specific questions of God, such as whether you should take a walk or drive one route or the other; instead, just try to live each day with an attitude of surrender rather than struggle. In your prayer times also ask God what you can do to better practice submission; you will discover ways to submit to God in matters large and small. These words from Richard Foster best describe our task:

> At the beginning of the day we wait, in the words of the hymn writer, "yielded and still" before Father, Son, and Holy Spirit. The first words of our day form the prayer of Thomas à Kempis, "As thou wilt; what thou wilt; when thou wilt." We yield our body, mind, and spirit for his purposes. Likewise, the day is lived in deeds of submission interspersed with constant ejaculations of inward surrender. As the first words of the morning are of submission, so are the last words of the night. We surrender our body, mind, and spirit into the hands of God to do with us as he pleases through the long darkness.[2]

Fearing God

So now, O Israel, what does the LORD your God require of you? Only to fear the LORD your God, to walk in all his ways, to love him, to serve the LORD your God with all your heart and with all your soul, and to keep the commandments of the LORD your God and his decrees that I am commanding you today, for your own well-being.

Deuteronomy 10:12–13

ISRAEL HERE LEARNS what covenant relationship entails. First is fear of the Lord. Fear here means neither abject terror nor simple respect. It involves recognition that God is our creator and we are totally dependent on him for our very life. We are to walk in all his ways. His way is a metaphor for his will in our lives. We are to love him. Like fear, love is an emotion, but in a covenant context it certainly refers to the feeling of gratitude and a commitment to stay in a relationship. Also, in the covenant God proclaims himself king and his people are his servants. Thus we are not surprised to learn that we are to serve him. On the basis of that relationship we are to obey his commandments.

Reflect on this prayer as you consider how submission is like fear of the Lord:

Take, Lord, and receive all my liberty, my memory,
my understanding, and my entire will.
All I have and call my own.
Whatever I have or hold, you have given me.
I return it all to you and surrender it wholly
to be governed by your will.
Give me only your love and your grace
and I am rich enough and ask for nothing more.

—St. Ignatius of Loyola, Spiritual Exercises

~ Your Will Be Done

Let It Be with Me According to Your Word

In the sixth month the angel Gabriel was sent by God to a town in Galilee called Nazareth, to a virgin engaged to a man whose name was Joseph, of the house of David. The virgin's name was Mary. And he came to her and said, "Greetings, favored one! The Lord is with you." But she was much perplexed by his words and pondered what sort of greeting this might be. The angel said to her, "Do not be afraid, Mary, for you have found favor with God. And now, you will conceive in your womb and bear a son, and you will name him Jesus. He will be great, and will be called the Son of the Most High, and the Lord God will give to him the throne of his ancestor David. He will reign over the house of Jacob forever, and of his kingdom there will be no end." Mary said to the angel, "How can this be, since I am a virgin?" The angel said to her, "The Holy Spirit will come upon you, and the power of the Most High will overshadow you; therefore the child to be born will be holy; he will be called Son of God. And now, your relative Elizabeth in her old age has also conceived a son; and this is the sixth month for her who was said to be barren. For nothing will be impossible with God." Then Mary said, "Here am I, the servant of the Lord; let it be with me according to your word." Then the angel departed from her.

Luke 1:26–38

MARY KNEW LITTLE of childbirth, marriage, or parenting when she learned that she would give birth to God's son. She did understand the disgrace she would probably suffer and was told early on, "A sword will pierce your own soul too" (2:35). The glorious prospect of becoming Jesus' mother held the promise of untold pain.

Try to place yourself in Mary's shoes. You are young and engaged. Gabriel appears. You become afraid, then ask Gabriel a question. Finally, you submit to the Lord. Try to recall a time in your life when you felt the Lord asking you to do something that you wanted to resist or that was outrageous by all the world's standards. What was your response?

No One Has Power Over the Wind

Whoever obeys a command will meet no harm, and the wise mind will know the time and way. For every matter has its time and way, although the troubles of mortals lie heavy upon them. Indeed, they do not know what is to be, for who can tell them how it will be? No one has power over the wind to restrain the wind, or power over the day of death; there is no discharge from the battle, nor does wickedness deliver those who practice it.

Ecclesiastes 8:5–8

It is easier to obey than to try to run our lives, for we mortals cannot know the proper course to take from our limited human perspective. We all feel the frustration of trying to keep control of life in a fallen world. But trying to control life is like trying to master the wind—impossible. Just take death—no one can delay it forever, no matter how hard they try. The Teacher who narrates Ecclesiastes ultimately concludes that we must "fear God, and keep his commandments; for that is the whole duty of everyone" (12:13b).

Many people are very nervous during airplane flights. For some, the nervousness is caused by having absolutely no control over what happens. Those who recognize this have two choices: either they can continue to be miserable, or they can release everything to God and submit to the expertise of the company who made the airplane, the abilities of the controller monitoring its flight path, and the experience of the flight crew to get them safely to their destination. Do you struggle with relinquishing control? What are some other problems we experience when we will not submit to those things that are unavoidable and inevitable? How can you help yourself to relinquish control, even a little bit at a time?

~ *Your Will Be Done*

If the Lord Wishes

Come now, you who say, "Today or tomorrow we will go to such and such a town and spend a year there, doing business and making money." Yet you do not even know what tomorrow will bring. What is your life? For you are a mist that appears for a little while and then vanishes. Instead you ought to say, "If the Lord wishes, we will live to do this or that."

James 4:13–15

JAMES WARNS THAT no human controls tomorrow and that life is dependent upon God. The look must always be beyond ourselves to God, with an appeal to God's graciousness and guidance. Requisite planning has its place; so do we have a place—humble before God, prudently seeking God's counsel for our lives.

How does the following quote increase your understanding of submitting to God's will?

"But it really would seem as if God's own children were more afraid of His will than of anything else in life—His lovely, lovable will, which only means loving-kindnesses and tender mercies, and blessings unspeakable to their souls! I wish only I could show to every one the unfathomable sweetness of the will of God. . . . He loves us—loves us, I say—and the will of love is always blessing for its loved one. Some of us know what it is to love, and we know that could we only have our way, our beloved ones would be overwhelmed with blessings. . . . And if this is the way of love with us, how much more must it be so with our God, who is love itself! Could we but for one moment get a glimpse into the mighty depths of His love, our hearts would spring out to meet His will and embrace it as our richest treasure; and we would abandon ourselves to it with an enthusiasm of gratitude and joy that such a wondrous privilege could be ours."

—Hannah Whitall Smith, *The Christian's Secret of a Happy Life*[3]

Israel Would Not Submit to Me

"Hear, O my people, while I admonish you;
   O Israel, if you would but listen to me!
There shall be no strange god among you;
   you shall not bow down to a foreign god.
I am the LORD your God,
   who brought you up out of the land of Egypt.
   Open your mouth wide and I will fill it.
But my people did not listen to my voice;
   Israel would not submit to me.
So I gave them over to their stubborn hearts,
   to follow their own counsels.
O that my people would listen to me,
   that Israel would walk in my ways!
Then I would quickly subdue their enemies,
   and turn my hand against their foes."

Psalm 81:8–14

THE CONTEXT OF this psalm signals a song used for a feast day, perhaps the fall Festival of Tabernacles. This is scheduled praise to celebrate God's saving power, particularly noting God's deliverance of Israel from Egypt. God invites the people to reap the benefits of his adequacy and generosity. Trust wholeheartedly, open wide, and you'll get all you need.

What seems to be meant by submission in this psalm? How was Israel defiant and unsubmissive to God? What lessons can we learn from its example for our nation? For our church? For our family? For ourselves?

Submit Yourselves Therefore to God

But he gives us all the more grace; therefore it says,
  "God opposes the proud,
    but gives grace to the humble."
Submit yourselves therefore to God. Resist the devil, and he will flee
from you. Draw near to God, and he will draw near to you. Cleanse
your hands, you sinners, and purify your hearts, you double-minded.
Lament and mourn and weep. Let your laughter be turned into mourning and your joy into dejection. Humble yourselves before the Lord,
and he will exalt you.

James 4:6–10

HUMBLING OURSELVES BEFORE the Lord places us in the position to
be freed from double-mindedness, a worldly and competitive spirit,
and a judgmental attitude toward others. The act of "drawing near" is
the proper response to God's invitation to receive the inner results of
forgiveness, acceptance, restoration, renewal, and guidance.

Reflect on these words as you seek to submit to God today. How does it
make you feel to think that you belong to God?

  "Every soul belongs to God and exists by His pleasure. God being who
and what He is, and we being who and what we are, the only thinkable
relation between us is one of full Lordship on His part and complete
submission on ours. We owe Him every honor that is in our power to give
Him. Our everlasting grief lies in giving Him anything less."

—A.W. Tozer, *The Pursuit of God*[4]

Denying Ourselves and Taking Up Our Cross

[Jesus] called the crowd with his disciples and said to them, "If any want to become my followers, let them deny themselves and take up their cross and follow me. For those who want to save their life will lose it, and those who lose their life for my sake, and for the sake of the gospel, will save it. For what will it profit them to gain the whole world and forfeit their life?"

Mark 8:34–36

ONCE WE HAVE made our confession of faith, we have only taken the first step. The second step is the lifelong journey of living our confession fully and authentically. Jesus tells us what kind of Messiah he has come to be and therefore what kind of life we are called to live: a life of service and sacrifice. Jesus requires self-denial and the taking up of our own crosses (not Jesus'). Discipleship is not for the faint-hearted!

What kind of a reaction do you have to Jesus' statement? What is the difference between self-denial and self-hatred? What does it mean to you to take up your cross? How has your practice of submission influenced your understanding?

Dear Lord, I want to follow you, but sometimes the flesh is so weak. Teach me what it means to deny myself and take up my cross. Give me the courage to stop being a slave to my own will. In your name I pray. Amen.

⟶ *Your Will Be Done*

Let This Cup Pass from Me

Then Jesus went with them to a place called Gethsemane; and he said to his disciples, "Sit here while I go over there and pray." He took with him Peter and the two sons of Zebedee, and began to be grieved and agitated. Then he said to them, "I am deeply grieved, even to death; remain here, and stay awake with me." And going a little farther, he threw himself on the ground and prayed, "My Father, if this is possible, let this cup pass from me; yet not what I want but what you want." Again he went away for the second time and prayed, "My Father, if this cannot pass unless I drink it, your will be done." Again he came and found [the disciples] sleeping, for their eyes were heavy. So leaving them again, he went away and prayed for the third time, saying the same words.

Matthew 26:36–39, 42–44

THE MATTHEAN GETHSEMANE story is a dramatic portrayal of Jesus wrestling with God's will and then finally accepting it. In Mark, readers are not told what Jesus said to God the second time he went away to pray. Here Jesus, on the first occasion, asks if it is possible for the cup (referring to the expression of God's judgment in and by the cross) to be removed from him, yet not as he wills, but as God wills. But on the second occasion he says, "If this cannot pass unless I drink it, your will be done." In both cases, Jesus addresses God in the most intimate terms as "my Father." During his third prayer, Jesus repeats the words of his second petition.

Father God, just as Jesus wrestled with submitting to your will, I too struggle with putting my own will aside. Give me the courage to follow Jesus' example and say, "Your will be done." In your name I pray. Amen.

Jesus' Reverent Submission

In the days of his flesh, Jesus offered up prayers and supplications, with loud cries and tears, to the one who was able to save him from death, and he was heard because of his reverent submission. Although he was a Son, he learned obedience through what he suffered; and having made himself perfect, he became the source of eternal salvation for all who obey him.

Hebrews 5:7–9

JESUS DID NOT seek his own glory, but offered prayers and supplications to God. Like all humans, he had to learn obedience from what he suffered. But unlike the Letter's intended recipients, and perhaps also unlike ourselves, Jesus did not become lax in faith, disbelieving, and hard-hearted. In all his trials and sufferings he reverently submitted to God and thus became both the model and means of salvation for us in our own trials and sufferings.

After your experience of trying to submit to God's will, which of the following descriptions best fits you? How has Jesus' example of reverent submission inspired and taught you?

"Some are led into the state of complete obedience by this well-nigh passive route, wherein God alone seems to be the actor and we seem to be wholly acted upon. And our wills are melted and dissolved and made pliant, being firmly fixed in Him, and He wills in us.

"But in contrast to this passive route to complete obedience most people must follow what Jean-Nicholas Grou calls the active way, where *we* must struggle and, like Jacob of old, wrestle with the angel until the morning dawns, the active way wherein the will must be subjected bit by bit, piecemeal and progressively, to the divine Will."

—Thomas R. Kelly, *A Testament of Devotion*[5]

Being Subject to One Another

Be subject to one another out of reverence for Christ.

Ephesians 5:21

SOMETIME WITHIN THE next ten days, choose one day in which you will try to practice the art of being "subject to others." This does not mean that you will give others license to walk all over you, but that you will choose to set aside your own will as is appropriate and practice subordination as Jesus did, being a servant to all, even those who are not honored by the rest of society. Voluntarily and lovingly submit to those around you, trying to place their best interests above your own. One discipline you may find especially helpful in your practice is silence. Richard Foster tells us that "usually the best way to handle most matters of submission is to say nothing."[6] Of course the important corollary to silence is listening. Listen respectfully to others; try to keep from arguing or adding your own two cents. In your practice of being subject to others, seek to keep love at the forefront of your being out of love and reverence for Christ, whose example you are trying to follow.

Spiritual Practice

Rules for a Christian Household

Wives, be subject to your husbands, as is fitting in the Lord. Husbands, love your wives and never treat them harshly.

Children, obey your parents in everything, for this is your acceptable duty in the Lord. Fathers, do not provoke your children, or they may lose heart. Slaves, obey your earthly masters in everything, not only while being watched and in order to please them, but wholeheartedly, fearing the Lord.

Colossians 3:18–22

THE ETHICAL PART of the Letter to the Colossians contains the so-called household code, rules for Christian households concerning husbands and wives, fathers and children, and masters and slaves. This is very controversial today mainly because of the implied patriarchy and the assumption of legitimacy given to slavery, although its enduring emphasis on the reciprocity of relationship illustrates that relationships always have the components of mutual commitment and mutual responsibility. It is also clear that the ethic of life together is not to be dismissed. Family and personal relations are not neutral, but must reflect the gospel ethic of love and forbearance.

What insight does this quote offer?

"It is astonishing that Paul called [wives, children, and slaves] to subordination since they were already subordinate by virtue of their place in first-century culture. The only meaningful reason for such a command was the fact that by virtue of the gospel message they had come to see themselves as free from a subordinate status in society. The gospel has challenged all second-class citizenships, and they knew it. Paul urged voluntary subordination not because it was their station in life, but because it was 'fitting in the Lord' (Col. 3:18)."

—Richard J. Foster, *Celebration of Discipline*[7]

Hear Your Father's Instruction

Hear, my child, your father's instruction,
  and do not reject your mother's teaching;
for they are a fair garland for your head,
  and pendants for your neck.

Proverbs 1:8–9

THE VIEW THAT young people should learn from both mothers and fathers is pervasive throughout Proverbs. In fact, Proverbs begins by pointing out the importance of a mother's and father's teachings. Our parents are often the first persons with whom we practice submission.

Reflect on your relationship with your mother and father. In what ways did you submit to their authority and in what ways did you reject it? What did they teach you about submission? Next, consider the best way to train children to be submissive and respectful. Why was this important in biblical times? Why is it important today? Seek to deliberately treat children respectfully today.

Obey Your Leaders

Obey your leaders and submit to them, for they are keeping watch over your souls and will give an account. Let them do this with joy and not with sighing—for that would be harmful to you.

Hebrews 13:17

THE LEADERS THE author of Hebrews is referring to are the leaders of the church. The goal of Christian leadership is to be vigilant over the spiritual welfare of believers. The message for us is that since our leaders are to have our best interests at heart, it is best to submit to them joyfully, trusting that they have God-given insight about what is best for us.

Do you find it easier or harder to submit to leaders in the church compared to family members, people you work with, or secular authorities? Why? When you have submitted to leaders in the church, what has been the result?

⌐ Being Subject to One Another

When Submission Becomes Destructive

For the Lord's sake accept the authority of every human institution, whether of the emperor as supreme, or of governors, as sent by him to punish those who do wrong and to praise those who do right. For it is God's will that by doing right you should silence the ignorance of the foolish. As servants of God, live as free people, yet do not use your freedom as a pretext for evil. Honor everyone. Love the family of believers. Fear God, honor the emperor.

1 Peter 2:13–17

IF WE SUBMIT to authorities, even those who will occasionally harm us, a higher purpose will be accomplished, that of reflecting the life of our Savior, who himself suffered unjustly for the sake of his enemies. This having been said, there is also a time when "submission" is simply wrong. The same Peter who here counsels submission to "every human institution" also told the Sanhedrin, "Whether it is right in God's sight to listen to you rather than to God, you must judge; for we cannot keep from speaking about what we have seen and heard" (Acts 4:19–20). Later, speaking to the high priest, he said flatly, "We must obey God rather than any human authority" (Acts 5:29). We see the same dual approach in the apostle Paul (see Rom 13:1; Acts 16:37). Were Peter and Paul opposing their own principle of submission? No. They simply understood that when the Spiritual Discipline of submission becomes destructive, it then becomes a denial of the law of love as taught by Jesus and is an affront to genuine biblical submission.

How do we know when submission becomes destructive?

"Of all the Spiritual Disciplines none has been more abused than the Discipline of submission. . . . Therefore, we must work our way through this Discipline with great care and discernment in order to ensure that we are the ministers of life, not death."

—Richard J. Foster, *Celebration of Discipline*[8]

Queen Vashti Refuses to Submit

On the seventh day, when the king was merry with wine, he commanded the seven eunuchs who attended him to bring Queen Vashti before the king, wearing the royal crown, in order to show the peoples and the officials her beauty; for she was fair to behold. But Queen Vashti refused to come at the king's command conveyed by the eunuchs. At this the king was enraged, and his anger burned within him.

Then Memucan said in the presence of the king and officials, "Not only has Queen Vashti done wrong to the king, but also to all the officials and all the peoples who are in all the provinces of King Ahasuerus. For this deed of the queen will be made known to all women, causing them to look with contempt on their husbands. If it pleases the king, let a royal order go out from him, and let it be written among the laws of the Persias and the Medes so that it may not be altered, that Vashti is never again to come before King Ahasuerus; and let the king give her royal position to another who is better than she."

This advice pleased the king and the officials, and the king did as Memucan proposed.

Esther 1:10–12, 16–17a, 19, 21

AFTER A WEEK-LONG drinking party, a public display of his wealth and power, the king, by now drunk, has in mind to bring Vashti before his fellows as the climactic display of his greatness. Her refusal is a refusal to be objectified by him. Such a refusal, of course, does not sit well with him, sending him into a hot rage and his officers into a panic. (What if their wives start undermining them as well?) The solution—not only dethroning and banishing Vashti, but also making her an object lesson for all the women of Persia—is extreme to the point of ridiculous. It leaves readers with little respect for anyone in chapter 1 except Vashti.

In your practice of submission to others, have you come across any situations where you knew submission would be wrong?

⁓ Being Subject to One Another

Human Power Posing as God

Then the Rabshakeh stood and called out in a loud voice in the language of Judah, "Hear the word of the great king, the king of Assyria! Thus says the king: 'Do not let Hezekiah deceive you, for he will not be able to deliver you out of my hand. Do not let Hezekiah make you rely on the LORD by saying, The LORD will surely deliver us, and this city will not be given into the hand of the king of Assyria.' Do not listen to Hezekiah; for thus says the king of Assyria: 'Make your peace with me and come out to me; then every one of you will eat from your own vine and your own fig tree, and drink water from your own cistern, until I come and take you away to a land like your own land, a land of grain and wine, a land of bread and vineyards, a land of olive oil and honey, that you may live and not die. Do not listen to Hezekiah when he misleads you by saying, The LORD will deliver us.'"

2 Kings 18:28–32

THE RABSHAKEH, AN Assyrian official, uses powerful imagery familiar to the Israelites to entice them to surrender and accept exile. They will eat from their own vines and fig trees (Mic 4:4). Fertile land will spread before them (Deut 8:7–9). Speaking for Sennacherib, this official mimics God, offering life for obedience, death for disobedience (Deut 30:15–20). Once again human power poses as God, stealing the language of security and well-being to entice humans to displace God and trust in lesser powers.

We are to submit to human authorities as long as this submission does not become destructive, but never to place them before God. The promises of the king of Assyria mimic the promises of God. We are often tempted to think that another person—spouse, friend, parent, pastor—can fulfill all our needs. This expectation can only lead to disappointment. Today ask yourself who in your life you are placing unfair expectations on. Instead, seek to fulfill a need of theirs.

Not Submitting to False Believers

But because of false believers secretly brought in, who slipped in to spy on the freedom we have in Christ Jesus, so that they might enslave us—we did not submit to them even for a moment, so that the truth of the gospel might always remain with you.

Galatians 2:4–5

THE GALATIANS WERE in danger of ingesting a toxic mix of self-help, outward religious observance, and lies about God. For some, the freedom we have in Christ to become the persons God created and redeemed us to be is too wild, too predictable, and too available. Surely, they said, God never intended to include anyone and everyone. We must have standards and controls. People have to do or know the right things in order to please God. This was the first in a long line of different gospels that continue even now to raise their ugly heads.

In this verse Paul cautions against submitting to false believers who try to take away our freedom in Christ. Has there been a time in your life when you submitted to a teaching that later turned out to be false? Which Spiritual Disciplines help us avoid being misled?

Clothe Yourselves with Humility

Now as an elder myself and a witness of the sufferings of Christ, as well as one who shares in the glory to be revealed, I exhort the elders among you to tend the flock of God that is in your charge, exercising the oversight, not under compulsion but willingly, as God would have you do it—not for sordid gain but eagerly. Do not lord it over those in your charge, but be examples to the flock. And when the chief shepherd appears, you will win the crown of glory that never fades away. In the same way, you who are younger must accept the authority of the elders. And all of you must clothe yourselves with humility in your dealings with one another, for

"God opposes the proud, / but gives grace to the humble."

1 Peter 5:1–5

PETER RAISES THE issue of authority, in this instance exhorting those who are younger to willingly submit to the authority of the elders in their local congregation. Submission to authority can be a difficult and dangerous business, particularly if the authorities in question are themselves self-deceived and inflated with a sense of their own importance, wisdom, and power. The safety net for submission and the safe exercise of authority is humility itself, a virtue Peter highlights throughout his Letter. And what is humility? A realistic and honest self-appraisal in which we acknowledge our strengths and weaknesses, our abilities and inabilities, the gifts that God has given us and those gifts we can receive only from others. In the final analysis, those who embrace humility openly admit that they are not the center of the universe and stand in dire need of Christ and Christ's Body, the Church.

Humbling ourselves before God is also gloriously freeing, as it allows us to cast our concerns upon him. Try to recall times that you have been especially aware that God cares for you. Did you feel more free to "cast" your anxieties on God then or during other times when his love didn't seem so close? What do you think causes these differences in feeling?

Humble Service

Do nothing from selfish ambition or conceit, but in humility regard others as better than yourselves. Let each of you look not to your own interests, but to the interests of others.

Philippians 2:3–4

PAUL PLEADS WITH his readers, appealing to their own tender care for him, to live in unity and humility. Paul's joy (and God's) is made complete when the Church is united in both head and heart (2:2). This unity is experienced through the practice of the discipline of humility: renouncing self-centered pursuits, actively regarding others in the best light possible, paying attention to the concerns and interests of others. As our hearts and minds are directed away from self and toward others in the practice of attentive, humble service, we begin to identify with one another; and before we know it, we find ourselves sharing the "same mind" with them.

Richard Foster writes, "In submission we are at last free to value other people. Their dreams and plans become important to us. We have entered into a new, wonderful, glorious freedom—the freedom to give up our own rights for the good of others. For the first time we can love people unconditionally. We have given up the right to demand that they return our love."[9]

Father God, thank you for the freedom I have found in submission. Give me more and more genuine love for the people in my life. Keep reminding me that as deeply as I can love and care for my fellow human beings, it is a mere shadow of the love you have for all of us. In your name I pray. Amen.

For more verses on submission and ideas on how to practice the discipline of submission, see the Responding exercises and Spiritual Disciplines Index in *The Life with God Bible*.

Sacrifice

Deliberately forsaking the security of satisfying our own needs with our resources in the faith and hope that God will sustain us

We first encounter biblical sacrifice early in the Old Testament as the offering of animals or grain to God. Grain offerings were gifts to God, either to recognize what came from God or to seek favor. Animal sacrifices were offerings of atonement, necessary to return the Israelites into right relationship with God after being separated by sin or impurity. It is important to remember that these sacrifices were about more than bloodletting. When the ancient Israelites gave the best of their food to God, they had to go without it. Their altar gifts were sacrifices in more ways than one. But not long after this practice was established we see many prophets decrying sacrifices as empty rituals, not because the sacrifices in themselves were wrong, but because when they were done without the proper commitment and sense of repentance, they lacked meaning.

Then Jesus turned the concept of sacrifice on its head by offering his own body on the cross—the ultimate act of obedience. We could spend many lifetimes pondering the meaning and magnificence of his gesture, but here let us simply say Jesus' atoning sacrifice forever released us from atoning with animals or crops. Now we are called to follow Jesus' example of sacrifice as we can, whether that means offering money or time or service. Through sacrifice we show our obedience to God. When we give of ourselves, when we offer to God things we need or want, we are recognizing that God is the one who provides for all our needs.

Present your bodies as a living sacrifice, holy and acceptable to God, which is your spiritual worship.

—Romans 12:1

Sacrifice

Small Sacrifices

For the bodies of those animals whose blood is brought into the sanctuary by the high priest as a sacrifice for sin are burned outside the camp. Therefore Jesus also suffered outside the city gate in order to sanctify the people by his own blood. Let us then go out to him outside the camp and bear the abuse he endured. Through him, then, let us continually offer a sacrifice of praise to God, that is, the fruit of lips that confess his name. Do not neglect to do good and to share what you have, for such sacrifices are pleasing to God.

Hebrews 13:11–13, 15–16

THIS PASSAGE CLEARLY ties together for us the meaning of sacrifice in the Old Testament, the way Jesus changed sacrifice forever, and finally, the way we can respond to his sacrifice. The tabernacle in the wilderness is a fitting metaphor of the spiritual life. In the first covenant, animals were sacrificed "outside the camp." Jesus likewise was crucified "outside the city gate." We, therefore, should also take our stand with Christ, bearing the abuse he endured, "outside the camp." The true spiritual life is formed and lived outside the promises and security of this world, accepting Jesus' mission and participating in his sufferings. To this end we are to make sacrifices, whether this entails sacrificing earthly comforts and security at times, offering a "sacrifice of praise," or simply doing good and sharing what we have, all of which belongs to God anyway.

For each of the next ten days find one small way you can make a sacrifice as an offering to God. For example, give all the money in your wallet to a homeless person. Your sacrifice could also include a form of service, which often involves a sacrifice of your time. Another idea is to sacrifice some sleep so that you can spend extra time in the morning or at night in prayer.

Think of each offering as a way of being obedient to God; that way your sacrifice will not be empty, but will show God honor and respect. As Richard Foster reminds us: "The greatest of God's demands is not for us to do heroic deeds or to make great sacrifices, but to obey."[1]

Spiritual Practice

Offering Ourselves

The LORD summoned Moses and spoke to him from the tent of meeting, saying: Speak to the people of Israel and say to them: When any of you bring an offering of livestock to the LORD, you shall bring your offering from the herd or from the flock.

If the offering is a burnt offering from the herd, you shall offer a male without blemish; you shall bring it to the entrance of the tent of meeting, for acceptance in your behalf before the LORD. You shall lay your hand on the head of the burnt offering, and it shall be acceptable in your behalf as atonement for you.

Leviticus 1:1–4

THE OPENING CHAPTERS of Leviticus are addressed to the whole faith community, the whole people of ancient Israel. The word used to describe the animals usually refers to domestic rather than wild animals. Those from the herd would be cattle, those from the flock sheep or goats. The sacrifice of these animals was costly for ancient Israelites. Meat was a rare luxury in that world; the offering was to be genuinely sacrificial. The ancient Israelite practice of animal sacrifice illustrates the sacrificial nature of a life of faith. Genuine faith is in a real sense a commitment, a giving of one's life to God—it is costly.

Reflect on this quotation as you decide on today's small sacrifice:

"In order for a lump of clay to be made into a beautiful vessel, it must be entirely abandoned to the potter, and must lie passive in his hands. And, similarly, in order for a soul to be made into a vessel unto God's honor, "sanctified and meet for the master's use, and prepared unto every good work," it must be utterly abandoned to Him, and must lie passive in His hands. . . . To a soul ignorant of God, this may look hard; but to those who know Him it is the happiest and most restful of lives. He is our Father, and He loves us, and He knows just what is best."

—Hannah Whitall Smith, *The Christian's Secret of a Happy Life*[2]

~ Small Sacrifices

A Living Sacrifice

I appeal to you therefore, brothers and sisters, by the mercies of God, to present your bodies as a living sacrifice, holy and acceptable to God, which is your spiritual worship.

Romans 12:1

IN THE PASSAGE before this verse, Paul has been dealing with complex matters; he has done his best by vigorous reasoning and devout meditation on Scripture to bring Gentiles and Jews into a mutual awareness of community. The word "therefore" signals a shift of emphasis. Are we, Jews and Gentiles, now on common ground? Are we, sinners all, brothers and sisters in Christ? Do we understand that Jesus is our Savior? Do we realize that we are all, every one of us, new creatures, resurrection men and women through the work of the Holy Spirit? Well, then—therefore!—let us live this new life to the hilt, placing our bodies simply, wholly, believingly on the altar, a daily offering so that God can work his will in us.

In commenting on this verse, Richard Foster says that the problem with a "living" sacrifice is that it always wants to get off the altar. Try preparing your heart by saying this prayer today as you offer your little sacrifice to God:

Father, I abandon myself / into Your hands. / Do with me what You will, / whatever You do, I will thank You. / I am ready for all, I accept all. / Let only Your will be done in me, / as in all Your creatures, / and I'll ask nothing else, my Lord. / Into your hands I commend my spirit; / I give it to You / with all the love of my heart, / for I love You, Lord, / and so need to give myself / to surrender myself into Your hands / with a trust beyond all measure, / because You are my Father.

—Charles de Foucauld, "Prayer of Abandonment to God"[3]

Restoring Relationship

The burnt offering shall be flayed and cut up into its parts. The sons of the priest Aaron shall put fire on the altar and arrange wood on the fire. Aaron's sons the priests shall arrange the parts, with the head and the suet, on the wood that is on the fire on the altar; but its entrails and its legs shall be washed with water. Then the priests shall turn the whole into smoke on the altar as a burnt offering, an offering by fire of pleasing odor to the LORD.

Leviticus 1:6–9

THE WHOLE BURNT offering symbolized the commitment of one's whole life to God and was an atoning sacrifice. Leviticus assumes that God and ancient Israel are in a covenant relationship, and that the relationship will be broken by the effects of sin and uncleanness. This sacrifice provides a possibility for restoring the relationship between people and God. The goal of the ritual is to give the offering, the pleasing aroma, to God in the hope of God's granting atonement. The concern of the text is to regulate the ritual so that it can be acceptable to God. These themes also appear in the New Testament: forgiveness (1 John 1:5–10) and total commitment (Matt 10:34–39; Heb 13:15–16). Also of central importance is the crucifixion as the ultimate sacrifice-effecting atonement (Mark 10:45; Eph 5:2; 1 Pet 1:18–19). Spiritual formation is about the deepening and maturation of one's relationship with God. Sin is the great hindrance to this relationship. As a result, repentance and forgiveness are important parts of our journey toward spiritual maturity.

Offer your small sacrifice today with a spirit of repentance and thankfulness for Jesus Christ's atoning sacrifice.

Jesus, without the cross we would be lost. The only response I know is to drop to my knees and ask forgiveness yet again for all the sins that still plague me. Help me to swallow my pride and repent one more time, ever grateful that your sacrifice makes forgiveness possible. Amen.

Giving God Our Best

Every firstling male born of your herd and flock you shall consecrate to the Lord your God; you shall not do work with your firstling ox nor shear the firstling of your flock. You shall eat it, you together with your household, in the presence of the Lord your God year by year at the place that the Lord will choose. But if it has any defect—any serious defect, such as lameness or blindness—you shall not sacrifice it to the Lord your God.

Deuteronomy 15:19–21

WHEN MAKING A sacrifice, not just any animal from the flock will do, only the firstling male. And the animal is to be whole, without defect. The unblemished quality of the animal demonstrates the seriousness of sacrifice. The principle here is that the best belongs to God, not what is left over. In this way we show how we love God with all our heart, mind, and body.

Today make the effort to offer a small sacrifice to God that represents your best and your first fruits. Dedicate your sacrifice with this prayer:

Lord, take as your right,
and receive as my gift,
all my freedom, my memory,
my understanding and my will.
Whatever I am and whatever I possess,
you have given it to me;
I restore it all to you again,
to be at your disposal,
according to your will.
Give me only a love for you,
and the gift of your grace;
then I am rich enough,
and ask for nothing more.

—St. Ignatius of Loyola

The Honor Due to God

A son honors his father, and servants their master. If then I am a father, where is the honor due me? And if I am a master, where is the respect due me? says the LORD of hosts to you, O priests, who despise my name. You say, "How have we despised your name?" By offering polluted food on my altar. And you say, "How have we polluted it?" By thinking that the LORD's table may be despised. When you offer blind animals in sacrifice, is that not wrong? And when you offer those that are lame or sick, is that not wrong? Try presenting that to your governor; will he be pleased with you or show you favor? says the LORD of hosts. Oh, that someone among you would shut the temple doors, so that you would not kindle fire on my altar in vain! I have no pleasure in you, says the LORD of hosts, and I will not accept an offering from your hands. For from the rising of the sun to its setting my name is great among the nations, and in every place incense is offered to my name, and a pure offering; for my name is great among the nations, says the LORD of hosts.

Malachi 1:6–11

HERE GOD CHALLENGES the spiritually indifferent priests to present their second-rate sacrifices to the Persian governor. If the civil ruler will not accept these, how much less will the jealous God? To offer the Almighty less than our costly and wholehearted devotion is to insult his majesty.

Take a moment to think of the person or thing you have been giving your best to: your spouse, your work, the book you are reading? Ask God for forgiveness for all the times you have not placed him first.

Lord God, you deserve my best. Forgive me for the times I have offered you only the dregs, whether it be half-heartedly muttered prayers or only the money I know I can do without. Help me to remember that there is no better resting place for my heart and indeed all my possessions than with you. Help me to trust and obey you more each day. In your name I pray. Amen.

Heartfelt Devotion

For you have no delight in sacrifice;
    if I were to give a burnt offering, you would not be pleased.
The sacrifice acceptable to God is a broken spirit;
    a broken and contrite heart, O God, you will not despise.
Do good to Zion in your good pleasure;
    rebuild the walls of Jerusalem,
then you will delight in right sacrifices,
    in burnt offerings and whole burnt offerings;
    then bulls will be offered on your altar.

Psalm 51:16–19

THE DANGER OF substituting ritual behavior for heartfelt devotion to God, for moral integrity, and for justice is always close at hand in those public practices that foster group solidarity and depend upon social approval. This is why the prophetic witness, reaffirmed by Jesus, always emphasizes mercy over sacrifice (Matt 9:13; 12:7). Mercy, you see, is of the heart, while sacrifice may or may not be. Sadly, there seems no limit to the perversion of heart that can exist alongside the reciting of creeds and the singing of hymns in sacred settings. What the great prophets relentlessly condemned—pious ritual without inward and outward transformation—was perhaps even worse in the days of Jesus, and it remains a terrible problem today. Just think how different our life would be if we actually lived the words we mouth in religious services. What a tremendous step forward in spiritual formation that would be!

Say this prayer today to help focus your heart as you make your small sacrifice:

Lord, all too often I find myself just going through the motions in church, in prayer, in my daily life. Help me to make my offering to you today with the right attitude of honor and respect. Help me to focus my heart and mind on you along with my actions and words. In your name I pray. Amen.

Sanctified Through Christ

Since the law has only a shadow of the good things to come and not the true form of these realities, it can never, by the same sacrifices that are continually offered year after year, make perfect those who approach. Otherwise, would they not have ceased being offered, since the worshipers, cleansed once for all, would no longer have any consciousness of sin? But in these sacrifices there is a reminder of sin year after year. For it is impossible for the blood of bulls and goats to take away sins. Consequently, when Christ came into the world, he said,

"Sacrifices and offerings you have not desired, / but a body you have prepared for me; / in burnt offerings and sin offerings / you have taken no pleasure, / Then I said, 'See, God, I have to come to do your will, O God.'"

He abolishes the first in order to establish the second. And it is by God's will that we have been sanctified through the offering of the body of Jesus Christ once for all.

Hebrews 10:1–7a, 9b–10

THE SELF-SACRIFICE OF Jesus was so perfect and effective that it rendered the first covenant "obsolete" (8:13), initiating the new and better covenant foreseen by the prophet Jeremiah (8:1–13). Jesus' sacrifice is also of special significance for the spiritual life. The essential element in spiritual formation is always spiritual transformation, which is effected by the acceptance of the redeeming sacrifice of Jesus. Progress in the spiritual life is not an automatic evolutionary process. Spiritual progress is the result of deliberate and discerning choices. Like a marriage, it is entered into by conscious commitment. We are to "lay aside every weight and the sin that clings so closely, and . . . run with perseverance the race that is set before us, looking to Jesus the pioneer and perfecter of our faith" (12:1–2).

Today pray for a fuller understanding of Jesus' death as a sacrifice for us.

Jesus: The Atoning Sacrifice for the World

My little children, I am writing these things to you so that you may not sin. But if anyone does sin, we have an advocate with the Father, Jesus Christ the righteous; and he is the atoning sacrifice for our sins, and not for ours only but also for the sins of the whole world.

1 John 2:1–2

THE KEY TO the Christian life is to know and love Christ, which is reflected both in our responsiveness to Jesus' guidance and in a readiness to confess times of failure. Jesus keeps the way clear for us to come to him. His death offers purification for the whole world, and now he prays to the Father for us, to keep us cleansed and filled with God's love. Jesus wants us close enough to actually live in him, and in this way we can walk with him and become more like him. We can live as we were created to live. Though this call to God's loving nature and ways has existed from the beginning, it has now assumed newness in its embodiment in Christ and in us as we abide in him. This is no theoretical belief system, but a dynamic and transforming embrace.

Offer this prayer today as you thank Jesus for his sacrifice and make your own small sacrifice in a recognition of his:

O Gracious God, I am fully aware that I am unworthy. I deserve to be a brother of Satan and not of Christ. But Christ, your dear Son, died and rose for me. I am his brother. He earnestly desires that I should believe him, without doubt and fear. I need no longer regard myself as unworthy and full of sin. For this I love and thank him from my heart. Praise be to the faithful Savior, for he is so gracious and merciful as are you and the Holy Spirit in eternity. Amen.

—Martin Luther, *Luther's Prayers*[4]

The Christ Way of Life

They are now justified by his grace as a gift, through the redemption that is in Christ Jesus, whom God put forward as a sacrifice of atonement by his blood, effective through faith. He did this to show his righteousness, because in his divine forbearance he had passed over the sins previously committed.

Romans 3:24–25

ALL THE ENERGY and action of the Christian life come from Jesus: God in Christ sets us right with himself. "Redemption" and "atonement" are gateway words into vast mysteries, words we cannot hope to completely comprehend, but ones we can spend the rest of our lives entering into and letting continuously expand our living space. The beyond-our-comprehension reality at the heart of the universe is that God in Christ on the cross has forgiven all our sins, set us right with him, and gathered us into his righteousness. We cannot comprehend it, but we can most certainly live it—a way of life in which everything about us is and continues to be formed in the likeness of Christ.

Say this prayer as you ask God for the strength and courage to sacrifice yourself to him:

Lord, I can never replicate Jesus' sacrifice, but just as Christ did, I too need to completely give myself to you, to allow you to shape me into the image of Christ. Help me to relinquish the illusion of control I clutch so tightly and to recognize you as the true master of my life. Amen.

Joyful and Lavish Giving

Now while Jesus was at Bethany in the house of Simon the leper, a woman came to him with an alabaster jar of very costly ointment, and she poured it on his head as he sat at the table. But when the disciples saw it, they were angry and said, "Why this waste? For this ointment could have been sold for a large sum, and the money given to the poor." But Jesus, aware of this, said to them, "Why do you trouble the woman? She has performed a good service for me. For you always have the poor with you, but you will not always have me. By pouring this ointment on my body she has prepared me for burial. Truly I tell you, wherever this good news is proclaimed in the whole world, what she has done will be told in remembrance of her."

Matthew 26:6–13

THE WOMAN OF this story has made the sacrifice of offering a very expensive gift to Jesus, so lavish that the disciples see it as wasteful. Jesus quickly corrects their understanding: nothing given to God is a waste. Yet today most of us still find ourselves guilty of skimping on, or at least second-guessing, our financial gifts—both to church and to charity. Like the widow who offered her two small copper coins (Mark 12:42; Luke 21:2), we too please God when we give to him something that requires us to go without.

Throughout the next ten days challenge yourself to give an extravagant gift, one that requires you to sacrifice in some way. To help you get in the proper frame of mind, try Richard Foster's advice and think of all your finances and possessions as already stamped with God's ownership. But lavish gifts are not limited to financial ones. Perhaps you feel that your financial giving is adequate and are guided to offer a gift of another kind, such as committing to attend a mission trip, certainly a gift of time and service. Whatever your gift may be, our prayer is that it may provide a source of spiritual renewal. As Foster writes, "If our spiritual vitality seems low, if Bible study produces only dusty words, if prayer seems hollow and empty, then perhaps a prescription of lavish and joyful giving is just what we need."[5]

Sacrificial Giving

That day Gad came to David and said to him, "Go up and erect an altar to the LORD on the threshing floor of Araunah the Jebusite." Following Gad's instructions, David went up, as the LORD had commanded. When Araunah looked down, he saw the king and his servants coming toward him; and Araunah went out and prostrated himself before the king with his face to the ground. Araunah said, "Why has my lord the king come to his servant?" David said, "To buy the threshing floor from you in order to build an altar to the LORD, so that the plague may be averted from the people." Then Araunah said to David, "Let my lord the king take and offer up what seems good to him; here are the oxen for the burnt offering, and the threshing sledges and the yokes of the oxen for the wood. All this, O king, Araunah gives to the king." And Araunah said to the king, "May the LORD your God respond favorably to you."

But the king said to Araunah, "No, but I will buy them from you for a price: I will not offer burnt offerings to the LORD my God that cost me nothing." So David bought the threshing floor and the oxen for fifty shekels of silver. David built there an altar to the LORD, and offered burnt offerings and offerings of well-being. So the LORD answered his supplication for the land, and the plague was averted from Israel.

2 Samuel 24:18–25

DAVID UNDERSTANDS THAT, although there is nothing that God needs from him, there is nonetheless an inescapable relationship between his spirituality and his level of giving. There is no benefit in giving back to God what does not press David to sacrifice something of his own cherished possessions. In our own age of unprecedented economic growth and prosperity, such sacrificial giving would be a healthy corrective to the Church.

Try to recall another biblical story that reinforces this teaching. How does this example help you to think about your own "joyful and lavish gift"?

⌐ Joyful and Lavish Giving

Two Copper Coins

[Jesus] sat down opposite the treasury, and watched the crowd putting money into the treasury. Many rich people put in large sums. A poor widow came and put in two small copper coins, which are worth a penny. Then he called the disciples and said to them, "Truly I tell you, this poor widow has put in more than all those who are contributing to the treasury. For all of them have contributed out of their abundance; but she out of her poverty has put in everything she had, all she had to live on."

Mark 12:41–44

IN THE MIDST of religious and political power brokers, surrounded by the large, impressive buildings of Jerusalem, a lone, poor widow makes her quiet way into the Temple and gives her two small coins. She is the towering example of faithfulness and generosity. This widow, who has so little materially, has great faith. She knows that her welfare depends on God and her neighbors, not her own resources.

As you reflect on the widow's example, consider how the sacrifice of money is a path to spiritual formation.

"Money is an effective way of showing our love to God because it is so much a part of us. One economist put it this way: 'Money as a form of power is so intimately related to the possessor that one cannot consistently give money without giving self.' In a sense, money is coined personality, so tied to who we are that when we give it we are giving ourselves. We sing, 'Take my life and let it be, consecrated, Lord, to Thee.' But we must flesh out that consecration in specific ways, which is why the next line of the hymn says, 'Take my silver and my gold, not a mite would I withhold.' We consecrate ourselves by consecrating our money."

—Richard J. Foster, *The Challenge of the Disciplined Life*[6]

Kingdom Rewards for Earthly Sacrifices

Then [a young man] came to [Jesus] and said, "Teacher, what good deed must I do to have eternal life? I have kept all [the commandments]; what do I still lack?" Jesus said to him, "If you wish to be perfect, go, sell your possessions, and give the money to the poor, and you will have treasure in heaven; then come, follow me." When the young man heard this word, he went away grieving, for he had many possessions.

Then Peter said in reply, "Look, we have left everything and followed you. What then will we have?" Jesus said to them, "Truly I tell you, at the renewal of all things, when the Son of Man is seated on the throne of his glory, you who have followed me will also sit on twelve thrones, judging the twelve tribes of Israel. And everyone who has left houses or brothers or sisters or father or mother or children or fields, for my name's sake, will receive a hundredfold, and will inherit eternal life."

Matthew 19:16, 20b–22, 27–29

A RICH PERSON is said to be able to enter God's realm or eternal life only by God's grace. In all cases, salvation is a divine action, not a human one. The theme of heavenly, or eschatological, reward is a regular one in wisdom literature. Jesus assures Peter that there are such rewards in the kingdom for those who have made sacrifices here.

As you think about making your own gift, consider all God's earthly gifts and heavenly promises. How have they made you feel about making sacrifices? Do they humble you? Do they make you want to give something, anything in return?

"The promises made by Jesus have one other excellent effect when duly considered. They tend to humble. That is one reason why the rewards of the kingdom of heaven are so great. God bestows His gifts so as at once to glorify the Giver and to humble the receiver."

Alexander Balmain Bruce, *Training of the Twelve*[7]

⌐ Joyful and Lavish Giving

In Giving We Receive

We want you to know, brothers and sisters, about the grace of God that has been granted to the churches of Macedonia; for during a severe ordeal of affliction, their abundant joy and their extreme poverty have overflowed in a wealth of generosity on their part. For as I can testify, they voluntarily gave according to their means, and even beyond their means, begging us earnestly for the privilege of sharing in this ministry to the saints.

The point is this: the ones who sows sparingly will also reap sparingly, and the one who sows bountifully will also reap bountifully. Each of you must give as you have made up your mind, not reluctantly or under compulsion, for God loves a cheerful giver. And God is able to provide you with every blessing in abundance, so that by always having enough of everything, you may share abundantly in every good work.

2 Corinthians 8:1–4; 9:6–8

IT IS IN giving that we receive. Giving outstrips receiving, because it strengthens and expands us, enabling us to experience the true scope of our power. Paul here is talking about philanthropy, but the point applies to other forms of giving as well. Those who are often on the receiving end of things eventually must reclaim their dignity by turning to giving themselves. Since what we have to give and what is needed constantly vary, there is little doubt that all can partake in the spiritual practice of giving if they train their eyes to see. The trick in giving is to give what is needed, not simply what one has in excess, whether money, advice, or even one's presence.

What will you receive from your planned gift?

Grant that we may not so much seek to be consoled as to console; to be understood as to understand; to be loved as to love. For it is in giving that we receive, it is in pardoning that we are pardoned, and it is in dying that we are born to eternal life. Amen.

—St. Francis of Assisi

Sacrificing to Obey God's Law

Naomi, her mother-in-law, said to [Ruth], "My daughter, I need to seek some security for you, so that it may be well with you. Now here is our kinsman Boaz, with whose young women you have been working. When he lies down, observe the place where he lies; then, go and uncover his feet and lie down; and he will tell you what to do."

So she went down to the threshing floor and did just as her mother-in-law instructed her. He said, "Who are you?" And she answered, "I am Ruth, your servant; spread your cloak over your servant, for you are next-of-kin." He said, "May you be blessed by the LORD, my daughter. And now, my daughter, do not be afraid. I will do for you all that you ask, for all the assembly of my people know that you are a worthy woman."

Ruth 3:1–2a, 4, 6, 9–10a, 11

BOAZ HAD MANY other commitments and responsibilities, but out of obedience to God's law he was willing to make the necessary sacrifices to take on Ruth and her mother-in-law, Naomi. The Hebrew community of faith was obligated by the stipulations of the Mosaic covenant to practice justice toward the disadvantaged—the poor, widows, orphans, resident aliens (Exod 22:22; Deut 24:14–22). Mosaic law also dictated that the male next-of-kin was to marry a widow in order to secure an inheritance for the dead husband (Deut 25:5–10). The Christian community of faith shoulders a similar responsibility, since Christ calls us to love our neighbors as ourselves (James 2:8). Such care for the socially disadvantaged is "religion that is pure and undefiled before God" (James 1:27).

Connect, for the moment, the Mosaic law in which a male next-of-kin marries a widow to secure an inheritance for the dead husband (Deut 25:5–10) to that of the command of Christ to "love your neighbor as yourself" (Matt 22:39). What sacrifices would the brother of a dead man have to make to marry his widow? What sacrifices do we have to make to love our neighbor? How similar are they?

Joyful and Lavish Giving

Sacrificing All

Abram was very rich in livestock, in silver, and in gold. Now Lot, who went with Abram, also had flocks and herds and tents, so that the land could not support both of them living together.

Then Abram said to Lot, "Let there be no strife between you and me, and between your herders and my herders; for we are kindred. Is not the whole land before you? Separate yourself from me. If you take the left hand, then I will go to the right; or if you take the right hand, then I will go to the left." Lot looked about him and saw that the plain of the Jordan was well watered everywhere like the garden of the LORD. So Lot chose for himself all the plain of the Jordan. Abram settled into the land of Canaan.

The LORD said to Abram, after Lot had separated from him, "Raise your eyes now, and look from the place where you are, northward and southward and eastward and westward; for all the land that you see I will give to you and to your offspring forever. I will make your offspring like the dust of the earth; so that if one can count the dust of the earth, your offspring can also be counted. Rise up, walk through the length and the breadth of the land, for I will give it to you."

Genesis 13:2, 5–6a, 8–10a, 11a, 12a, 14–17

ALL CAN LEARN from the pattern of submission and sacrifice that made Abraham's faith possible. His willingness to sacrifice his belongings, his relationships, his security, and even his child allowed God the room to act in his life. Faith often means taking a voluntary step from the known into the unknown in response to God's leading. And faith often requires a voluntary giving away of persons, positions, or possessions in response to God's nudging. It can involve acts of great sacrifice.

Ponder this quote as you work to practice sacrificial submission:
"As thou wilt, what thou wilt, when thou wilt."

—Thomas à Kempis, *The Imitation of Christ*

Training in Godliness

Do you not know that in a race the runners all compete, but only one receives the prize? Run in such a way that you may win it. Athletes exercise self-control in all things; they do it to receive a perishable wreath, but we an imperishable one. So I do not run aimlessly, nor do I box as though beating the air; but I punish my body and enslave it, so that after proclaiming to others I myself should not be disqualified.

1 Corinthians 9:23–27

AFTER MEETING CHRIST on the Damascus road Paul prayed and fasted for three days. Shortly after his conversion he spent a long period of time, thought to be three years, in solitude in the Arabian desert. Throughout his years of ministry and travel Paul spent time in fasting and prayer, both alone and with his ministry partners. He modeled continual self-sacrifice, simplicity, frugality, and service. He worked to support his ministry life and gracefully endured imprisonment and beatings. He often went without food, sleep, or adequate clothes, and he dealt in love and perseverance with those who took him for granted. Paul asked his fellow Christians to imitate him and "train . . . in godliness" (1 Tim 4:7), as he was doing, in a way similar to physical training.

Today let the example of Paul inspire you in your own joyful and lavish gift or sacrifice.

"Paul and his Lord were people of immense power, who saw clearly the wayward ways the world considered natural. With calm premeditation and clear vision of a deeper order, they took their stand always among those 'last who shall be first' mentioned repeatedly in the Gospels. With their feet planted in the deeper order of God, they lived lives of utter self-sacrifice and abandonment, seeing in such a life the highest possible personal attainment."

—Dallas Willard, *The Spirit of the Disciplines* [8]

_____

Joyful and Lavish Giving

Do Justice

"With what shall I come before the LORD,
   and bow myself before God on high?
Shall I come before him with burnt offerings,
   with calves a year old?
Will the LORD be pleased with thousands of rams,
   with ten thousands of rivers of oil?
Shall I give my firstborn for my transgression,
   the fruit of my body for the sin of my soul?"
He has told you, O mortal, what is good;
   and what does the LORD require of you
but to do justice, and to love kindness,
   and to walk humbly with your God?

Micah 6:6–8

THESE WORDS ARE the best known of Micah's prophecy. The Lord despises empty religious rituals. For their part, God's people must uphold the rights of the poor and downtrodden in society, embody good-heartedness and mercy in relation to others, and live in close communion with God. Christian spiritual formation ought not and, indeed, cannot be divorced from compassionate social engagement.

Another way we can make sacrifices is to try to put the needs of our neighbors before our own, to practice the spirit of justice and kindness in our lives. What are some ways you have done so in the past? What are some ways you can do so now? How will your "joyful and lavish gift" benefit others?

— Joyful and Lavish Giving

Feed My Sheep

When they had finished breakfast, Jesus said to Simon Peter, "Simon son of John, do you love me more than these?" He said to him, "Yes, Lord; you know that I love you." Jesus said to him, "Feed my lambs." A second time he said to him, "Simon son of John, do you love me?" He said to him, "Yes, Lord; you know that I love you." Jesus said to him, "Tend my sheep." He said to him the third time, "Simon son of John, do you love me?" Peter felt hurt because he said to him the third time, "Do you love me?" And he said to him, "Lord, you know everything; you know that I love you." Jesus said to him, "Feed my sheep. Very truly, I tell you, when you were younger, you used to fasten your own belt and to go wherever you wished. But when you grow old, you will stretch out your hands, and someone else will fasten a belt around you and take you where you do not wish to go." (He said this to indicate the kind of death by which he would glorify God.) After this he said to him, "Follow me."

John 21:15–19

IN OTHER VERSES in John, Jesus talks about laying down his life (10:11), Peter says he is willing to lay down his life for Jesus (13:37), and Jesus says, "No one has greater love than this, to lay down one's life for one's friends" (15:13). What else can we do in response to Jesus' act of love and sacrifice but to respond with love to others? This narrative's many themes challenge us—genuine love, laying down one's life, and shepherding (10:11–18; 13:36–38; 21:15–17). What a wonder that Jesus commissions us to do his work even though we love so inadequately!

Jesus, I am so humbled when I think of your death on the cross. Truly there could be no greater act of love. Please help me to honor your sacrifice by sacrificing when and where I can. Show me the ways in which I can feed your sheep. In your name I pray. Amen.

For more verses on sacrifice and ideas on how to practice the discipline of sacrifice, see the Responding exercises and Spiritual Disciplines Index in *The Life with God Bible*.

Silence

Closing off the inner self from "sounds," whether noise, music, or words, so that we may better still the chatter and clatter of our noisy hearts and be increasingly attentive to God

Many of us spend our lives without so much as a hint of silence. All the background noise in our lives makes it very difficult for us to hear even our own innermost thoughts, let alone God. It may be worth asking ourselves why we need so much entertaining.

To practice the discipline of silence is to turn it all off in order to better listen to God. Certainly it is helpful to try to be alone in a place of external quiet to practice silence; silence is closely tied with solitude. Yet silence does not require being alone or even the absence of words. As Richard Foster explains, "Though silence sometimes involves the absence of speech, it always involves the act of listening. Simply to refrain from talking, without a heart listening to God, is not silence."[1] Our aim is to cultivate an inner silence, so that we can turn our hearts to God even while we hear background noise or converse with others.

Silence also involves the judicious use of words. So many times in conversing with others, we are not truly listening, but instead thinking about what we will say next. The practice of silence teaches us to control our tongue, so that we can listen to others as well as to God. Yet this does not mean that we should never speak. As Mordecai told Esther when he asked her to help him fight the king's edict to kill all the Jews, "If you keep silence at such a time as this, relief and deliverance will rise for the Jews from another quarter, but you and your father's family will perish" (Esther 4:14a). If we do not speak up when we should, we are not practicing the Spiritual Discipline of silence.

For God alone my soul waits in silence, / for my hope is from him.
—Psalm 62:5

Silence

Be Still, and Know That I Am God

"Be still, and know that I am God!
   I am exalted among the nations,
   I am exalted in the earth."

Psalm 46:10

FOR EACH OF the next ten days seek to spend at least fifteen minutes in silence. It is hard to find complete silence anymore. You will probably not be able to completely get away from the noises of electronics, traffic, or people in the vicinity. But try to find the quietest place you can, and make sure that you honor the silence by not speaking, playing music, having the TV on, or bringing your phone. Begin each time of silence with a short prayer asking the Lord to help you block out any extra noise, so that you can focus on God. You may want to spend some of the time studying Scripture or praying, but mostly seek to quietly listen for whatever God may tell you. Write in your journal any insights that come to you from your silent times. Take as inspiration these words from Dietrich Bonhoeffer: "Let none expect from silence anything but a direct encounter with the Word of God, for the sake of which he has entered into silence. But this encounter will be given to him. The Christian will not lay down any conditions as to what he expects or hopes to get from this encounter. If he will simply accept it, his silence will be richly rewarded."[2]

Spiritual Practice

A Sound of Sheer Silence

[The angel of the LORD] said, "Go out and stand on the mountain before the LORD, for the LORD is about to pass by." Now there was a great wind, so strong that it was splitting mountains and breaking rocks in pieces before the LORD, but the LORD was not in the wind; and after the wind an earthquake, but the LORD was not in the earthquake; and after the earthquake a fire, but the LORD was not in the fire; and after the fire a sound of sheer silence. When Elijah heard it, he wrapped his face in his mantle and went out and stood at the entrance of the cave. Then there came a voice to him that said, "What are you doing here, Elijah?" He answered, "I have been very zealous for the LORD, the God of hosts; for the Israelites have forsaken your covenant, thrown down your altars, and killed your prophets with the sword. I alone am left, and they are seeking my life, to take it away." Then the LORD said to him, "Go, return on your way to the wilderness of Damascus; when you arrive, you shall anoint Hazael as king over Aram. Also you shall anoint Jehu son of Nimshi as king over Israel; and you shall anoint Elisha son of Shaphat of Abel-meholah as prophet in your place."

1 Kings 19:11–16

WORN OUT AND frightened by his ministry and the very real threat against his life, Elijah has hidden in a cave, where he is visited by the angel of the Lord. Through this experience Elijah found that Yahweh was not in the earthquake, wind, or fire, but in the silence. Moses experienced divine fireworks and Elijah experienced "sheer silence," but both experienced God. This is a vital teaching for us. God may come to us in the dramatic and spectacular or in the hidden and the ordinary. However God comes, we are to hear and obey.

Dallas Willard writes, "Silence is frightening because it strips us as nothing else does, throwing us upon the stark realities of our life."[3] Are you frightened to begin your practice of silence? Why or why not?

⟶ Be Still, and Know That I Am God

My Soul Waits in Silence

For God alone my soul waits in silence;
   from him comes my salvation.
He alone is my rock and my salvation,
   my fortress; I shall never be shaken.
For God alone my soul waits in silence,
   for my hope is from him.

Psalm 62:1–2, 5

PSALM 62 IS a strong call to trust in God alone. Too many times we take the attitude that it is a waste of time to "wait" on the Lord, much less quiet our soul while waiting. But the psalmist waits for God and quiets his soul, because he recognizes that God fulfills all of his needs and hopes.

Consider how waiting on God while quieting your soul changes your perception of God's provision; then set aside ten minutes to try it. What did you experience?

In Quietness and in Trust
Shall Be Your Strength

For thus said the Lord GOD, the Holy One of Israel;
In returning and rest you shall be saved;
   in quietness and in trust shall be your strength.

Isaiah 30:15

THE LINES OF this verse constitute what is probably the most significant affirmation of the prophet Isaiah in the eighth century BCE. Both Isaiah 7:9 and this text urge complete reliance upon Yahweh as the alternative to frantic, anxious military and political posturing. Isaiah is not a pacifist; rather, he believes that trust in Yahweh is the taproot of security. All trust in armaments and alliances, he reasons, is an act of mistrust and idolatry that will only lead to destruction. The assurance of faith is the conviction that anxious self-securing does not work in the real world. The phrase "returning and rest" is an affirmation that faith is quiet confidence, which is decisive for being safe and well in the world.

This verse has the same feel as Psalm 46:10, "Be still, and know that I am God." We are often so frantic today, running this way and that to secure our finances, our job prospects, our children's futures. But, instead, God calls us to quietness—in quiet and in trust we will find our strength. Meditate on these words for a few moments. How do they speak to your life?

— Be Still, and Know That I Am God

I Will Keep a Muzzle on My Mouth

I said, "I will guard my ways / that I may not sin with my tongue; /
I will keep a muzzle on my mouth / as long as the wicked are in my
presence." / I was silent and still; / I held my peace to no avail; / my
distress grew worse, / my heart became hot within me. / While I
mused, the fire burned; / then I spoke with my tongue. / "Lord, let
me know my end, / and what is the measure of my days; / let me
know how fleeting my life is. / And now, O Lord, what do I wait
for? / My hope is in you. / Deliver me from my transgressions. / Do
not make me the scorn of the fool. / I am silent; I do not open my
mouth, / for it is you who have done it."

Psalm 39:1–4, 7–9

THE PSALMS AND the rest of the Bible warn us that our mouths can
get us in a lot of trouble. The singer here has worked hard to avoid
that, even shutting down whatever damning words he would like to say
about the wicked. But then anguished questions spill out, some echoing
the language of Ecclesiastes. Life is so fragile, so short, like a puff of air,
a passing shadow. How long do I have? What does it mean anyway? But
the singer also hopes in God and seeks deliverance from sin. Loose-end
questions and hope in God often exist together in the one who seeks a
life with God.

Can you relate to the struggle of the singer? Have you ever tried to keep
words back that you feared would damage your relationship with someone? With God? Are there questions that you are afraid to ask God? Is
this a case in which talking to God is better than saying nothing?

⁀ Be Still, and Know That I Am God

He Did Not Open His Mouth

He was oppressed, and he was afflicted,
    yet he did not open his mouth;
like a lamb that is led to the slaughter,
    and like a sheep that before its shearers is silent,
    so he did not open his mouth.

Isaiah 53:7

THESE FAMILIAR WORDS about how the servant would suffer in silence are from one of the Servant Songs in Isaiah. These verses were understood by the early Church as an anticipatory reference to Jesus Christ, who would suffer in saving and redemptive ways. That particular connection of this imagery to Jesus is explicit in Acts (see 8:32–35). There Isaiah 53:7–8 is quoted and Philip the evangelist offers an interpretation that specifically connects the Isaiah text to Jesus.

Reflect on the silence of the sheep before the shearers and the lamb led to slaughter. What light do these images shed on Jesus' sacrifice? What is the significance of suffering in silence?

Dear Lord, Jesus took on the sins of the world in silence, yet I have trouble even spending a few minutes that way. I ask for strength to continue my practice of silent time with you, that I may continue to learn from Jesus' example of letting his actions speak louder than his words. In your name I pray. Amen.

❧ Be Still, and Know That I Am God

Silence in Heaven

When the Lamb opened the seventh seal, there was silence in heaven for about half an hour. And I saw the seven angels who stand before God, and seven trumpets were given to them.

Another angel with a golden censer came and stood at the altar; he was given a great quantity of incense to offer with the prayers of all the saints on the golden altar that is before the throne.

Revelation 8:1–3

AT THE BEGINNING of Revelation 8, we are at the moment when, quite literally, all hell is about to break loose. But heaven does not prepare for holy war with bombastic speeches or missiles and bombs. Instead, a hush falls over the heavenly court, the calm before the storm. The prayers of the faithful are placed upon the altar. At long last those noiseless cries for justice are about to be answered.

Just as sheer silence announced God's presence to Elijah, here we see silence in heaven. Why do you think God chooses silence? When you spend your time today in silence, try to imagine the thick, profound silence described in the verse.

~ Be Still, and Know That I Am God

Waiting Quietly

The steadfast love of the LORD never ceases, / his mercies never come to an end; / they are new every morning; / great is your faithfulness. / "The LORD is my portion," says my soul, / "therefore I will hope in him." / The LORD is good to those who wait for him, / to the soul that seeks him. / It is good that one should wait quietly / for the salvation of the LORD. / It is good for one to bear / the yoke in youth, / to sit alone in silence / when the Lord has imposed it, / to put one's mouth to the dust / (there may yet be hope), / to give one's cheek to the smiter / and be filled with insults.

Lamentations 3:22–30

THE BOOK OF Lamentations is a collection of poetry mourning the horribly cataclysmic destruction of Jerusalem in 587 BCE. Yet even in the middle of its soul-searing lament, there is this section of doxology, of praise. Is this statement of God's love only a pious fraud? Does this grieving community really feel that God is loving, merciful, and faithful? Perhaps it is only after honest, heartfelt grief that we are able to sing doxology. Perhaps the People of God have found these truths about God's good reiterated when they were able to wait quietly, to sit alone in silence. Here, in the middle of Lamentations, is an extraordinary statement of faith, faith that is born of doubt, despair, and tears. Perhaps that is the best sort of faith.

Have you ever been able to wait quietly for the Lord in times of trouble and grief or when you could not hear him? Think about your time of silence today as waiting for the Lord. How does God meet you?

~ *Be Still, and Know That I Am God*

In Quiet Resting Places

Until a spirit from on high is poured out on us
    and then the wilderness becomes a fruitful field,
    and the fruitful field is deemed a forest.
Then justice will dwell in the wilderness,
    and righteousness abide in the fruitful field.
The effect of righteousness will be peace,
    and the result of righteousness, quietness and trust forever.
My people will abide in a peaceful habitation,
    in secure dwellings, and in quiet resting places.

Isaiah 32:15–18

AGAIN IT IS promised, after so much judgment and punishment, that the ultimate outcome for God's people will be justice and righteousness and peace. Quiet is an important component of this happy future. The earlier part of the chapter had imagined that this would come through the Davidic dynasty. In these verses, however, there is no mention of such a king. It is simply the case that God will work such a newness and such a goodness; the People of God are urged to have confidence to wait for the good gifts that God will yet give in the future.

What does it mean for righteousness to result in quietness? Close your eyes. Picture the complete quietness of your soul. Feel the peace settling over you, a glimpse of the kingdom to come. How can you better cultivate quietness throughout your day?

Quieting the Soul

O Lord, my head is not lifted up,
    my eyes are not raised too high;
I do not occupy myself with things
    too great and too marvelous for me.
But I have calmed and quieted my soul,
    like a weaned child with its mother;
    my soul is like the weaned child that is with me.
O Israel, hope in the Lord
    from this time on and forevermore.

Psalm 131:1–3

Psalm 131 is an ode to humility and a quiet soul. One of the core obstacles to spiritual maturity and life at its best is overreaching ambition. The need to run the world, to control what happens, saps our energy and sabotages our ability to trust.

What have you learned about what surroundings are necessary to achieve a calm and quiet soul? How can these be cultivated?

"In quiet and silence the faithful soul makes progress, the hidden meanings of the Scripture become clear, and the eyes weep with devotion every night. Even as one learns to grow still, he draws closer to the Creator and father from the hurly-burly of the world. As one divests himself of friends and acquaintances, he is visited by God and his holy angels."

—Thomas à Kempis, *The Imitation of Christ*[4]

Listening

When you are disturbed, do not sin;
   ponder it on your beds, and be silent.

Psalm 4:4

GOD CALLS US to silence. A large part of pondering in silence is listening for God's guiding word. Yet in prayer and in life we tend to talk more than we listen. Sometime in the next ten days, try to spend an entire day in relative silence, speaking as little as possible, leaving off the radio, music player, and TV. Make a concentrated effort to listen, to God and others. See what God chooses to show you about the familiar world around you when you eliminate some of the distractions that are usually a part of your life. Be especially aware of your interactions with other people. Practicing silence with others does not mean never speaking, but rather choosing your words carefully and listening to the words of others. Your practice may show you some surprising insights about how little you listen on a regular basis.

Spiritual Practice

Be Silent Before the Lord

Be silent before the Lord GOD!
For the day of the LORD is at hand;
the LORD has prepared a sacrifice,
he has consecrated his guests.

Zephaniah 1:7

THE SUMMONS TO be silent is a call to listen and acknowledge the Lord. Activity can preclude hearing what God is saying and doing. Busyness and being driven by a culture that overvalues what can be achieved, where worth is associated by what is done, can hinder believers' "being" with God. The call to silence is a contemplative call to pay attention to God, to be still in the midst of life's activities, and to draw near to the One in whom "we live and move and have our being" (Acts 17:28).

Lord, teach me to listen. The times are noisy and my ears are weary with the thousand raucous sounds which continually assault them. Give me the spirit of the boy Samuel when he said to Thee, "Speak, for Thy servant heareth." Let me hear Thee speaking in my heart. Let me get used to the sound of Thy voice, that its tones may be familiar when the sounds of earth die away and the only sound will be the music of Thy speaking voice. Amen.

—A.W. Tozer, *The Pursuit of God*[5]

― Listening

Let All the Earth Keep Silence

What use is an idol
    once its maker has shaped it—
    a cast image, a teacher of lies?
For its maker trusts in what has been made,
    though the product is only an idol that cannot speak!
Alas for you who say to the wood, "Wake up!"
    to silent stone, "Rouse yourself!"
    Can it teach?
See, it is gold and silver plated
    and there is no breath in it at all.
But the LORD is in his holy temple;
    let all the earth keep silence before him!

Habakkuk 2:18–20

IN CONTRAST TO the idol that is silent and cannot speak or answer us, God calls *us* to silence. "Let all the earth keep silence before him!" Silence before God is the appropriate response to God's holiness. It is a Spiritual Discipline of the first order.

Before you embark on your day of silence, reflect on this quote:

"Silence is the simple stillness of the individual under the Word of God. We are silent before hearing the Word because our thoughts are already directed to the Word, as a child is quiet when he enters his father's room. We are silent after hearing the Word because the Word is still speaking and dwelling within us. We are silent at the beginning of the day because God should have the first word, and we are silent before going to sleep because the last word also belongs to God."

—Dietrich Bonhoeffer, *Life Together*[6]

An Intelligent Person Remains Silent

Whoever belittles another lacks sense,
    but an intelligent person remains silent.
A gossip goes about telling secrets,
    but one who is trustworthy in spirit keeps a confidence.

Proverbs 11:12–13

SILENCE IS A Spiritual Discipline to be practiced not just in meditation when we are alone and listening for God's guiding voice, but also when we are with others and need to hold back words that are harsh, hurtful, or boastful.

Meditate on this quote for a few minutes, and as you go about your day try to be especially aware of ways in which you might need to practice silence in your relationships:

"The mark of solitude is silence, as speech is the mark of community. Silence and speech have the same inner correspondence and difference as do solitude and community. One does not exist without the other. Right speech comes out of silence, and right silence comes out of speech."

—Dietrich Bonhoeffer, *Life Together*[7]

Taming the Tongue

Not many of you should become teachers, my brothers and sisters, for you know that we who teach will be judged with greater strictness. For all of us make many mistakes. Anyone who makes no mistakes in speaking is perfect, able to keep the whole body in check with a bridle. If we put bits into the mouths of horses to make them obey us, we guide their whole bodies. Or look at ships: though they are so large that it takes strong winds to drive them, yet they are guided by a very small rudder wherever the will of the pilot directs. So also the tongue is a small member, yet it boasts of great exploits.

How great a forest is set ablaze by a small fire! And the tongue is a fire. For every species of beast and bird, of reptile and sea creature, can be tamed and has been tamed by the human species, but no one can tame the tongue—a restless evil, full of deadly poison. With it we bless the Lord and Father, and with it we curse those who are made in the likeness of God. From the same mouth come blessing and cursing. My brothers and sisters, this ought not to be so. Does a spring pour forth from the same opening both fresh and brackish water?

James 3:1–6a, 7–11

SINCE SINS OF speech are so prevalent in human interaction, James offers wisdom to church leaders and members on how these can be avoided in their fellowship. Those who teach must weigh their words with care. But all Christians must be careful with the use of the tongue. A Christian's speech should bless, not berate or abuse. The tongue betrays the world that is in one's heart; it is a microcosm of the inner self.

Father God, show me where I hide behind words or fill silences with them. Help me to know when to speak and when to keep silent, during my day of silence and throughout my life. In your name I pray. Amen.

A Word Fitly Spoken

Those who guard their mouths preserve their lives;
  those who open wide their lips come to ruin.
A fool takes no pleasure in understanding,
  but only in expressing personal opinion.
The words of the mouth are deep waters;
  the fountain of wisdom is a gushing stream.
A fool's lips bring strife,
  and a fool's mouth invites a flogging.
The mouths of fools are their ruin,
  and their lips a snare to themselves.
The words of a whisperer are like delicious morsels;
  they go down into the inner parts of the body.
Death and life are in the power of the tongue,
  and those who love it will eat its fruits.
A word fitly spoken
  is like apples of gold in a setting of silver.

Proverbs 13:3; 18:2, 4, 6–8, 21; 25:11

A NUMBER OF sayings in Proverbs emphasize the dangers of the unguarded tongue, such as insensitivity to others and foolishly expressing an opinion without listening. The language used, for example, "death and life are in the power of the tongue," make it clear that what we say and do not say is extremely important.

Statements such as these show the old nursery rhyme, "Sticks and stones will break my bones, but words will never hurt me," to be patently untrue. Why do you think careless speech is such a focus of wisdom literature in books like Proverbs? In your own life, when have thoughtless words caused lasting damage? Or when have carefully chosen words "fitly spoken" made a positive difference?

Listening

No One Spoke a Word

Now when Job's three friends heard of all these troubles that had come upon him, each of them set out from his home—Eliphaz the Temanite, Bildad the Shuhite, and Zophar the Naamathite. They met together to go and console and comfort him. When they saw him from a distance, they did not recognize him, and they raised their voices and wept aloud; they tore their robes and threw dust in the air upon their heads. They sat with him on the ground seven days and seven nights, and no one spoke a word to him, for they saw that his suffering was very great.

Job 2:11–13

JOB HAS LOST his children, all that he owns, and is now covered head to foot with "loathsome sores" (2:7). The friends come to Job in his need. They weep with him and sit quietly with him. Their quiet ministry of presence speaks loudly to those who think that only words heal.

In times of tragedy in your life, have you appreciated the ministry of presence of your friends? If so, how did it make you feel? Why do you think we are often so quick to try to offer words of comfort and support rather than just being with our friends and loved ones when they suffer great loss?

Teach Me, and I Will Be Silent

"Teach me, and I will be silent;
    make me understand how I have gone wrong."

Job 6:24

IN THE PREVIOUS reading we saw how Job's friends had come to be with him in his agony. They sat with him in silence for seven days and seven nights and then listened to Job agonize and rail against God over the loss of his family and all he owned. Now these words of Job's reveal a heart willing to listen to his friends.

How willing are we to receive teaching that points out our mistakes and misconceptions? Are we more prone to make excuses than to accept the teaching in silence? If today or in the next few days someone points out a mistake you have made or an idea of yours that might be wrong, make a concerted effort to remain silent and not offer excuses.

Listen Carefully to My Words

"Look, my eye has seen all this,
  my ear has heard and understood it.
What you know, I also know;
  I am not inferior to you.
But I would speak to the Almighty,
  and I desire to argue my case with God.
As for you, you whitewash with lies;
  all of you are worthless physicians.
If you would only keep silent,
  that would be your wisdom!
Hear now my reasoning,
  and listen to the pleadings of my lips.
Listen carefully to my words,
  and let my declaration be in your ears."

Job 13:1–6, 17

JOB AND HIS friends are not listening to one another, but each has so much to say. One of the reasons God may be silent so long in the book is that, since they are not listening to one another, why intervene? Something about pain requires it to be fully expressed and fully heard before healing occurs. We say in English that a person needs to be "all talked out," but where are the listeners?

Here Job chastises Eliphaz, Bildad, and Zophar for not listening. But we get the sense that Job is not listening fully to the words of his three companions either. Continue to concentrate on listening, really listening, to those you talk with today. What stirrings did you feel in your spirit?

Quick to Listen, Slow to Speak

You must understand this, my beloved: let everyone be quick to listen, slow to speak, slow to anger.

James 1:19

JAMES ADVISES BELIEVERS about the need to listen carefully, to speak considerately, and to be of a calm demeanor. Most of us are so intent on thinking about what we are going to say during a conversation that we fail to listen to the other person.

What has your practice of silence during these past days taught you about yourself? About your relationships?

Father God, I long for inner silence, so that I can hear you more clearly. Teach me to turn everything off, including my pinballing thoughts. Help me control my tongue and focus on listening to and loving those around me. Show me when my words are needed, and when I wish to speak, keep me from feeling the need to impress or fill the silence. In your name I pray. Amen.

For more verses on silence and ideas on how to practice the discipline of silence, see the Responding exercises and Spiritual Disciplines Index in *The Life with God Bible*.

Simplicity

The inward reality of single-hearted focus upon God and his kingdom, which results in an outward lifestyle of modesty, openness, and unpretentiousness and which disciplines our hunger for status, glamour, and luxury

Simplicity for spiritual formation is putting our love and energies into God rather than into material goods and the pursuit of social status. An inward focus on God will lead to simplicity in our outward lifestyle—in the way we speak, spend money, dress, and share what we have.

Throughout the Bible we see warnings about the accumulation of wealth and the oppression of the poor. The institution of the year of jubilee required all ancestral land to revert back to its original owner every fifty years. Such a system was intended to prevent the extreme disparities in income that are such a part of our modern world. Proverbs 11:28 warns us that the person who trusts in riches will wither. In the New Testament, Jesus spoke more about economics than any other social issue. He announced that the poor were blessed and that the rich had already received their consolation (Luke 6:20, 24). He told his listeners that no servant could serve both God and mammon (Luke 16:13). The message is clear and consistent: wealth does not bring security or happiness. Only God can do that. Instead of seeking to amass wealth and social status we should be aware that our treasure, the only lasting thing about this life, is our relationship with God and life in community.

So how do we practice simplicity? First and most important, we seek the kingdom of God. All other priorities will fall into place when we deliberately place ourselves under God's reign. Simplicity is the result.

We brought nothing into the world, so that we can take nothing out of it.

—*1 Timothy 6:7*

Simplicity

Do Not Worry

[Jesus] said to his disciples, "Therefore I tell you, do not worry about your life, what you will eat, or about your body, what you will wear. For life is more than food, and the body more than clothing. Consider the ravens: they neither sow nor reap, they have neither storehouse nor barn, and yet God feeds them. Of how much more value are you than the birds! And can any of you by worrying add a single hour to your span of life? If then you are not able to do as small a thing as that, why do you worry about the rest? And do not keep striving for what you are to eat and what you are to drink, and do not keep worrying. For it is the nations of the world that strive after all these things, and your Father knows that you need them. Instead, strive for his kingdom, and these things will be given to you as well."

Luke 12:22–26, 29–31

Spiritual Practice

FOR THE NEXT ten days, as much as possible seek to strive for God's kingdom and to take your focus off material things. You can do this by thinking of all your resources as belonging to God and weighing carefully any purchase that you make, however small. Take advantage of those activities in your community that are shared and free—parks, libraries, scenic walks. Pay attention to any addictions that you might have—to coffee, TV, your cell phone—and try to reduce or eliminate your use of any of these items. As much as possible try to stop or at least take a break from worrying about your finances, holding before you the example of the ravens that God cares for so exquisitely. As Martin Luther writes:

> The sinful worship of Mammon does not consist in eating and drinking and wearing clothes . . . for the needs of this life and of the body make food and clothing a requirement. But the sin consists in being concerned about it and making it the reliance and confidence of your heart . . .[1]

He Must Not Acquire

When you have come into the land that the LORD your God is giving you, and have taken possession of it and settled in it, and you say, "I will set a king over me, like all the nations that are around me," you may indeed set over you a king whom the LORD your God will choose. One of your own community you may set as king over you; you are not permitted to put a foreigner over you, who is not of your own community. Even so, he must not acquire many horses for himself, or return the people to Egypt in order to acquire more horses, since the LORD has said to you, "You must never return that way again." And he must not acquire many wives for himself, or else his heart will turn away; also silver and gold he must not acquire in great quantity for himself.

Deuteronomy 17:14–17

ISRAEL IS PERMITTED to have a king, but the king has certain restrictions. After all, he is not the ultimate king, and he must know his place. The Israelite kingship is not a place for personal aggrandizement. Leadership of the covenant people is not to be done for one's own benefit, but out of service for God and for those led. Israelite history is peppered with kings who fall far short of this divine prescription for proper rule (especially Solomon) and so, unfortunately, is the modern Church.

This passage records God's warning to future kings of Israel against acquiring the trappings associated with wealth. This warning, however, did not deter David and later Solomon from acquiring great wealth. Today we all know stories of contemporary leaders who take office with good intentions, but whose service is later compromised by money. What is so seductive about money and what it can buy? How does it keep you from living a life of simplicity?

Solomon's Riches

The weight of gold that came to Solomon in one year was six hundred sixty-six talents of gold, besides that which came from the traders and from the business of the merchants, and from all the kings of Arabia and the governors of the land. King Solomon made two hundred large shields of beaten gold; six hundred shekels of gold went into each large shield. He made three hundred shields of beaten gold; three minas of gold went into each shield; and the king put them in the House of the Forest of Lebanon. The king also made a great ivory throne, and overlaid it with the finest gold.

1 Kings 10:14–18

SOLOMON'S SINGLE-MINDED FOCUS on God and his spiritual leadership of the nation began to wane as he became increasingly engaged with his various building projects, his wealth, his notoriety, and his relationships with hundreds of foreign wives. His success became too much for him, and Solomon's passions overwhelmed his commitment to the one true God. Any love he originally had for God was nearly smothered by all of his earthly loves. Note that Solomon's gold is used to ornament buildings on display to courtiers and visiting dignitaries. The remainder of 1 Kings 10 shows Solomon amassing his wealth. Deuteronomy warns against those who exalt themselves, believing that their own efforts have brought them wealth. This self-aggrandizement will come, Deuteronomy warns, "when you have eaten your fill and have built fine houses and live in them . . . and your silver and gold is multiplied"; then the self-impressed will be tempted to forget God (8:12–17).

What are the financial or social things you place your trust in?

Father God, I work to build up possessions and assets, believing that they will keep me safe. Forgive me for putting my trust in anything but you. Help me to realize the limits of wealth and to use what I have for your purposes, not my own. In your name I pray. Amen.

The Lover of Money

The lover of money will not be satisfied with money; nor the lover of wealth, with gain. This is also vanity.

Ecclesiastes 5:10

MANY PEOPLE TODAY try to find their satisfaction in life by making a lot of money. The Teacher, the narrator of Ecclesiastes, has gone before us and tells us that wealth in itself does not bring contentment. Money is not the source of ultimate contentment—or ultimate meaning. Those who love money will never have enough, and they will wear themselves out before they ever come close to being satisfied.

The Teacher wrote that we will not be satisfied if we love money, and Paul advised Timothy that "the love of money is a root of all kinds of evil" (1 Tim 6:10). Yet most of us tend to agree with the American tycoon John D. Rockefeller, who when reportedly asked how much money was enough, replied, "Just a little more." Perhaps we feel because we do not spend a great deal of money that we live in simplicity. But hoarding money can be just as challenging a problem spiritually. Simplicity is about breaking the hold money has on us, not necessarily saving more or spending less. In what direction—spending or hoarding—does money hold allure for you? What can you do to change the pattern?

You Never Have Your Fill

Thus says the Lord of hosts: These people say the time has not yet come to rebuild the Lord's house. Then the word of the Lord came by the prophet Haggai, saying: Is it a time for you yourselves to live in your paneled houses, while this house lies in ruins? Now therefore thus says the Lord of hosts: Consider how you have fared. You have sown much, and harvested little; you eat, but you never have enough; you drink, but you never have your fill; you clothe yourselves, but no one is warm; and you that earn wages earn wages to put them into a bag with holes.

Thus says the Lord of hosts: Consider how you have fared. Go up to the hills and bring wood and build the house, so that I may take pleasure in it and be honored, says the Lord. You have looked for much, and lo, it came to little; and when you brought it home, I blew it away. Why? says the Lord of hosts. Because my house lies in ruins, while all of you hurry off to your own houses.

Haggai 1:2–9

THE PEOPLE HAVE put off building the Temple, but have built houses for themselves (paneled ones, suggesting wealth). The metaphor of earning wages but putting them into "a bag with holes" suggests that the people's efforts will be wasted until they construct the Temple, since they have apparently worked, but still have not fared well. This message calls us to replace our self-concern with right worship.

The Lord here reprimands the People of God for putting their money and resources in their own homes, their own interests. Where in your life have you invested for yourself what belongs to God? Are you giving enough of what you have to the community and to the work of the Lord?

All Was Vanity

I said to myself, "Come now, I will make a test of pleasure; enjoy your-self." But again, this also was vanity. I said of laughter, "It is mad," and of pleasure, "What use is it?" I searched with my mind how to cheer my body with wine—my mind still guiding me with wisdom—and how to lay hold on folly, until I might see what was good for mortals to do under heaven during the few days of their life. I made great works; I built houses and planted vineyards for myself; I made myself gardens and parks, and planted in them all kinds of fruit trees. I made myself pools from which to water the forest of growing trees. I bought male and female slaves, and had slaves who were born in my house; I also had great possessions of herds and flocks, more than any who had been before me in Jerusalem. I also gathered for myself silver and gold and the treasure of kings and of the provinces; I got singers, both men and women, and delights of the flesh, and many concubines.

Then I considered all that my hands had done and the toil I had spent in doing it, and again, all was vanity and a chasing after wind, and there was nothing to be gained under the sun.

Ecclesiastes 2:1–8, 11

THE TEACHER OF Ecclesiastes tries to find ultimate meaning and satisfaction in the pursuit of pleasure. He explores different forms of pleasure, some of them sensual (alcohol and women) and some of them from achievements and possessions (building great houses, acquiring slaves and livestock). His final conclusion, though, is that pleasure does not satisfy. Money, sex, power, position, human wisdom, even our at-tempts to become righteous—all are "vanity of vanities" (1:2). Nothing satisfies. Nothing delivers the goods. Nothing fulfills. Nothing. It is only when we have genuinely given up on everything, absolutely every-thing, that we become candidates for growth in grace.

How has the Teacher's lesson revealed itself in your life?

Give Your Rewards to Someone Else

Then Daniel was brought in before the king. The king said to Daniel, "So you are Daniel, one of the exiles of Judah, whom my father the king brought from Judah? I have heard of you that a spirit of the gods is in you, and that enlightenment, understanding, and excellent wisdom are found in you. Now the wise men, the enchanters, have been brought in before me to read this writing and tell me its interpretation, but they were not able to give the interpretation of the matter. But I have heard that you can give interpretations and solve problems. Now if you are able to read the writing and tell me its interpretation, you shall be clothed in purple, have a chain of gold around your neck, and rank third in the kingdom."

Then Daniel answered in the presence of the king, "Let your gifts be for yourself, or give your rewards to someone else!"

Daniel 5:13–17a

WHAT KING BELSHAZZAR can give is nothing compared to what God has given. Daniel remembers who the source of all blessings is. Daniel rejects the king's offers of costly clothing, jewelry, and influence in his community. He must have been tempted by some or all of the offers, but Daniel understood that material possessions (and certainly professional success) can get in the way of our relationship with God.

Father God, it is so tempting to be defined by what others think of us, especially when they heap up with praise and honor. Teach me to follow Daniel's example and tame my desire for earthly recognition. Help me to remember that my blessings come from you alone, that power and success will wither just as earthly riches. In your name I pray. Amen.

Storing Up Treasures

And [Jesus] said to them, "Take care! Be on your guard against all kinds of greed; for one's life does not consist in the abundance of possessions." Then he told them a parable: "The land of a rich man produced abundantly. And he thought to himself, 'What should I do, for I have no place to store my crops?' Then he said, 'I will do this: I will pull down my barns and build larger ones, and there I will store all my grain and my goods. And I will say to my soul, Soul, you have ample goods laid up for many years; relax, eat, drink, be merry.' But God said to him, 'You fool! This very night your life is being demanded of you. And the things you have prepared, whose will they be?' So it is with those who store up treasures for themselves but are not rich toward God."

Luke 12:15–21

WE OFTEN CONSIDER this story in the light of material possessions— too many cars, too many TVs, too many clothes, too big a house, too much in the bank—since that was certainly the rich man's problem. But Jesus' comment at the end does not specify money or possessions: "So it is with those who store up treasures for themselves but are not rich toward God." We might consider friendships or children or physical health to be our greatest possessions. We might even store up spiritual treasure after spiritual treasure. We can make a god out of prayer and spiritual formation and solitude. We can live for our experiences rather than God, who is the source of them. We can hoard what we have learned and never share with others who are struggling. Our richness should be in God himself, not in the ways we enjoy worshiping him.

Simplicity is not only about our attitude toward material goods. It is easy to become too insular in our focus on a particular Spiritual Discipline or to feel secretly superior about some spiritual practice we have done successfully. What is your greatest possession? Is there a spiritual treasure in your life that you are hoarding or becoming prideful about?

Be Rich in Good Works

As for those who in the present age are rich, command them not to be haughty, or to set their hopes on the uncertainty of riches, but rather on God who richly provides us with everything for our enjoyment. They are to do good, to be rich in good works, generous, and ready to share, thus storing up for themselves the treasure of a good foundation for the future, so that they may take hold of the life that really is life.

1 Timothy 6:17–19

NOT ALL OF the earliest Christians were poor. Note that the rich are instructed last, after more pressing concerns for the most vulnerable are addressed—the first shall be last (Matt 20:16). From those to whom much has been given much will be required (Luke 12:48). Our full, affluent churches must admit that riches are not spiritually neutral. Scripture is clear that those with riches are in a vulnerable position as far as their souls are concerned (Matt 19:24). Money is a spiritual issue. Spiritual formation and renovation for those who have material goods means quite specific responsibilities—"They are to do good, to be rich in good works, generous, and ready to share."

Most of us qualify as rich by biblical standards. We have enough to eat and clothe ourselves; we have a roof over our head. Jesus tells us in Luke 12:48, "From everyone to whom much has been given, much will be required." If you are "rich" in the present age, how well are you meeting the guidelines set out in the last verse above? How has your practice these last several days affected your attitude? How could you do better?

You Have Lived on the Earth in Luxury

Come now, you rich people, weep and wail for the miseries that are coming to you. Your riches have rotted, and your clothes are moth-eaten. Your gold and silver have rusted, and their rust will be evidence against you, and it will eat your flesh like fire. You have laid up treasure for the last days. Listen! The wages of the laborers who mowed your fields, which you kept back by fraud, cry out, and the cries of the harvesters have reached the ears of the Lord of hosts. You have lived on the earth in luxury and in pleasure; you have fattened your hearts in a day of slaughter.

James 5:1–5

THE PROBLEM OF rich and poor is treated again, this time in a radical rebuke against those whose wealth and affluence, gained by unfairness, oppression, and fraud, are arrogantly used. God's judgment against such sins is announced. James cautions employers against defrauding or treating those who work for them unfairly. Arrogant violation of the righteous invites divine judgment, because their sure recourse is God's justice.

Father God, we, too, are complicit in the disparity between rich and poor that exists in our world. As I seek your kingdom, teach me to be more generous and judicious with my own resources. Give me an inward focus upon you and your kingdom. In your name I pray. Amen.

Giving to Everyone

"From anyone who takes away your coat do not withhold even your shirt. Give to everyone who begs from you; and if anyone takes away your goods, do not ask for them again."

Luke 6:29b–30

PART OF LIVING a lifestyle of simplicity is recognizing when possessions become too important in our lives. If we find ourselves becoming too attached to something, the best course is to give it away. Sometime within the next ten days, consider whether there is a material possession in your life that is starting to assume too prominent a place in your heart. Give it to a thrift organization or to someone you know who could use it. If you cannot think of one thing in particular, sort through some of your possessions—clothes, books, toys, kitchen appliances, and challenge yourself to give many of them away. Focusing on the needs of others will help focus your heart upon God and his kingdom. "Truly I tell you, just as you did it to one of the least of these who are members of my family, you did it to me" (Matt 25:40).

Spiritual Practice

Do Not Love the World

Do not love the world or the things in the world. The love of the Father is not in those who love the world; for all that is in the world—the desire of the flesh, the desire of the eyes, the pride in riches—comes not from the Father but from the world. And the world and its desire are passing away, but those who do the will of God live forever.

1 John 2:15–17

THERE IS NO place for complacency. It is easy to become self-centered and drawn away from God by the glamour of sensuality, status, and riches, even though these things will not last. In contrast, those who remain on our pilgrimage with God will live forever. The author reminds us that we must choose; we can have only one master.

Father, I want to know Thee, but my cowardly heart fears to give up its toys. I cannot part with them without inward bleeding, and I do not try to hide from Thee the terror of the parting. I come trembling, but I do come. Please root from my heart all those things which I have cherished so long and which have become a very part of my living self, so that Thou mayest enter and dwell there without a rival. Then shalt Thou make the place of Thy feet glorious. Then shall my heart have no need of the sun to shine in it, for Thyself wilt be the light of it, and there shall be no night there. In Jesus' name. Amen.

—A.W. Tozer, *The Pursuit of God*[2]

Giving to Everyone

Disciples Travel Light

[Jesus] called the twelve and began to send them out two by two, and gave them authority over the unclean spirits. He ordered them to take nothing for their journey except a staff; no bread, no bag, no money in their belts; but to wear sandals and not to put on two tunics. He said to them, "Wherever you enter a house, stay there until you leave the place. If any place will not welcome you and they refuse to hear you, as you leave, shake off the dust that is on your feet as a testimony against them." So they went out and proclaimed that all should repent. They cast out many demons, and anointed with oil many who were sick and cured them.

Mark 6:7–13

THE WAY OF training disciples in Jesus' day was deceptively simple: disciples were to listen to the teacher's words and watch his actions and then try to say and do what he did. We can learn in the same way today. As we mature spiritually, we give ourselves more and more fully to God's care and keeping. Our security is not found in possessions, but in belonging to God. We continue the mission of the first disciples as we proclaim the good news of Jesus and work for healing and wholeness in individuals and groups. Disciples travel light, realizing their interdependence with others and, most of all, their dependence upon God.

How do you think traveling light enhanced the disciples' ministry?

"There is the danger and the temptation to you, of drawing your minds into your business, and clogging them with it; so that ye can hardly do anything to the service of God . . . and your minds will go into the things, and not over the things. . . . And then, if the Lord God cross you, and stop you by sea and land, and take [your] goods and customs from you, that your minds should not be cumbered, then that mind that is cumbered will fret, being out of the power of God."

—George Fox, *Works*[3]

Treasures on Earth

"Do not store up for yourselves treasures on earth, where moth and rust consume and where thieves break in and steal; but store up for yourselves treasures in heaven, where neither moth nor rust consumes and where thieves do not break in and steal. For where your treasure is, there your heart will be also.

"No one can serve two masters; for a slave will either hate the one and love the other, or be devoted to the one and despise the other. You cannot serve God and wealth."

Matthew 6:19–21, 24

JESUS URGES THE disciples not to store up resources on earth, but rather in heaven. His point relates to what we place our trust in and where our security lies. Jesus stresses that two masters, God and money, cannot both be served. In light of this passage, it is ironic that U.S. currency says, "In God we trust."

As you prepare to give away some of your possessions, remind yourself of their finite nature.

Father God, help me to break my addiction to material things. Help me to identify and rid myself of those things that are keeping me from fully serving you—not only the goods, but my vanity, my pride, my selfish ambition. Teach me what true simplicity is. In your name I pray. Amen.

Limited Possessions

Share in suffering like a good soldier of Christ Jesus. No one serving in the army gets entangled in everyday affairs; the soldier's aim is to please the enlisting officer.

2 Timothy 2:3–4

JESUS CAME TO us, preached words of life, and showed us the way, and we crucified him for it. His way is the narrow way that seems, no matter how charmingly and beguilingly we try to put the gospel, to involve suffering. Few of us North American Christians find ourselves in circumstances where we are persecuted for our faith, yet millions of Christians are persecuted and martyred still because of their commitment to Christ. It cannot be that we have at last found a society in which no one can be hurt following Jesus. More likely, our Church has settled in comfortably with the powers; we have scaled the gospel down to some message that never offends; we have practiced the faith in ways that never present a rebuke to the ways of the world.

Unlike most of our lives, soldiers' lives are the epitome of simplicity. Their possessions are limited to personal effects and clothes, since all of their energies must be focused on their job. Try to imagine a life pared down to such bare essentials. How does ridding ourselves of possessions make it easier to shun the status quo and seek first God's kingdom and its righteousness, the "central point for the Discipline of simplicity," as Richard Foster writes in *Celebration of Discipline*?[4]

Do Not Set Your Heart on Riches

Those of low estate are but a breath,
   those of high estate are a delusion;
in the balances they go up;
   they are together lighter than a breath.
Put no confidence in extortion,
   and set no vain hopes on robbery;
   if riches increase, do not set your heart on them.

Psalm 62:9–10

GOD THE ROCK is far more trustworthy than people, rich or poor, who are "lighter than a breath." The psalm even warns those who may be tempted to be self-reliant as they grow prosperous. The Spiritual Discipline of simplicity helps focus attention and reliance on God.

Father in Heaven! What are we without You? . . . What is all our striving, could it ever encompass a world, but a half-finished work if we do not know You: You the One, who is one thing and who is all!
   So may you give to the intellect
      wisdom to comprehend that one thing;
   to the heart,
      sincerity to receive this understanding;
   to the will
      purity that wills only one thing.
   In prosperity, may you grant
      perseverance to will one thing;
   amid distractions,
      collectedness to will one thing;
   in suffering,
      patience to will one thing.
      —Søren Kierkegaard, *Purity of Heart Is to Will One Thing*[5]

The Rich Will Wither Away

Let the believer who is lowly boast in being raised up, and the rich in being brought low, because the rich will disappear like a flower in the field. For the sun rises with its scorching heat and withers the field; its flower falls, and its beauty perishes. It is the same way with the rich; in the midst of a busy life, they will wither away.

James 1:9–11

WEALTH IS A major preoccupation of James's Letter. If poor or disadvantaged, we are advised not to seek wealth as an ultimate good, and if rich, we are not to hoard wealth and enjoy privileges as if these can be possessed eternally. Although the "lowly" are lacking in relation to others who have much, there should be pride in having been "raised" higher in Christ; the "rich" are charged to remember how temporary the material side of life really is.

James writes that "in the midst of a busy life," the rich will wither away. Implicit in his statement is the time and energy we must devote to accumulating wealth and material possessions. This stands in stark contrast to Jesus' instructions to us in Luke 12:22: "Therefore, I tell you, do not worry about your life, what you will eat, or about your body, what you will wear." Today try to be aware of all the time you spend thinking about or caring for either your finances or your possessions. What did you learn?

Superficial Signs of Wealth

"I know your works; you are neither cold nor hot. I wish that you were either cold or hot. So, because you are lukewarm, and neither cold nor hot, I am about to spit you out of my mouth. For you say, 'I am rich, I have prospered, and I need nothing.' You do not realize that you are wretched, pitiable, poor, blind, and naked."

Revelation 3:15–17

FOCUSING ON THE superficial signs of wealth and health blocks our awareness of spiritual reality. We feel safe and secure as long as we have money in the bank, cars in the garage, and plenty of credit cards. But these do not feed the deepest longings of our spirit, which may be starving in the midst of apparent plenty.

List ways that wealth can work against living a simple life, both inwardly and outwardly. Choose one problem in this area of your life, for example, trusting in money more than God for security. Hold it before God and quietly give it to God in prayer. See what you learn.

To Whom Do You Belong?

If with Christ you died to the elemental spirits of the universe, why do you live as if you still belonged to the world?

Colossians 2:20a

REFUSING TO DEFINE ourselves as "consumers" may help orient our attention toward God and away from material goods. The Amish rejection of modern conveniences and Roman Catholic vows of "chastity, poverty, and obedience" focus attention on God's providence. Tithing is comparable as a Spiritual Discipline too, insofar as it decreases self-indulgence and raises our awareness that everything we have is God's gift.

What other Spiritual Disciplines can help us practice simplicity and remember that we belong to God, not to the world?

Content with Whatever I Have

I rejoice in the Lord greatly that now at last you have revived your concern for me; indeed, you were concerned for me, but had no opportunity to show it. Not that I am referring to being in need; for I have learned to be content with whatever I have. I know what it is to have little, and I know what it is to have plenty. In any and all circumstances I have learned the secret of being well-fed and of going hungry, of having plenty and of being in need. I can do all things through him who strengthens me. In any case, it was kind of you to share my distress.

Philippians 4:10–14

ONE OF THE lessons of spiritual maturity is the secret of living well, whatever our means. Paul shares this lesson as he thanks the Philippians for their financial support. Although he is grateful for their generosity, Paul wants the Church to know that in Christ he can be satisfied with any standard of living, even in prison.

In defining simplicity, Richard Foster writes that it is "an inward reality that results in an outward lifestyle."[6] According to Paul, what is the outward reality? After your experience of practicing simplicity, how close are you to experiencing it in your life? What can you do to encourage it?

Lord, please continue to teach me to be content with whatever I have. Help me to experience the true simplicity that comes from placing my trust only in you. In your name I pray. Amen.

For more verses on simplicity and ideas on how to practice the discipline of simplicity, see the Responding exercises and Spiritual Disciplines Index in *The Life with God Bible*.

Celebration

Utter delight and joy in ourselves, our life, and our world as a result of our faith and confidence in God's greatness, beauty, and goodness

Celebration is perhaps the most overlooked discipline. For many of us, celebration has a ring of the hedonistic; it does not fit with our image of what a Spiritual Discipline should be. But God calls his people to celebrate, with festivals or with spontaneous and joyful praise, such as Miriam and the Israelites singing and playing tambourines after God parted the Red Sea (Exod 15), David dancing and leaping before the ark of the Lord (2 Samuel 6), or the shepherds glorifying and praising God after they see Jesus in the manger (Luke 2:20). The Psalms are filled with praise and celebration. But celebration can also be as simple as enjoying life. John tells us that Jesus attended a wedding in Cana, where he performed the ultimate party trick of turning water into wine (2:1–10).

According to Dallas Willard, "We engage in celebration when we enjoy ourselves, our life, our world, *in conjunction with* our faith and confidence in God's greatness, beauty, and goodness. We concentrate on *our* life and world as God's work and as God's gift to us." Thus celebration is inextricably linked with worship. Willard continues by describing celebration as "the completion of worship, for it dwells on the greatness of God as shown in his goodness *to* us."[1]

Perhaps celebration is most clearly defined by its central emotion: joy. Jesus tells his disciples that one of his purposes in teaching is to pass on his joy: "I have said these things to you so that my joy may be in you, and that your joy may be complete" (John 15:11).

Rejoice in the Lord always; again I will say, Rejoice.

—*Philippians 4:4*

Celebration

Singing to the Lord a New Song

Then Moses and the Israelites sang this song to the LORD:
"I will sing to the LORD, for he has triumphed gloriously;
   horse and rider he has thrown into the sea.
The Lord is my strength and my might,
   and he has become my salvation;
this is my God, and I will praise him,
   my father's God, and I will exalt him."
Then the prophet Miriam, Aaron's sister, took a tambourine in her
hand; and all the women went out after her with tambourines and with
dancing.

Exodus 15:1–2, 20

THROUGHOUT THE BIBLE we see God's people thank and celebrate
him by singing, by reciting his deeds, by remembering how wonderful
he is. Each of the festivals celebrated by the Israelites revolved around
some particular deed for which they were offering thanks, for example,
for delivering them from Egypt at Passover, for delivering them from
Haman's plan at Purim. Other times we see spontaneous recitations of
God's character and work on the people's behalf. Those who recite the
words often seem to bubble over with joy, to rejoice, even to dance.

For this exercise, write down the things you want to praise God for,
such as your health, family, security, friends. Then read or sing your
praise aloud. Tomorrow add more things to the celebration list, perhaps
expanding your view to thank God for Jesus or for things he has done
for the world, the country you live in, your town, and so forth. Continue adding to or refining this list over the next ten days, reflecting on
how you feel that day. The Bible makes it clear that music and musical
instruments were an important part of celebrations. Consider listening
to or playing a favorite praise song before or during the reading or singing of your list. Remember that your act of reading or singing is a way
of celebrating, praising God for all he has done and all he is. Allow joy
to bubble up in you as you think about all the blessings in your life.

Spiritual Practice

Awake, Awake, Utter a Song!

Then Deborah and Barak son of Abinoam sang on that day, saying: /
"When locks are long in Israel, / when the people offer themselves
willingly— / bless the LORD! / Hear, O kings; give ear, O princes; /
to the LORD I will sing, / I will make melody to the LORD, the God
of Israel. / Lord, when you went out from Seir, / when you marched
from the region of Edom, / the earth trembled, / and the heavens
poured, / the clouds indeed poured water. / The mountains quaked
before the LORD, the One of Sinai, / before the LORD, the God of
Israel. / Awake, awake, Deborah! / Awake, awake, utter a song!"

Judges 5:1–5, 12a

CONSIDERED BY MANY a beautiful literary work, this song praises
God for his deliverance and for the people's cooperation with God.
Deborah's prayer of praise holds as much gratitude for the turning of
the people's hearts toward God as for the turning of the battle to Israel's
favor. Deborah rejoices to see the Israelites once again worshiping God
and placing themselves in his hands.

Allow Deborah's exuberant praise to inspire your own song of
celebration.

Lord, as you awaken us to delight in your praise,
grant that we may know you,
call on you, and praise you;
for you have made us for yourself,
and our hearts are restless
until they find their rest in you. Amen.

—St. Augustine

~ Singing to the Lord a New Song

Clap Your Hands, All You Peoples

Clap your hands, all you peoples; / shout to God with loud songs of
joy. / For the LORD, the Most High, is awesome, / a great king over
all the earth. / He subdued peoples under us, / and nations under
our feet. / He chose our heritage for us, / the pride of Jacob whom
he loves. / God has gone up with a shout, / the LORD with the sound
of a trumpet. / Sing praises to God, sing praises; / sing praises to
our King, sing praises. / For God is the king of all the earth; / sing
praises with a psalm. / God is king over the nations; / God sits on
his holy throne. / The princes of the peoples gather / as the people of
the God of Abraham. / For the shields of the earth belong to God; /
he is highly exalted.

Psalm 47:1–9

THIS IS ONE of the "enthronement psalms," songs that celebrate God's
rule as "king of all the earth." Just as Israel rejoices that Yahweh rules
over all, so it calls all people to join in "loud songs of joy." To gladly
acknowledge this unrivaled King puts us in a place where we can feel
secure, learn, and hope.

Does the assurance that God is in charge make you want to celebrate?
Why or why not?

"St. Augustine [says] that God has taught us to praise Him, in the
Psalms, not in order that He may get something out of this praise, but
in order that we might be made better by it. Praising God in the words
of the Psalms, we can come to know Him better. Knowing Him better
we love Him better, loving Him better we find our happiness in Him."

—Thomas Merton, *Praying the Psalms* [2]

Celebrate Your Festivals

Look! On the mountains the feet of one
    who brings good tidings,
    who proclaims peace!
Celebrate your festivals, O Judah,
    fulfill your vows,
for never again shall the wicked invade you;
    they are utterly cut off.

Nahum 1:15

FEASTS AND FESTIVALS of faith are important components in the life of believers. God's people gather together to hear stories of faith, remember the acts of God, offer thanksgiving, and renew vows (Isa 40:9). One of the most important festivals of the Jewish calendar year is Passover, the celebration of the deliverance of the People of God from slavery in ancient Egypt. At the seder, or special meal, celebrants eat particular kinds of food, each with its own significance, and read aloud passages from Exodus. Observing the Christian calendar, with its various feasts and saints' days, festivals and seasons, is a building block of faith.

As you sing or recite your praise today, consider adding something to it about Christmas, Easter, or other special days on which we remember God together.

Lord God, thank you for the beautiful rhythm of the church year. Help me to honor you as I remember and celebrate all the ways you have been with me. As I reflect on the wonder of Jesus' birth, death, and resurrection, help me to learn more about you and your ways. What better cause for celebration than the knowledge that Jesus rose again! In your name I pray. Amen.

─● *Singing to the Lord a New Song*

Thanking God

You shall count seven weeks; begin to count the seven weeks from the time the sickle is first put to the standing grain. Then you shall keep the festival of weeks to the LORD your God, contributing a freewill offering in proportion to the blessing that you have received from the LORD your God. Rejoice before the LORD your God—you and your sons and your daughters, your male and female slaves, the Levites resident in your town, as well as the strangers, the orphans, and the widows who are among you—at the place that the LORD your God will choose as a dwelling for his name. Remember that you were a slave in Egypt, and diligently observe these statutes.

You shall keep the festival of booths for seven days, when you have gathered in the produce from your threshing floor and your wine press. Rejoice during your festival, you and your sons and your daughters, your male and female slaves, as well as the Levites, the strangers, the orphans, and the widows resident in your towns. Seven days you shall keep the festival to the LORD your God at the place that the LORD will choose; for the LORD your God will bless you in all your produce and in all your undertakings, and you shall surely celebrate.

Deuteronomy 16:9–15

THREE TIMES A year Israelites were to appear before the Lord to offer him thanks for agricultural bounty and, in some cases, for historical deliverance (for the reference to Passover, see 16:1–8). He saved them from Egypt and now provides the crops that sustain them.

Today, look back in the past to thank God for Jesus, the Passover Lamb, who saves us and provides for us (1 Cor 5:6–8).

Jesus, thou soul of all our joys, / For whom we now lift up our voice, / And all our strength exert, / Vouchsafe the grace we humbly claim, / Compose into a thankful frame, / And tune thy people's heart.

—Charles Wesley, "Jesus, Thou Soul of All Our Joys"[3]

Blow the Trumpets

The LORD spoke to Moses, saying: Make two silver trumpets; you shall make them of hammered work; and you shall use them for summoning the congregation and for breaking camp. Also on your days of rejoicing, at your appointed festivals, and at the beginning of your months, you shall blow the trumpets over your burnt offerings and over your sacrifices of well-being; they shall serve as a reminder on your behalf before the LORD your God: I am the LORD your God.

Numbers 10:1–2, 10

GOD USED TRUMPETS to coordinate the movements of the people. They were God's instruments for bringing about order and discipline. The whole community was directed by their sound. Numbers describes God's work in teaching and organizing the Israelites and shaping them, once slaves in Egypt, into a great nation. That he would make for them beautiful-sounding silver trumpets shows God's attention to detail, his loving care and concern for directing the Israelites in their wilderness journey. We pay homage to this tradition in our churches today when we have a procession, prelude, or special music to summon people for worship.

Today consider singing or reciting your song of praise with musical accompaniment, such as piano or an instrumental CD.

"[Medieval German abbess Hildegard of Bingen] believed that many times a day, we fall out of sorts, lose our way or find ourselves off center. Music was the sacred technology which could best tune humanity, redirect our hearts toward heaven and put our feet back onto the wholesome ways of God. . . . In singing and playing music, we integrate mind, heart and body, heal discord between us, and celebrate heavenly harmony here on earth. According to Hildegard, this becomes our 'opus'—the epitome of good work in the service of God."

—Nancy Fierro, *Hildegard of Bingen*[4]

Singing to the Lord a New Song

Celebrating the Jubilee

You shall count off seven weeks of years, seven times seven years, so that the period of seven weeks of years gives forty-nine years. Then you shall have the trumpet sounded loud; on the tenth day of the seventh month—on the day of atonement—you shall have the trumpet sounded throughout all your land. And you shall hallow the fiftieth year and you shall proclaim liberty throughout the land to all its inhabitants. It shall be a jubilee for you: you shall return, every one of you, to your property and every one of you to your family. The fiftieth year shall be a jubilee for you: you shall not sow, or reap the aftergrowth, or harvest the unpruned vines. For it is a jubilee, it shall be holy to you: you shall only eat what the field itself produces.

Leviticus 25:8–12

THE JUBILEE IS associated with the sound of trumpets announcing liberty throughout the land. All people get a new start. This practice is a remarkable witness to hope and God's justice.

Did you try reading or singing your praise with music? How did it affect your experience?

Blow, ye the trumpet, blow!
The gladly solemn sound
Let all the nations know,
To earth's remotest bound,
The year of jubilee is come!
The year of jubilee is come!
Return, ye ransomed sinners, home.

—William Walker[5]

Make a Joyful Noise

Make a joyful noise to the LORD, all the earth.
>Worship the LORD with gladness;
>come into his presence with singing.
Know that the LORD is God.
>It is he that made us, and we are his;
>we are his people, and the sheep of his pasture.
Enter his gates with thanksgiving,
>and his courts with praise.
>Give thanks to him, bless his name.
For the LORD is good;
>his steadfast love endures forever,
>and his faithfulness to all generations.

Psalm 100:1–5

THIS IS A joyous, universal call to praise and thanksgiving. Its old hymn setting captures its gladness: "Him serve with mirth, his praise forthtell." The call to joyful noise includes relaxing and being creatures who are well tended by the Creator-Shepherd. When we accept our place and trust God's goodness, we take a giant step toward wholeness. Entering into worship with deep gladness and living with liberating trust takes root here. Confessing that God's steadfast love and faithfulness will never fail opens the way to joy.

Have you found that your practice of celebrating has enhanced and completed your enjoyment of God? Consider these words:

"I think we delight to praise what we enjoy because the praise not merely expresses but completes the enjoyment; it is its appointed consummation."

—C. S. Lewis, *Reflections on the Psalms*[6]

David Dances Before the Lord

It was told King David, "The LORD has blessed the household of Obed-edom and all that belongs to him, because of the ark of God." So David went and brought up the ark of God from the house of Obed-edom to the city of David with rejoicing; and when those who bore the ark of the LORD had gone six paces, he sacrificed an ox and a fatling. David danced before the LORD with all his might; David was girded with a linen ephod. So David and all the house of Israel brought up the ark of the LORD with shouting, and with the sound of the trumpet.

As the ark of the LORD came into the city of David, Michal daughter of Saul looked out of the window, and saw King David leaping and dancing before the LORD; and she despised him in her heart.

David returned to bless his household. But Michal the daughter of Saul came out to meet David, and said, "How the king of Israel honored himself today, uncovering himself today before the eyes of his servants' maids, as any vulgar fellow might shamelessly uncover himself!" David said to Michal, "It was before the LORD, who chose me in place of your father and all his household, to appoint me as prince of Israel, the people of the LORD, that I have danced before the LORD. I will make myself yet more contemptible than this, and I will be abased in my own eyes; but by the maids of whom you have spoken, by them I shall be held in honor."

2 Samuel 6:12–16, 20–22

AS WAS THE case for the journey, the settling of the ark is accompanied by sacrifice and then also blessing and a feast, all of which will be echoed later in the eucharistic meal celebrated in Christian worship after the resurrection of Jesus. In the dangerous presence of Yahweh there is, for those whose motives are pure, great joy and happiness—a reason to rejoice. Undoubtedly this is why David desires to have the ark nearby.

As you recite your praise again, do not hold back. Ask the Lord to give you the courage to be a fool for him, no matter who's watching.

Mary's Spirit Rejoices

And Mary said, / "My soul magnifies the Lord, / and my spirit rejoices in God my Savior, / for he has looked with favor on the lowliness of his servant. / Surely, from now on all generations will call me blessed; / for the Mighty One has done great things for me, / and holy is his name. / His mercy is for those who fear him / from generation to generation. / He has shown strength with his arm; / he has scattered the proud in the thoughts of their hearts. / He has brought down the powerful from their thrones, / and lifted up the lowly; / he has filled the hungry with good things, / and sent the rich away empty. / He has helped his servant Israel, / in remembrance of his mercy, / according to the promise he made to our ancestors, / to Abraham and to his descendants forever."

Luke 1:46–55

AFTER MARY RECEIVED the unbelievable news that she was to bear the Son of God, she responded by rejoicing in God her Savior. Mary approached her nearly unthinkable role with great emotion, with awe. At first she simply stood perplexed at what would be; then she sat amazed at the Child's coming and the confirmation from hosts of heaven, the shepherds, and learned foreigners. She pondered the words of the angel and the testimony of the shepherds, and as the story of Jesus unfolded before her, she treasured each piece in her heart (2:19). Mary knew she had been the site of a holy miracle, the habitation of divinity.

Mary's song of praise reflected her feelings after the strange and wonderful visit from Gabriel. How is your song like hers and how is it different? What has writing your own song and celebrating with it each day taught you?

Rejoicing Together

Set apart a tithe of all the yield of your seed that is brought in yearly from the field. In the presence of the LORD your God, in the place that he will choose as a dwelling for his name, you shall eat the tithe of your grain, your wine, and your oil, as well as the firstlings of your herd and flock, so that you may learn to fear the LORD your God always. But if, when the LORD your God has blessed you, the distance is so great that you are unable to transport it, because the place where the LORD your God will choose to set his name is too far away from you, then you may turn it into money. With the money secure in hand, go to the place that the LORD your God will choose; spend the money for whatever you wish—oxen, sheep, wine, strong drink, or whatever you desire. And you shall eat there in the presence of the LORD your God, you and your household rejoicing together.

Deuteronomy 14:22–26

IF ANY BIBLE passage turns on its ear the thought of a dour God who does not want his people to enjoy life, here it is. God instructs those who are not able to travel to Jerusalem to spend the money on whatever they want and throw a party, "rejoicing together." So that's what you are to do. Sometime in the next ten days, have a gathering of friends and family and celebrate together. You might want to tie your party to a particular event, or perhaps you just want to celebrate your friends and some good food. Play some music you enjoy. Rejoice in the blessings God has given you. Let everyone who comes know that you are thankful for them and for their friendship. Enjoy yourselves!

Spiritual Practice

The Joy of Jerusalem

Now at the dedication of the wall of Jerusalem they sought out the Levites in all their places, to bring them to Jerusalem to celebrate the dedication with rejoicing, with thanksgivings and with singing, with cymbals, harps, and lyres. The companies of the singers gathered together from the circuit around Jerusalem. Then I brought the leaders of Judah up onto the wall, and appointed two great companies that gave thanks and went in procession. One went to the right on the wall to the Dung Gate with the musical instruments of David the man of God, and the scribe Ezra went in front of them. The other company of those who gave thanks went to the left, and I followed them with half of the people on the wall. They offered great sacrifices that day and rejoiced, for God had made them rejoice with great joy; the women and children also rejoiced. The joy of Jerusalem was heard far away.

Nehemiah 12:27–28a, 31, 36b, 38a, 43

FOUR AND A half centuries before Jesus (445 BCE) the people living in Jerusalem were crushed and broken. The population had dwindled to only a few thousand people, and the walls and the gates of the city were piles of ash and broken stones. Nehemiah, a cupbearer for King Artaxerxes I in the city of Susa, gained permission from the king to return to his hometown of Jerusalem and lead the people in rebuilding the walls. Here the task is finally finished, and the people are beside themselves with joy. Can you hear the music and dancing, the laughter and singing? Pious Ezra, priest and scribe, with a grin from ear to ear, dances a jig on the wall overlooking the Temple. The reserved Nehemiah lifts his hands and voice in praise as he nears the sacred area. The people, after long days and nights of toil and labor, are delirious with joy. God is in their midst. Time for celebration, time for singing.

When have you rejoiced the way the Israelites did at the dedication of the wall?

Lost and Found

"But while [the younger son] was still far off, his father saw him and was filled with compassion; he ran and put his arms around him and kissed him. Then the son said to him, 'Father, I have sinned against heaven and before you; I am no longer worthy to be called your son.' But the father said to his slaves, 'Quickly, bring out a robe—the best one—and put it on him; put a ring on his finger and sandals on his feet. And get the fatted calf and kill it, and let us eat and celebrate; for this son of mine was dead and is alive again; he was lost and is found!' And they began to celebrate.

"Now his elder son became angry and refused to go in. His father came out and began to plead with him. Then the father said to him, 'Son, you are always with me, and all that is mine is yours. But we had to celebrate and rejoice, because this brother of yours was dead and has come to life; he was lost and has been found.'"

Luke 15:20b–24, 25a, 28b, 31–32

IN THE PARABLE of the prodigal son, neither of the two sons can do anything to save himself. The younger, having thrown away his inheritance, cannot force his father to take him back, even as a hired man. The older brother, crippled by jealousy and bitterness, cannot force himself over the threshold to welcome his brother back to life. Only the father can be the catalyst of resurrection for them both. The father goes out to both of them. He is not concerned about how it looks. The great patriarch kisses the younger renegade, who has dishonored him, and pleads with the older renegade, who has also dishonored him. Love does not care if it looks foolish. Love only asks that it be allowed to love at whatever cost. In this one story, fashioned from the mind of Christ, we find the very essence of the gospel.

Lord God, we were lost and now we are found. Let us praise and celebrate together! Amen.

Celebrating as a Community

Haman son of Hammedatha the Agagite, the enemy of all the Jews, had plotted against the Jews to destroy them, and had cast Pur—that is "the lot"—to crush and destroy them; but when Esther came before the king, he gave orders in writing that the wicked plot that he had devised against the Jews should come upon his own head, and that he and his sons should be hanged on the gallows. Therefore these days are called Purim, from the word Pur. The Jews established and accepted as a custom for themselves and their descendants and all who joined them, that without fail they would continue to observe these two days every year, as it was written and at the time appointed.

Esther 9:24–26a, 27

As a direct response to the experience of deliverance "from sorrow into gladness and from mourning into a holiday" (9:22), Purim focuses not on the dread and sorrow of the ordeal, but the joyful astonishment of the reversal of fortune. Haunted as it is by so many true stories in which the Hamans of the world succeed, Purim is nonetheless commanded to be joyous and festive. As a response to this deliverance, Purim is not only a time of feasting, but also a time of giving to one another and to the poor. Community celebrations need not turn us inward. As with Purim, they may open us up to the larger society of which we are a part.

When you host your party, consider following the example of Purim and sharing your celebration with those less fortunate by making or buying an extra cake or main course to donate to your local shelter. If this is not an option for you, you may want to remember the poor at your celebration with the following prayer:

Lord God, when we celebrate all that you have given us, help us to remember those who are less fortunate, who lack the food or the money or the freedom to celebrate as we do. Turn our hearts outward so we can share your joy with everyone we meet. In your name we pray. Amen.

Our Mouth Was Filled with Laughter

When the Lord restored the fortunes of Zion,
    we were like those who dream.
Then our mouth was filled with laughter,
    and our tongue with shouts of joy;
then it was said among the nations,
    "The Lord has done great things for them."
The Lord has done great things for us,
    and we rejoiced.
Restore our fortunes, O Lord,
    like the watercourses in the Negeb.
May those who sow in tears
    reap with shouts of joy.
Those who go out weeping,
    bearing the seed for sowing,
shall come home with shouts of joy,
    carrying their sheaves.

Psalm 126:1–6

THIS PSALM REFLECTS, perhaps, the return of the exiles from Babylon. In any event, it bursts with joy when the too-good-to-be-true actually comes true. Laughter, full of surprise and wonder, brims over and spills out over lips filled with song. God's marvels on our behalf deserve extravagant celebration.

"What soap is to the body, so laughter is to the soul," says a Yiddish proverb. How does laughter cleanse your soul? If you have already had your celebration, reflect on how your soul was affected by the joy and laughter.

A Royal Wedding

My heart overflows with a goodly theme; / I address my verses to
the king; / my tongue is like the pen of a ready scribe. / You are the
most handsome of men; / grace is poured upon your lips; / therefore God has blessed you forever. / Gird your sword on your thigh,
O mighty one, / in your glory and majesty. / Hear, O daughter,
consider and incline your ear; / forget your people and your father's
house, / and the king will desire your beauty. / Since he is your lord,
bow to him; / the people of Tyre will seek your favor with gifts, /
the richest of the people with all kinds of wealth. / The princess is
decked in her chamber with gold-woven robes; / in many-colored
robes she is led to the king; / behind her the virgins, her companions, follow. / With joy and gladness they are led along / as they
enter the palace of the king.

Psalm 45:1–3, 10–15

TAKEN LITERALLY, THIS song celebrates a king's wedding. We can
readily imagine the pomp and circumstance surrounding this royal
wedding—the groom decked out in his best clothes, the bride wearing a gold gown and accompanied by her attendants as they process to
the palace. All the while joy and gladness permeate the air. The king
is handsome, strong, righteous, rich, and even fragrant (45:2–9). The
bride should and will yield to him gladly, much to her own good. As
with the Song of Solomon, this psalm has often come to be interpreted
allegorically: Christ as King receives the Church as his bride.

It's easy to think of a wedding as a time of celebration, but as Richard
Foster writes, "God's normal means of bringing his joy is by redeeming
and sanctifying the ordinary junctures of human life."[7] As you go about
your normal routine today, be especially aware of God's redeeming
presence in the most menial job. Then at the end of the day, reflect on
how that brought joy into your life.

Rejoicing in Our Sexuality

Let him kiss me with the kisses of his mouth!
For your love is better than wine,
    your anointing oils are fragrant,
your name is perfume poured out;
    therefore the maidens love you.
Draw me after you, let us make haste.
    The king has brought me into his chambers.
We will exult and rejoice in you;
    we will extol your love more than wine;
    rightly do they love you.

Song of Solomon 1:1–4

WHAT A WONDERFUL way of celebrating God has given us with his good gift of sexuality! The Song is an incarnational celebration of our spirituality. It is a sensuous book, reveling in God's good gifts of both spiritual and physical intimacy. All the senses participate in the description of the pleasures of love. Wine is a sensuous liquid, leaving a long aftertaste on the tongue, like the kisses of one's beloved. More than that, love and wine both leave one lightheaded.

The entire book of Song of Solomon is a beautiful description of young lovers taking great joy in one another. Consider writing down or telling your spouse or another loved one just how much you delight in and appreciate her or him.

Celebrating in Times of Suffering

Awake, awake, put on strength, / O arm of the LORD! / Awake, as
in days of old, / the generations of long ago! / Was it not you who
cut Rahab in pieces, / who pierced the dragon? / Was it not you
who dried up the sea, / the waters of the great deep; / who made
the depths of the sea a way / for the redeemed to cross over? / So
the ransomed of the LORD shall return, / and come to Zion with
singing; / everlasting joy shall be upon their heads; / they shall
obtain joy and gladness, / and sorrow and sighing shall flee away.

Isaiah 51:9–11

THESE WORDS ARE written to Israel in exile. In this time of suffering
and hardship, the poet calls upon God and remembers God's great
deeds on his people's behalf, such as the parting of the Red Sea in the
exodus. The poet proclaims that the people will return, that joy and
gladness are in their future. Celebration may well be the most overlooked of the Spiritual Disciplines, but it is indeed a discipline meant
to be practiced. Reaching for everlasting joy through singing, dancing,
and praising is essential even and perhaps especially in times of sadness, because it returns our focus to God.

It may be that now is a time in which you do not feel like celebrating.
Reflect on this quote and prayerfully consider holding your celebration
anyway:

"Celebration heartily done makes our deprivations and sorrows
seem small, and we find in it great strength to do the will of our God
because his goodness becomes so real to us."

—Dallas Willard, *The Spirit of the Disciplines*[8]

Joy in Christ

I thank my God every time I remember you, constantly praying with joy in every one of my prayers for all of you, because of your sharing in the gospel from the first day until now.

Rejoice in the Lord always; again I will say, Rejoice.

Philippians 1:3–5; 4:4

PAUL'S LETTER TO the Philippians is full of joy. Paul not only remembers them joyfully in prayers, but rejoices at the proclamation of the gospel. Elsewhere in the Letter Paul identifies the aim of his ministry as their "progress and joy in faith" (1:25). Here he encourages the Philippians to take on the disciplines of rejoicing and prayer. This is the third time Paul tells the community to rejoice (2:18; 3:1). Their concerns (and ours) are to be addressed not by worrying about them, but by developing habits of prayer and rejoicing, as Paul has done. Late in his ministry—having endured hardships and opposition from all sides—Paul expresses joy. Here is spiritual maturity: when Paul had every reason to be tired and bitter, he responded to life with joy. This is the fruit of a life lived in close relationship with God, the fruit of a life formed in Christ.

When, if ever, have you felt this kind of joy in the Lord?

"Our Lord sometimes causes in the soul a certain jubilation and a strange and mysterious kind of prayer. If He bestows this grace on you, praise him fervently for it; I describe it so that you may know that it is something real. I believe that the faculties of the soul are closely united to God but that He leaves them at liberty to rejoice in their happiness together with the senses, although they do not know what they are enjoying nor how they do so. This may sound nonsense but it really happens. So excessive is its jubilee that the soul will not enjoy it alone but speaks of it to all around so that they may help it to praise God, which is its one desire."

—St. Teresa of Avila, *The Interior Castle*[9]

Praise the Lord!

Praise the LORD!
Praise God in his sanctuary;
  praise him in his mighty firmament!
Praise him for his mighty deeds;
  praise him according to his surpassing greatness!
Praise him with trumpet sound;
  praise him with lute and harp!
Praise him with tambourine and dance;
  praise him with strings and pipe!
Praise him with clanging cymbals;
  praise him with loud clashing cymbals!
Let everything that breathes praise the LORD!
Praise the LORD!

Psalm 150:1–6

IN CONCLUDING THE Psalter, this call to praise describes how praise is to be offered. It basically says, "Be unrestrained and rambunctious. Let it all out!" "Praise him according to his surpassing greatness" suggests that big bands, drums, and dancing may not even be exuberant enough. When our own worship traditions aren't quite cut-loose enough, we can still enter such praise with bursting hearts, full voices, clapping hands, and joyful feet as we listen and join musical settings of the psalm from great chorales to Duke Ellington's "Praise God and Dance." "Let everything that breathes praise the LORD!" Oh, yes!

Lord, help me to be unrestrained and exuberant in my praise. Remove from me all fear of embarrassment, all concern about how I look to others. Bring me to my feet, shouting and clapping your praises. Thank you, Lord! Amen.

For more verses on celebration and ideas on how to practice the discipline of celebration, see the Responding exercises and Spiritual Disciplines Index in *The Life with God Bible.*

Acknowledgments

Grateful acknowledgment is made for permission to reprint from the following sources:

Excerpts taken from *Hearing God: Developing a Conversational Relationship with God* by Dallas Willard. Copyright © 1999 by Dallas Willard. Used by permission of the InterVarsity Press, PO Box 1400, Downers Grove, IL 60515. www.ivpress.com.

Excerpts from *The Pursuit of God* by A.W. Tozer, copyright © 1948, 1982, 1993 by Zur Ltd. Used by permission of WingSpread Publishers, a division of Zur Ltd. 800.884.4571.

Excerpts from *Life Together* by Dietrich Bonhoeffer. Copyright © 1954, by Harper & Row Publishers, Inc.; from *Celebration of Discipline* by Richard J. Foster. Copyright © 1978, 1988, 1998 by Richard J. Foster; from *Prayers from the Heart* by Richard J. Foster. Copyright © 1994 by Richard J. Foster; from *The Challenge of the Disciplined Life* by Richard J. Foster. Copyright © 1985 by Richard J. Foster; from *The Spirit of the Disciplines* by Dallas Willard. Copyright © 1988 by Dallas Willard. Used by permission of HarperCollins Publishers.

Notes

The With-God Life
1. Dallas Willard, *The Spirit of the Disciplines* (San Francisco: Harper & Row, 1988), p. 138.

Prayer
1. Richard J. Foster, *Prayer: Finding the Heart's True Home* (San Francisco: HarperSanFrancisco, 1992), p. 8.
2. Richard J. Foster, *Prayers from the Heart* (San Francisco: HarperSanFrancisco, 1994), p. 4.
3. Simone Weil, "Concerning the Our Father," in Richard J. Foster and Emilie Griffin, eds., *Spiritual Classics* (San Francisco: HarperSanFrancisco, 2000), p. 51.
4. Dallas Willard, *The Spirit of the Disciplines* (San Francisco: Harper & Row, 1988), p. 185.
5. Etty Hillesum, "Prayer from Auschwitz," trans. Otto Pomerans, in Mary Ford-Grabowsky, *WomanPrayers* (San Francisco: HarperSanFrancisco, 2003), p. 132.
6. George Buttrick, "A Simple Regimen of Private Prayer," in Richard J. Foster and James Bryan Smith, eds., *Devotional Classics* (San Francisco: HarperSanFrancisco, 1993), pp. 89–90.
7. Father Gilbert Shaw, in *Celtic Daily Prayer: Prayers and Readings from the Northumbria Community* (San Francisco: HarperSanFrancisco, 2002), p. 402.
8. Agnes Sanford, *The Healing Light*, in Foster and Griffin, *Spiritual Classics*, pp. 38–39.
9. Martin Luther, "What a Great Gift We Have in Prayer," in Foster and Smith, *Devotional Classics*, p. 118.
10. Foster, *Prayers from the Heart*, p. 80.

11. Agnes Sanford, *The Healing Light,* in Foster and Griffin, *Spiritual Classics,* p. 39.

12. Foster, *Prayers from the Heart,* p. 24.

13. Andre Louf, *Teach Us to Pray,* in Foster and Griffin, *Spiritual Classics,* p. 33.

Study

1. Richard J. Foster and others, eds., *The Life with God Bible* (San Francisco: HarperSanFrancisco, 2005), p. xxvi.

2. Foster and others, *The Life with God Bible,* pp. xxv, xxvi.

3. Foster and others, *The Life with God Bible,* p. xxviii.

4. David Watson, *Fear No Evil: A Personal Struggle with Cancer* (London: Hodder and Stoughton, 1984), p. 39.

5. Abraham Lincoln, available at http://www.keyway.ca/htm2002/biblquot .htm.

6. Dallas Willard, *The Divine Conspiracy: Rediscovering Our Hidden Life in God* (San Francisco: HarperSanFrancisco, 1998), pp. 271–72.

7. Willard, *The Divine Conspiracy,* p. 272.

8. *Francis and Clare: The Complete Writings,* trans. Regis J. Armstrong and Ignatius C. Brady, Classics of Western Spirituality Series (New York: Paulist, 1982), pp. 38–39.

9. A. W. Tozer, *The Knowledge of the Holy* (New York: Harper, 1961), p. 13.

Confession

1. St. Alphonsus Liguori, "A Good Confession," in *To Any Christian* (London: Burnes & Oates, 1964), p. 192.

2. Richard J. Foster, *Celebration of Discipline,* rev. ed. (San Francisco: HarperSanFrancisco, 1988), p. 145.

3. Foster, *Celebration of Discipline,* p. 148.

4. Dallas Willard, *The Spirit of the Disciplines* (San Francisco: Harper & Row, 1988), p. 189.

5. Frederick Buechner, *Beyond Words* (San Francisco: HarperSanFrancisco, 2004), p. 65.

6. Foster, *Celebration of Discipline,* pp. 149–50.

7. Søren Kierkegaard, *The Living Thoughts of Kierkegaard,* ed. W. H. Auden (New York: NYRB Classics, 1999), p. 237.

8. Dietrich Bonhoeffer, *Life Together* (New York: Harper, 1954), p. 116.

9. Martin Luther, *Luther's Prayers,* ed. Herbert F. Brokering (Minneapolis, MN: Augsburg Fortress, 1994), p. 19.

Worship

1. Richard J. Foster, *Celebration of Discipline*, rev. ed. (San Francisco: HarperSanFrancisco, 1988), p. 158.
2. Foster, *Celebration of Discipline*, p. 162.
3. William Temple, in Foster, *Celebration of Discipline*, p. 158.
4. Frederick Buechner, *Beyond Words* (San Francisco: HarperSanFrancisco, 2004), pp. 414–15.
5. Dallas Willard, *The Spirit of the Disciplines* (San Francisco: Harper & Row, 1988), p. 178.
6. Eugene H. Peterson, *A Long Obedience in the Same Direction* (Downers Grove, IL: InterVarsity, 2000), p. 54.
7. Thomas R. Kelly, *The Eternal Promise* (New York: Harper & Row, 1966), p. 72.
8. Foster, *Celebration of Discipline*, pp. 161–63.

Service

1. Paul Achtemeier, ed., *HarperCollins Bible Dictionary* (San Francisco: HarperSanFrancisco, 1996), 1000–1001.
2. Dallas Willard, *The Spirit of the Disciplines* (San Francisco: Harper & Row, 1988), p. 183.
3. Willard, *The Spirit of the Disciplines*, p. 184.
4. Richard J. Foster, *Celebration of Discipline*, rev. ed. (San Francisco: HarperSanFrancisco, 1988), p. 126.
5. Richard J. Foster, *The Challenge of the Disciplined Life* (San Francisco: Harper & Row, 1985), p. 229.
6. Foster, *Celebration of Discipline*, pp. 128–30.

Secrecy

1. John of the Cross, *The Dark Night of the Soul*, in Richard J. Foster and James Bryan Smith, eds., *Devotional Classics* (San Francisco: HarperSanFrancisco, 1993), p. 34.
2. Dallas Willard, *The Spirit of the Disciplines* (San Francisco: Harper & Row, 1988), p. 173.
3. *Meister Eckhart: Selections from His Essential Writings*, ed. Emilie Griffin, HarperCollins Spiritual Classics (San Francisco: HarperSanFrancisco, 2005), p. 45.
4. Willard, *The Spirit of the Disciplines*, p. 174.
5. Andrew Murray, *Humility* (New Kensington, PA: Whitaker), p. 123.
6. Murray, *Humility*, p. 60.

7. Martin Luther, *Luther's Prayers,* ed. Herbert F. Brokering (Minneapolis, MN: Augsburg Fortress, 1994), p. 83.
8. Thomas à Kempis, *The Imitation of Christ,* in Irwin Edman, ed., *The Consolations of Philosophy* (New York: Random House, Modern Library, 1943), p. 177.

Guidance

1. Dallas Willard, *Hearing God* (Downers Grove, IL: InterVarsity, 1999), p. 18.
2. E. Stanley Jones, "For Sunday of Week 41," *Victorious Living* (Nashville, TN: Abingdon, 1938), p. 281.
3. Willard, *Hearing God,* p. 36.
4. Virgil Vogt, in Richard J. Foster, *Celebration of Discipline,* rev. ed. (San Francisco: HarperSanFrancisco, 1988), p. 187.
5. Ignatius of Loyola, *Rules for the Discernment of Spirits,* in Richard J. Foster and Emilie Griffin, eds., *Spiritual Classics* (San Francisco: HarperSanFrancisco, 2000), pp. 292–96.
6. Willard, *Hearing God,* p. 96.
7. Willard, *Hearing God,* pp. 10–11.

Meditation

1. Joyce Huggett, *Learning the Language of Prayer,* in Richard J. Foster and Emilie Griffin, eds., *Spiritual Classics* (San Francisco: HarperSanFrancisco, 2000), p. 11.
2. Richard J. Foster, *Celebration of Discipline,* rev. ed. (San Francisco: HarperSanFrancisco, 1988), p. 30.
3. *John and Charles Wesley: Selected Prayers, Hymns, and Sermons,* ed. Emilie Griffin, HarperCollins Spiritual Classics (San Francisco: HarperSanFrancisco, 2004), pp. 22–23.
4. Lilias Trotter, *The Way of the Sevenfold Secret,* in Foster and Griffin, *Spiritual Classics,* p. 89.
5. Bonhoeffer, *The Way to Freedom* (New York: Harper & Row, 1966), p. 59.
6. Madame Guyon, *Experiencing the Depths of Jesus Christ,* as quoted in Richard J. Foster and James Bryan Smith, eds., *Devotional Classics* (San Francisco: HarperSanFrancisco, 1993), p. 303.
7. Martin Luther, *Luther's Prayers,* ed. Herbert F. Brokering (Minneapolis, MN: Augsburg Fortress, 1994), p. 66.
8. A. W. Tozer, *The Knowledge of the Holy* (New York: Harper, 1961), p. 14.

9. Madame Guyon, *Experiencing the Depths of Jesus Christ*, as quoted in Foster and Smith, *Devotional Classics*, p. 305.

10. Huggett, *Learning the Language of Prayer*, in Foster and Griffin, *Spiritual Classics*, p. 11.

11. Frederick W. Faber, in Tozer, *The Knowledge of the Holy*, p. 12.

12. Charles de Foucauld, in *Celtic Daily Prayer: Prayers and Readings from the Northumbria Community* (San Francisco: HarperSanFrancisco, 2002), p. 652.

Solitude

1. *Celtic Daily Prayer: Prayers and Readings from the Northumbria Community* (San Francisco: HarperSanFrancisco, 2002), p. 62.

2. Thomas Merton, *A Year with Thomas Merton*, ed., Jonathan Montaldo (San Francisco: HarperSanFrancisco, 2004), p. 8.

3. Emilie Griffin, *Wilderness Time* (San Francisco: HarperSanFrancisco, 1997), p. 17.

4. Anne Morrow Lindbergh, *Gift from the Sea* (New York: Random House, 1978), p. 42.

5. Henri J. M. Nouwen, *Clowning in Rome*, in *Celtic Daily Prayer*, p. 341.

6. Madeleine L'Engle, *A Circle of Quiet* (New York: Farrar, Straus & Giroux, 1972), p. 4.

7. Thomas Merton, in Montaldo, ed., *A Year with Thomas Merton*, p. 8.

8. Thomas à Kempis, *The Imitation of Christ*, trans. William C. Creasy (Notre Dame, IN: Ave Maria Press, 2004), p. 50.

Fellowship

1. Dietrich Bonhoeffer, *Life Together* (New York: Harper, 1954), p. 39.

2. H. Richard Niebuhr, *Christ and Culture* (New York: Harper & Row, 1951), p. 222.

3. Bonhoeffer, *Life Together*, p. 23.

4. Richard J. Foster and others, eds., *The Life with God Bible* (San Francisco: HarperSanFrancisco, 2005), p. 260.

5. Richard J. Foster, *Prayer: Finding the Heart's True Home* (San Francisco: HarperSanFrancisco, 1992), p. 200.

Fasting

1. Martin Luther, *Luther's Prayers*, ed. Herbert F. Brokering (Minneapolis, MN: Augsburg Fortress, 1994), p. 97.

2. Edith Schaeffer, L'Abri, available at http://dailychristianquote.com/dcq fasting.html.

3. Dallas Willard, *The Spirit of the Disciplines* (San Francisco: Harper & Row, 1988), p. 167.

4. Augustine, in Richard J. Foster and Emilie Griffin, eds., *Spiritual Classics* (San Francisco: HarperSanFrancisco, 2000), p. 69.

5. Richard J. Foster, *Celebration of Discipline*, rev. ed. (San Francisco: Harper-SanFrancisco, 1988), p. 55.

6. John Piper, available at http://dailychristianquote.com/dcqfasting.html.

Chastity

1. Dallas Willard, *The Spirit of the Disciplines* (San Francisco: Harper & Row, 1988), p. 170.

2. Richard J. Foster, *The Challenge of the Disciplined Life* (San Francisco: Harper & Row, 1985), p. 109.

3. Foster, *The Challenge of the Disciplined Life*, p. 99.

4. Kathleen Norris, *The Cloister Walk* (New York: Riverhead, 1996), p. 118.

5. David Allan Hubbard, "Love and Marriage," *The Covenant Companion*, January 15, 1969, p. 4.

6. Foster, *The Challenge of the Disciplined Life*, pp. 161–62.

7. Willard, *The Spirit of the Disciplines*, p. 172.

Submission

1. Richard J. Foster, *The Challenge of the Disciplined Life* (San Francisco: Harper & Row, 1985), p. 113.

2. Richard J. Foster, *Celebration of Discipline*, rev. ed. (San Francisco: Harper-SanFrancisco, 1988), p. 122.

3. Hannah Whitall Smith, *The Christian's Secret of a Happy Life* (Old Tappan, NJ: Fleming Revell, 1942), p. 35.

4. A. W. Tozer, *The Pursuit of God* (Camp Hill, PA: Wingspread, 1993), p. 96.

5. Thomas R. Kelly, *A Testament of Devotion* (New York: Harper, 1941), p. 32.

6. Foster, *Celebration of Discipline*, p. 112.

7. Foster, *Celebration of Discipline*, p. 118.

8. Foster, *Celebration of Discipline*, p. 110.

9. Foster, *Celebration of Discipline*, p. 112.

Sacrifice

1. Richard J. Foster, *The Challenge of the Disciplined Life* (San Francisco: Harper & Row, 1985), p. 230.

2. Hannah Whitall Smith, *The Christian's Secret of a Happy Life* (Old Tappan, NJ: Fleming Revell, 1942), pp. 34–35.

3. Charles de Foucauld, "Prayer of Abandonment to God," in *Celtic Daily Prayer: Prayers and Readings from the Northumbria Community* (San Francisco: HarperSanFrancisco, 2002), p. 49.

4. Martin Luther, *Luther's Prayers*, ed. Herbert F. Brokering (Minneapolis, MN: Augsburg Fortress, 1994), p. 11.

5. Foster, *The Challenge of the Disciplined Life*, p. 43.

6. Foster, *The Challenge of the Disciplined Life*, p. 43.

7. Alexander Balmain Bruce, *Training of the Twelve*, available at http://www.ccel.org/ccel/bruce/twelve.xix.ii.html.

8. Willard, *The Spirit of the Disciplines*, pp. 106–7.

Silence

1. Richard J. Foster, *Celebration of Discipline*, rev. ed. (San Francisco: HarperSanFrancisco, 1988), p. 98.

2. Dietrich Bonhoeffer, *Life Together* (New York: Harper, 1954), pp. 80–81.

3. Dallas Willard, *The Spirit of the Disciplines* (San Francisco: Harper & Row, 1988), p. 163.

4. Thomas à Kempis, *The Imitation of Christ*, in Richard J. Foster and Emilie Griffin, eds., *Spiritual Classics* (San Francisco: HarperSanFrancisco, 2000), p. 150.

5. A. W. Tozer, *The Pursuit of God* (Camp Hill, PA: Wingspread, 1993), p. 78.

6. Bonhoeffer, *Life Together*, p. 79.

7. Bonhoeffer, *Life Together*, p. 78.

Simplicity

1. Martin Luther, *The Place of Trust*, in Richard J. Foster and Emilie Griffin, eds., *Spiritual Classics* (San Francisco: HarperSanFrancisco, 2000), pp. 120, 123–124.

2. A. W. Tozer, *The Pursuit of God*, in Foster and Griffin, *Spiritual Classics*, p. 115.

3. George Fox, *Works*, Vol. 8 (Philadelphia, 1831), p. 126, Epistle 131.

4. Richard J. Foster, *Celebration of Discipline*, rev. ed. (San Francisco: HarperSanFrancisco, 1988), p. 86.

5. Søren Kierkegaard, *Purity of Heart Is to Will One Thing*, in Richard J. Foster, *Prayers from the Heart* (San Francisco: HarperSanFrancisco, 1994), p. 53.

6. Foster, *Celebration of Discipline*, p. 79.

Celebration

1. Dallas Willard, *The Spirit of the Disciplines* (San Francisco: Harper & Row, 1988), p. 179.
2. Thomas Merton, *Praying the Psalms* (Collegeville, MN: Liturgical, 1956), p. 12.
3. *John and Charles Wesley: Selected Prayers, Hymns, and Sermons,* ed. Emilie Griffin, HarperCollins Spiritual Classics (San Francisco: HarperSanFrancisco, 2004), p. 86.
4. Nancy Fierro, *Hildegard of Bingen: Symphony of the Harmony of Heaven,* available at http://www.staff.uni–mainz.de/horst/hildegard/music/music.html.
5. William Walker, available at http://www.ccel.org/ccel/walker/harmony2.vi.c.html.
6. C. S. Lewis, *Reflections on the Psalms* (New York: Harvest/Harcourt Brace Jovanovich, 1958), p. 95.
7. Richard J. Foster, *Celebration of Discipline,* rev. ed. (San Francisco: HarperSanFrancisco, 1988), p. 193.
8. Willard, *The Spirit of the Disciplines,* p. 181.
9. Teresa of Avila, *The Interior Castle,* available at http://www.ccel.org/ccel/teresa/castle2.x.vii.html.

Further Reading

The With-God Life

Foster, Richard J., and Kathy Helmers. *Life with God: Reading the Bible for Spiritual Transformation*. San Francisco: HarperOne, 2008.

Foster, Richard J., and others, eds. *The Life with God Bible*. San Francisco: HarperSanFrancisco, 2005.

Graybeal, Lynda L., and Julia L. Roller. *Connecting with God*. San Francisco: HarperOne, 2006.

——. *Learning from Jesus*. San Francisco: HarperOne, 2006.

——. *Living the Mission*. San Francisco: HarperOne, 2007.

——. *Prayer and Worship*. San Francisco: HarperOne, 2007.

Prayer

Brother Lawrence. *The Practice of the Presence of God*. Translated by John J. Delaney. New York: Doubleday, 1977.

Foster, Richard J. *Prayer: Finding the Heart's True Home*. San Francisco: HarperSanFrancisco, 1992.

Grou, Jean-Nicholas. *How to Pray*. Cambridge: Lutterworth, 2008. (Many editions available.)

Hallesby, O. *Prayer*. Minneapolis, MN: Augsburg, 1994. (Many editions available.)

Laubach, Frank C. *Prayer, The Mightiest Force in the World: Thoughts for an Atomic Age*. Whitefish, MT: Kessinger, 2007. (Many editions available.)

Sanford, Agnes. *The Healing Light*. Rev. ed. New York: Ballantine, 1983.

Study

Willard, Dallas. *The Divine Conspiracy*. San Francisco: HarperSanFrancisco, 1998.

Confession

The Confessions of St. Augustine. Grand Rapids, MI: Revell, 2008. (Many editions available.)

Luther, Martin. *Luther's Prayers.* Edited by Herbert F. Brokering. Minneapolis, MN: Augsburg Fortress, 1994.

Worship

Steere, Douglas V. *Prayer and Worship.* Richmond, IN: Friends United, 1988.

Tozer, A. W. *Worship: The Missing Jewel of the Evangelical Church.* Harrisburg, PA: Christian Publications, 1992.

Underhill, Evelyn. *Worship.* Eugene, OR: Wipf & Stock, 2002. (Many editions available.)

Webber, Robert E. *Worship Is a Verb.* Nashville, TN: Word, 1985.

Service

Day, Dorothy. *The Long Loneliness.* San Francisco: HarperSanFrancisco, 1996.

Greenleaf, Robert K. *Servant Leadership.* Mahwah, NJ: Paulist, 2002.

Secrecy

Muller, George. (Also spelled Mueller.) *The Autobiography of George Muller.* New Kensington, PA: Whitaker House, 1984.

Thomas à Kempis. *The Imitation of Christ.* Translated by William C. Creasy. Notre Dame, IN: Ave Maria, 1989. (Many editions available.)

Guidance

Huggett, Joyce. *Listening to God.* London: Hodder & Stoughton, 2006.

Ignatius of Loyola. *The Spiritual Exercises of Ignatius of Loyola.* (Many editions available.)

Peterson, Eugene H. *The Wisdom of Each Other.* Grand Rapids, MI: Zondervan, 1998.

Willard, Dallas. *Hearing God.* Westmont, IL: InterVarsity, 1999.

Meditation

Guyon, Madame Jeanne. *Experiencing the Depths of Jesus Christ.* Jacksonville, FL: Christian Books, Seedsowers, 1981.

Huggett, Joyce. *Learning the Language of Prayer.* New York: Crossroad, 1997.

Merton, Thomas. *What Is Contemplation?* Springfield, IL: Templegate, 1981.

Solitude

Chryssavgis, John. *In the Heart of the Desert: The Spirituality of the Desert Fathers and Mothers*. Rev. ed. Bloomington, IN: World Wisdom, 2008.

Griffin, Emilie. *Wilderness Time: A Guide to Spiritual Retreat*. San Francisco: HarperSanFrancisco, 1997.

Lindbergh, Anne Morrow. *Gift from the Sea*. New York: Vintage, 1978.

Fellowship

Bonhoeffer, Dietrich. *Life Together*. New York: Harper, 1954.

Nouwen, Henri J. M. *The Road to Daybreak*. New York: Doubleday/Image, 1988.

Vanier, Jean. *Community and Growth*. Mahwah, NJ: Paulist, 1989.

Fasting

Smith, David R. *Fasting: A Neglected Discipline*. Fort Washington, PA: Christian Literature Crusade, 1976.

Wallis, Arthur. *God's Chosen Fast*. Fort Washington, PA: Christian Literature Crusade, 1986. (Many editions available.)

Chastity

Foster, Richard J. *The Challenge of the Disciplined Life*. San Francisco: Harper & Row, 1985.

Submission

Caussade, Jean-Pierre de. *The Sacrament of the Present Moment*. San Francisco: Harper & Row, 1982.

Murray, Andrew. *Humility*. New Kensington, PA: Whitaker House, 1982.

Smith, Hannah Whitall. *The Christian's Secret of a Happy Life*. Old Tappan, NJ: Fleming Revell, 1942.

Yoder, John Howard. *The Politics of Jesus*. Grand Rapids, MI: Eerdmans, 1994.

Sacrifice

Bonhoeffer, Dietrich. *The Cost of Discipleship*. New York: Simon & Schuster/Touchstone, 1995.

Willard, Dallas. *The Spirit of the Disciplines*. San Francisco: Harper & Row, 1988. (See Sacrifice section in "Some Main Disciplines for the Spiritual Life.")

Silence

Doherty, Catherine de Hueck. *Poustinia*. Washington, DC: Madonna House, 2000.

Merton, Thomas. *Dialogues with Silence*. San Francisco: HarperSanFrancisco, 2001.

O'Connor, Elizabeth. *Search for Silence*. Philadelphia: Innisfree, 1986.

Simplicity

Brother Ugolino di Monte Santa Maria. *Little Flowers of St. Francis of Assisi*. New York: Cosimo, 2007. (Many editions available.)

Foster, Richard J. *Freedom of Simplicity*. Rev. ed. San Francisco: HarperSanFrancisco, 2005.

Celebration

Campolo, Tony. *The Kingdom of God Is a Party*. Nashville, TN: Thomas Nelson, 1992.

Foster, Richard J. *Celebration of Discipline*. Rev. ed. San Francisco: HarperSanFrancisco, 1988.

The Spiritual Disciplines

The following books contain chapters on several of the disciplines listed above:

Foster, Richard J., and Emilie Griffin, eds. *Spiritual Classics*. San Francisco: HarperSanFrancisco, 2000.

Johnson, Jan. *Spiritual Disciplines Companion*. Downers Grove, IL: InterVarsity, 2009.

Whitney, Donald S. *Spiritual Disciplines for the Christian Life*. Colorado Springs,

What Is RENOVARÉ?

RENOVARÉ (from the Latin, meaning "to renew") is an infrachurch movement committed to the renewal of the Church of Jesus Christ in all its multifaceted expressions. Founded by best-selling author Richard J. Foster, RENOVARÉ is Christian in commitment, international in scope, and ecumenical in breadth.

In *The Life with God Bible* (originally published as *The Renovaré Spiritual Formation Bible*) we observe how God spiritually formed his people through historical events and the practice of Spiritual Disciplines; this is the "with-God life." RENOVARÉ continues this emphasis on spiritual formation by placing it within the context of the two-thousand-year history of the Church and six great Christian traditions we find in its life—Contemplative: The Prayer-Filled Life; Holiness: The Virtuous Life; Charismatic: The Spirit-Empowered Life; Social Justice: The Compassionate Life; Evangelical: The Word-Centered Life; and Incarnational: The Sacramental Life. This balanced vision of Christian faith and witness was modeled for us by Jesus Christ and was evident in the lives of countless saints: Antony, Francis of Assisi, Susanna Wesley, Phoebe Palmer, and more. The with-God life of the People of God continues on today as Christians participate in the life and practices of local churches and look forward to spending eternity in that "all-inclusive community of loving persons with God himself at the very center of this community as its prime Sustainer and most glorious Inhabitant."

In addition to offering a balanced vision of the spiritual life, RENOVARÉ promotes a practical strategy for people seeking renewal by helping facilitate small spiritual formation groups; national, regional, and local conferences; one-day seminars; personal and group retreats; and readings from devotional classics that can sustain a long-term commitment to renewal. RENOVARÉ Resources for Spiritual Renewal, books published by HarperOne, seek to integrate historical, scholarly, and inspirational materials in practical, readable formats. These resources can be used in a variety of settings: small groups, private and organizational retreats, individual devotions, church-school classes, and more. Written and edited by people committed to the renewal of the Church, all of the materials present a balanced vision of Christian life and faith coupled with a practical strategy for spiritual growth and enrichment.

For more information about RENOVARÉ and its mission, please log on to its website (www.renovare.us) or write RENOVARÉ, 8 Inverness Drive East, Suite 102, Englewood, CO 80112, U.S.A.

A Sample Essay from *The Life with God Bible*

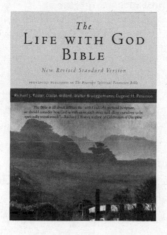

The People of God
in Prayer and Worship

DALLAS WILLARD

The aim of God in history is the creation of an all-inclusive community of loving persons with God himself at the very center of this community as its prime Sustainer and most glorious Inhabitant (Eph 2:19–22; 3:10). The Bible traces the formation of this community from the creation in the Garden of Eden all the way to the new heaven and the new earth. Come, join us as we explore the many dimensions of this with-God history—from individual to family to tribe to people to nation to all humanity—and apply what we learn to our own spiritual formation.

In the Psalms we see and hear the ways God nurtures the nation of Israel and continues to form an all-inclusive community through the development of liturgical praise and prayer.

GOD'S ACTION

Psalms is a book of praise and prayer. The psalmist sings to us that God is "enthroned on the praises of Israel" and addresses God as "you who answer prayer" (22:3, 65:2). Praise and prayer—these two spiritual practices articulate our most fundamental relationship to God. The Psalter expresses, with more immediacy and completeness than any other part of the Bible, how the People of God are formed spiritually. This is because it gathers up the historical and corporate experiences of the Israelites—as well as very intimate, personal experiences of individuals—and then expresses those experiences in the full depth and richness of poetry, classically understood as public reading and remembrance.

Ideally, the Psalms were performed in suitable and architectural and liturgical settings, beginning with the tabernacle in the wilderness and continuing up through the glorious Temple of Jesus' day. Undoubtedly they were simply read or chanted without any accompaniment, but indications are that their performance was at times replete with musical instruments, choir, and dance. The Psalms are works of art that skillfully and vigorously embody what cannot simply be stated or said. No doubt their primary use was in public worship, but individuals also utilized them frequently, and both of these practices continue in our own day. The language and images conveyed by the Psalms are unsurpassed for powerfully forming our spiritual life.

The Psalms are primary instruments for forming the inner life of the faithful, but much of their effectiveness derives from the fact that they are also about how this formation occurs. They speak forth, in suitable poetic tones, of how God and human beings interact to shape the inner and outer life of individuals and groups. Though the Psalms do teach, most of their power for forming our inner life and character lies in their beauty and capacity to penetrate our emotions, our body, our social relations—indeed, our entire life.

Praise and prayer are the pulse beat of the Psalms. The praise or adulation often looks like proclamation (Pss 1; 23; the Song of Moses and Miriam in Exod 15), but poetic proclamation is our natural response when we have entered into surpassing magnificence—the Person and the Creation of the Lord God, the Almighty. We simply *must* bear witness to it, proclaim it, shout it from the rooftops as an essential part of engaging, enjoying, and being faithful to it.

With regard to content, the Psalms move between two poles; on one side is the desperate condition of human beings when left to stand on their own, and on the other, the unlimited greatness and goodness of God. From those two poles there emerges, strangely but beautifully, the greatness of humanity under God and within God's life and cosmic plan. This is the result of God's salvation or deliverance, which in psalm after psalm is remembered, praised, and anticipated. "God-with-us" is the essence of deliverance regardless of the specific circumstance.

The book of Psalms graphically depicts the desperate human condition: our natural weakness, transience, insignificance, isolation, foolishness, inner wickedness, outer wickedness, oppression of others, oppression by others—indeed, our overall hopelessness. Now, this is raw realism about human existence wherever it may be. Who can deny it?

Yet, at the same time, the goodness and greatness of God are seen and celebrated: in God's covenant with Israel, in the lives of Israel's great ones, in the beauty and strength of the Torah, in the great historical acts of national and individual deliverance, in magnificent Jerusalem and the glorious Temple, in the unsurpassed works of nature, in righteous judgment, in the searching of the inmost heart, and in God's majestic rule over all—including all the nations of the earth. All this, and more, is held before the faithful in poetic performance to impress upon them what life with God is like and to lead them ever more deeply into that life. And finally, the practices and the character of godly persons are described, illustrated, and glorified.

HUMAN REACTION

The attraction of the Psalter is great and obvious. It is a "natural" form for expressing the drama of life: our precarious human condition and God's gracious offer of life-giving relationship with himself. The combination of poetic form, historical narrative, and profound insight makes the Psalms attractive even to unbelievers. Their sweeping vision and accurate reflection of the common experiences of human life provide a framework for the interpretation of human existence that has few, if any, rivals.

In the individual and corporate enactment of the Psalms a public form of life takes shape. In reality, the Psalter is a prayer book—or, better, a soul book—that correctly represents God and the life that we can have in him. This explains the huge role that the book of Psalms actually played in the Jewish religion, and later, in the life of the Church. In the Christian era the apostle Paul's emphasis upon singing is genuinely remarkable: "Be filled with the Spirit, as you sing psalms and hymns and spiritual songs among yourself, singing and making melody to the Lord in your hearts" (Eph 5:18–19). And more recently, from the Protestant Reformation on, great advances and renewals in Christendom have often been times of great singing. Beyond all doubt, singing is a most powerful force in our spiritual formation.

BLESSINGS AND BENEFITS
FOR OUR FORMATION

In the Psalter the language of praise, adoration, thanksgiving, intercession, petition, complaint, disappointment, remembrance, anger, relinquishment, and repentance is beautifully and memorably available. Ordinary persons like ourselves simply cannot come up with such language on our own, but we can enter into it if it is presented in a suitable context. And these inspired poetic expressions can, under God, be the locus of great joy and character transformation as we allow them to sink deep into our heart.

If we enter into the Psalms honestly and faithfully, they can induce experiences and actions within us that truly reflect the words expressed. This, in turn, will reshape our inner being and character into the state God would have it. And maintain it! The testimony of the People of God throughout the ages, even up to our day, confirms this. Nothing on earth matches the Psalter as a public exercise for cultivating a right heart in relation to God.

LIMITS AND LIABILITIES
FOR OUR FORMATION

But for all the glory and power of the Psalms, our response to them can have serious limitations. Any activity can become mere performance. As we have seen with the law, the limitation of liturgical language and ritual is that it can remain external and not touch the heart. This is true even though the content of the Psalms themselves flatly opposes it. We can sing "Search me, O God, and know my heart" (139:23), and even enjoy the thought expressed, but avoid the reality like the plague. Merely singing about God's searching our heart can also leave us with the mistaken impression that by virtue of the singing we have participated in its reality. The same is true for all the great expressions of the Psalter.

When the practices of praise and worship remain external, they can also bind our devotion to God to specific times and places ("church work"), to legalism, or to culture (ethnicity). When this happens, our religion becomes a performance—or worse yet, turns us into being merely spectators of a performance. Worship of God can be replaced by worship of beauty or merely "propriety" and even become simply entertainment.

Worship without heart is what the prophetic witness had to combat during the heyday of religious practices in the First Temple and in Samaria: "I hate, I despise your festivals, and I take no delight in your solemn assemblies" (Amos 5:21). "I cannot endure solemn assemblies with iniquity. Your new moons and your appointed festivals my soul hates;. . .Even though you make many prayers, I will not listen; your hands are full of blood" (Isa 1:13–15).

In addition, merely external worship leaves us incapable of devotion when the "props" are taken away. We then are at a loss about how we can "sing the LORD's song in a foreign land" (Ps 137:4). By contract, Paul and Silas in a Philippian jail pray and sing hymns at midnight and bring God's life to their fellow prisoners, indeed, to the jail keeper himself (Acts 16:25–34).

Externalization is *not* inevitable. By being aware of it and guarding against it we can appropriate the richness of the Psalms for great benefit to our inner life. Moving from the surface experience into the depths of our mind, will, and heart, we reach the place of true formation and being the transformation of character that God intends.

The danger of substituting ritual behavior for heartfelt devotion to God, for moral integrity, and for justice is always close at hand in those public practices that foster group solidarity and depend upon social approval. This is why the prophetic witness, reaffirmed by Jesus, always emphasizes mercy over sacrifice (Matt 9:13; 12:7). Mercy, you see, is of the heart, while sacrifice may or may not be. Sadly, there seems no limit to the perversion of heart that can exist alongside the reciting of creeds and the singing of hymns in sacred settings. What the great prophets relentlessly condemned—pious ritual without inward and outward transformation—was perhaps even worse in the days of Jesus, and it remains a terrible problem today. Just think how different our life would be if we actually lived the words we mouth in religious services. What a tremendous step forward in spiritual formation that would be!

INSIGHTS AND INSTRUCTIONS
FOR OUR FORMATION

Liturgical and ritual performance can be a source of great strength and direction in our spiritual formation, but it must be used and used well. Frankly, there is no such thing as purely inward religion. That would defy the reality of our embodied selves and the significance of the body and behavior in our godly formation. The contribution of poetry and ritual to the formation of the heart and life in corporate as well as individual worship is indispensable to all robust formation in Christlikeness. The Psalms and the forms of life they represent are a great gift to the People of God—really, to all humanity. We are to read and sing them *from the heart*. And the Psalms themselves show us in exquisite detail just how we can do exactly that—how we can "with gratitude in [our] hearts sing psalms, hymns, and spiritual songs to God" (Col 3:16).

Excerpt from The Life With God Bible, *Richard J. Foster, Editor; Gayle Beebe, Lynda L. Graybeal, Thomas C. Oden, and Dallas Willard, General Editors,* © *Copyright 2005 by Renovaré, Inc.*

You're Invited into a
Deeper and More Authentic

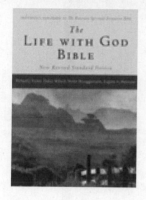

Life with God

"The Bible is all about human life 'with God.' As we read Scripture, we should consider how God is with us in each story and allow ourselves to be spiritually transformed."

—*Richard J. Foster*

The Life with God Bible
Leather-Like
Also available in paperback

The Life with God Bible with the Deuterocanonical Books
Leather-Like

Life with God: Reading the Bible for Spiritual Transformation
Richard J. Foster

Available Wherever Books Are Sold

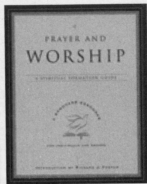